America and the Persian Gulf

The Third Party Dimension in World Politics

STEVE A. YETIV

PRAEGER

Westport, Connecticut
London

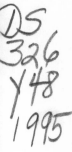

DS
326
Y48
1995

Library of Congress Cataloging-in-Publication Data

Yetiv, Steve A.
    America and the Persian Gulf : the third party dimension in world
politics / Steve A. Yetiv.
        p.   cm.
    Includes bibliographical references.
    ISBN 0–275–94973–7 (alk. paper)
    1. Persian Gulf Region—Foreign relations—United States.
2. United States—Foreign relations—Middle East.   3. Middle East—
Politics and government—1979–   4. Persian Gulf Region—Strategic
aspects.   I. Title.
DS326.Y48   1995
956.05—dc20   94–44171

British Library Cataloguing in Publication Data is available.

Library of Congress Catalog Card Number: 94–44171
ISBN: 0–275–94973–7

First published in 1995

Praeger Publishers, 88 Post Road West, Westport, CT 06881
An imprint of Greenwood Publishing Group, Inc.

Printed in the United States of America

The paper used in this book complies with the
Permanent Paper Standard issued by the National
Information Standards Organization (Z39.48–1984).

10 9 8 7 6 5 4 3 2 1

Copyright Acknowledgment

Parts of Chapter 5 are reprinted with permission from *Political Science Quarterly* 107 (Summer
1992): 195–212.

Parts of Chapter 4 first appeared in *Asian Affair: An American Review* 17(2) pp. 62–81, Summer
1990. Reprinted With Permission Of The Helen Dwight Reid Educational Foundation. Published
By Heldref Publications, 1319 18th Street, N.W. Washington, D.C. 20036–1802. Copyright 1990.

CONTENTS

LIST OF TABLES

LIST OF ABBREVIATIONS

AWACS	Airborne Warning and Air Control System
CBO	Congressional Budget Office
CDSP	*Current Digest of the Soviet Press*
CENTCOM	Central Command
CRS	Congressional Research Service
DoD	Department of Defense
DSB	*Department of State Bulletin*
FBIS	Foreign Broadcast Information Service
FY	Fiscal Year
GAO	General Accounting Office
GCC	Gulf Cooperation Council
GPO	Government Printing Office
IAEA	International Atomic Energy Agency
JPRS	Joint Publications Research Service
KUNA	Kuwait News Agency
MEA	Middle East and Africa
MECS	*Middle East Contemporary Survey*
MEED	*Middle East Economic Digest*
MEES	*Middle East Economic Survey*
MENA	Middle East and North Africa
MPS	Maritime Prepositioning Ship
NATO	North Atlantic Treaty Organization
NENA	Near East and North Africa
NESA	Near East and South Asia
NSIAD	National Security and International Affairs Division
NTPS	Near-term Prepositioned Ship
RDF	Rapid Deployment Force

SAVAK	Iranian Secret Police
UAE	United Arab Emirates
U.N.	United Nations
USCENTCOM	U.S. Central Command
WEU	Western European Union
YAR	Yemen Arab Republic

ACKNOWLEDGMENTS

I would like to thank the many people in the Middle East and United States for their help on this book, particularly those who consented to interviews. Most of the American and Middle Eastern officials and policymakers interviewed chose to remain anonymous. Therefore, no particular attributions were made on their behalf. However, the information they graciously provided proved as useful as other sources.

Special thanks also go to the Center for Middle Eastern Studies at Harvard University where I conducted post-doctoral research on this book and to Harvard's Center for International Affairs where I was a research affiliate in 1992–93. In particular, I thank Professors Bill Graham and Joseph Nye, the respective directors of these centers, who provided an excellent environment within which to conduct research.

Additional thanks for comments on parts of this manuscript go to Lenore Martin, Ambassador Richard Murphy, Malik Mufti, Dona Phares, Juliet Thompson, Saadia Touval, and Pia Wood; to a number of anonymous referees; and to policymakers who prefer to remain nameless. Finally, Elaine Dawson of Old Dominion University offered excellent computer support and camera-ready work for which I am also very grateful.

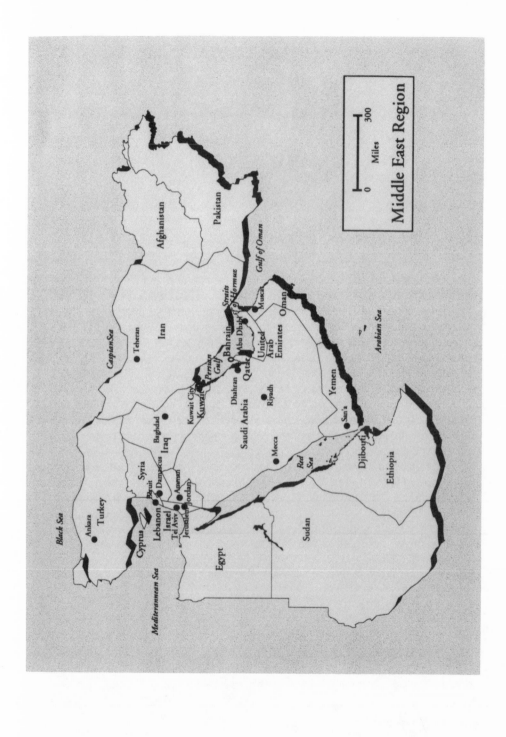

Middle East Region

1

CONFLICT AND CONSEQUENCE IN WORLD POLITICS

Wars in the Middle East, as in other regions of the world, are tragic events. They not only produce devastating human and economic costs but also often reflect the failure of reason to control events and emotion. Wars in the Middle East, however, were more than tragic armed struggles between organized groups. They were fundamental agents of political change, which produced some intriguing, paradoxical, and significant twists in the history and politics of this oil-rich, turbulent region.

This book explains the paradox of regional wars. At the same time, it illustrates and applies a basic approach to the study of conflict, which has not received enough attention by analysts of world politics. This approach helps illuminate conflict and also facilitates the development of general insights for policymaking and evaluation, and theory building. Hence, scholars and interested observers of economic, political, and military conflict may benefit from this approach and apply it in their own particular contexts.

With regard to the Middle East context, few observers would have predicted prior to the Soviet intervention in Afghanistan (1979–1988), the Iran-Iraq war (1980–1988), and Iraq's invasion of Kuwait (August 1990) that these conflicts would produce changes that would strengthen U.S. security in the Persian Gulf region. In fact, they probably would have guessed the opposite. After all, on what theoretical or logical basis could they have predicted that U.S. security would be enhanced by conflicts that greatly challenged its domestic, regional, and international interests? This would have made little or no sense.

The paradox is that these three wars, their disheartening bloodshed aside, did not undermine U.S. regional security. Rather, they did for the United States, and for others that count on it regionally and globally, what little else could have: these wars produced numerous unintended and unforeseen consequences that mixed in the crucible of history to yield an unexpected result. Over time, they put in motion numerous developments that reversed the United States' trajectory toward regional decline and made it much more able to protect the security of a region critical to the functioning of the entire international economy.

Some observers might argue that no other outcome was possible in the historical process. They might say that the rise of U.S. power in the Persian Gulf and the enhancement of regional security over time made perfect sense. How could anything else have occurred, after all? As Richard Ned Lebow, a noted political scientist, has pointed out, evidence suggests that humans are predisposed to believe in hindsight that things could not have been very different, that events had to unfold the way they did. Other factors in the historical process that could have led to different outcomes tend to be downplayed in retrospect as one's explanation of the outcome flows backward from the outcome. This compelling backward flow makes the course of observed history seem eminently sensible.[1]

Yet, in reality, conflict in the Middle East could have produced innumerable outcomes in regional history. It is conceivable that Iraq or Iran could have ended up dominating the region. Saudi Arabia might have collapsed. Iraq and Iran might have joined hands temporarily to undermine the "Great Satan," otherwise known as the United States, before resuming their own rivalry for regional domination. Or, more likely, the United States might have remained a regional power, but one seriously weakened by conflict. Indeed, prior to the eruption of regional conflicts, the Iranian revolution and other events in the Middle East had undermined U.S. standing in the Persian Gulf and set the United States on a very dubious historical course. The trend for Washington in 1979 was clearly toward regional decline.

This book shows not only that conflicts strengthened U.S. regional security and reversed this trend, but how and why this occurred and what this finding means more generally. The third-party approach to the study of conflict, which is discussed later in this chapter, is heuristic in this regard and might be of some use in the study of conflicts in other contexts as well.

At the surface, the argument that conflicts reversed U.S. decline in the Persian Gulf region smacks of dispassion. Wars, after all, are nasty things. They are rarely preferable to peaceful inter-state interaction. However, the argument shows just how counterproductive it was for the Soviet Union, Iraq, and Iran to initiate or pursue the use of force. Had these nations chosen to deal with their security problems peacefully, they would not have triggered conflicts that would, through a number of bizarre twists and turns, strengthen their principal outside adversary, the United States.

How in particular did wars affect the regional and international politics of the Middle East? How did they alter the evolution of U.S. security in the Persian Gulf region? Why did wars in the Middle East region not undermine U.S. regional standing? We lack answers to these questions largely because they have not been asked with vigor. While much valuable work has been done on U.S. security in the Persian Gulf,[2] few analysts have examined how these wars affected U.S. regional security in the short and longer term.[3] To be sure, some books have explored the issue of whether Operations Desert Shield and Desert Storm succeeded, but many have argued that it was a failure or a "hollow victory."[4] Although there is some truth to this view, it is largely a misreading of history.

Contrary to the comments of many observers, even Iraq's menacing movement of militarized divisions toward the Kuwaiti border in October 1994 did not reflect the failure of Desert Storm. Quite the contrary, Desert Storm and the U.N. resolutions against Iraq, which followed Desert Storm, had weakened Iraq so much that such desperate acts by Iraq against Kuwait were in ways understandable. Saddam's troop movements in October did not reflect power and strength. They reflected weakness—an economy in shambles, a country isolated in the region and worldwide, and a leader whose power position was increasingly in question.

The goal of this book is not to offer a rich historical analysis of how conflict affected the politics of the Middle East from 1978 to 1993. Rather, it is to present the relevant facts necessary to showing how regional conflict, through its impact on the Middle East and on world politics, affected U.S. security and power in the Persian Gulf region.

However, by explaining how the Iranian revolution and subsequent wars affected the evolution of U.S. security in the wider scheme of Middle Eastern politics, it is possible to put contemporary regional politics in perspective. Indeed, it is difficult to understand modern Middle Eastern politics, including Iraq's aggressive military moves toward Kuwait in October 1994, without comprehending the role of conflict in the historical process. This is because key features of Middle Eastern politics, such as the distribution of regional power, the nature of inter-state relations, the foreign policies of states, the appeal of democratic and Islamic forces, the role of outside powers, and the politics of peace, are either directly or indirectly linked to war. It is in this sense that wars in the Middle Eastern region were more than just military struggles. They were critical agents of political change, which shaped key features of the regional political-security landscape.

Tracing the evolution of any feature of world politics whether it be the rise of Japanese economic power, the growing influence of the European Union, the appeal of liberal-democratic ideas, or, as in this case, U.S. security in the Persian Gulf region, raises some interesting challenges. One of them is history itself.

The effects put in motion by the Afghanistan, Iran-Iraq, and Persian Gulf (1991) wars will continue to play themselves out in the historical process. Therefore, as with the study of the evolution of any phenomenon, this book is perforce incomplete; it cannot predict the outcome of regional history *a fortiori*. However, it does provide analysis of the impact of the Iranian revolution and conflicts on U.S. security during the period from 1979 to 1993, a basic perspective for judging the impact of future regional events on U.S. security and power, and a conceptual approach to the study of conflict in general.

Examining how regional events are linked across time also raises the interesting question of when to stop attempting to determine the longer-term consequences of events. World War II, for instance, is probably linked to the

Gulf crisis in certain ways, yet few analysts would care to show how and why. Although there are no definite answers to this question, logic suggests that longer-term analyses should be terminated when our ability to establish correlations between an event and its longer-term consequences becomes increasingly tenuous. Ultimately, the analyst must identify this point, and the reader must judge whether longer-term correlations between events identified by the analyst are plausible.

In this chapter, I present the third-party framework of the book, define U.S. security in the Persian Gulf, and explain how we can examine U.S. regional security with some confidence. In addition, I provide a background review of the conflicts explored herein and discuss the book in relation to major theoretical debates in international relations. In chapter 2, I develop the book's central argument and discuss some of its broader implications.

THE THIRD-PARTY DIMENSION OF CONFLICT

In examining the evolution of U.S. regional security, the third-party framework alerts us to something often forgotten: Conflicts take place in a broader political context that shapes their evolution and is shaped by them. While it is useful to focus on the two primary antagonists in any conflict, it is also important to view conflict within its broader context. One critical type of actor in this broader context is the third party. Its welfare is often affected by conflict in the short and longer term. The impact of conflict on the third party does not end when the conflict ends. The consequences of conflict continue to play themselves out in the historical process long after conflicts end. The security, power, and standing of the third party, in turn, continue to be affected long after conflict subsides.

The term "third party" is common in the literature and in basic parlance. Lawyers, for instance, are often referred to as third parties because they are drawn into conflict between two others, even though they are not initially involved in it. However, this book conceptualizes the third party in a manner different from traditional approaches.

In the study of world politics, analysts examine the third party in two basic ways. The first way is to explore the political role of third parties as diplomatic intermediaries who contribute to conflict avoidance or resolution.[5] The United States played such a role in brokering peace between Israel and Egypt. Washington helped the two antagonists resolve a long-standing conflict by offering its diplomatic services and financial support.

In the second approach, analysts explore the political and military role of third parties during an actual conflict. How do third parties react to conflict? Do they align with one side over another or attempt to frustrate both sides? Why so? These questions are often dealt with by analysts who study balance of power and alliances in world politics.

This book, however, approaches the third party from another perspective, which has not received much attention by analysts. As lenses through which we filter reality, perspectives are critical to understanding. They help determine how we view the world, what we see as important, and how we interpret what we see as important. The present perspective is no different. It draws attention to some phenomena that otherwise might be downplayed and helps alert us to connections in the historical process that might otherwise go unnoticed. The third-party framework is composed of six different parts.

1. The first part requires that we identify a particular third party on which to focus. The framework is inapplicable if the researcher does not have one particular third-party actor in mind. Naturally, choosing this actor depends at a minimum on the analyst's research agenda and goals. But no matter what these goals are, the third party, by definition will be an actor not initially involved in conflict but one that is affected by it directly or indirectly.

2. The second part of the third-party framework involves broadening the scope of analysis. While the framework focuses on one particular third-party actor, other third parties to conflict are not ignored. Quite the contrary, understanding how one third party, such as the United States, is affected by conflict requires inquiry into how a range of third parties are affected. This is because the fortunes of any one third party are often linked to that of other third parties. Thus, if conflict strengthens Saudi Arabia, this benefits the United States because the two actors often must co-operate to protect regional security.

   The analysis is also broadened to consider how non-state actors and political and military processes are affected by conflict. Doing so enhances understanding of the long-term effects of conflict on the third party. This is important because these broader effects, such as changes in the balance of power or in the role of an international organization, can play a major role in altering the power and position of the third party. For instance, U.S. interests in the Persian Gulf are more secure when Iran and Iraq are weaker as opposed to stronger.

3. The third part of the framework emphasizes a particular objective. In contrast to the two traditional approaches to third-party analysis, much less emphasis is placed on understanding the role of the third party as an intermediary to conflict or as an ally of one of the antagonists. Rather, attention focuses on whether conflict between two actors leaves the third party weaker or stronger once the conflict is over, and how and why this occurs. In other words, the third-party framework focuses on how and why conflict affects the position, welfare, and trajectory of the third party in the historical process. It is a dynamic rather than a static conceptual framework. It seeks to understand and explain change over time, long after the conflict that initially captured the analyst's attention is over.

To be sure, the third party can come in many forms. The United States is a major, Western third party with wide-ranging global interests, significant involvement in international organizations, strong allies, a powerful military, and a developed economic and democratic system. Other third parties to potential conflict may be weaker, lack a global role, and be more vulnerable to manipulation by major powers. The nature and geopolitics of a third party will affect how it reacts to any particular conflict and how conflict affects its security in the short and long terms.

However, the third party need not be a great power to be of interest. Conflict is as likely to affect the security of weak states in the short and long terms as it is major powers. While weak states are less able and likely to intervene in conflict between others than are great powers, they are also more likely to be vulnerable to its effects. This is because their fortunes are often dictated more by events in world politics than are those of greater powers. Exceptions of course exist. In the Persian Gulf context, for example, the United States' fortunes were very much affected by the behavior of other actors. But, by and large, smaller states are more sensitive to conflict than are larger states. Their security is less assured, and they are easier targets for opportunism.

4. The first three parts of the approach focus on identifying how the third party is affected by conflict in the short and longer term. By contrast, in the fourth part of the approach, the goal is to interpret the long-term political and security implications of changes in the power and security of the third party. Did these changes make peace or war more likely? Were international institutions strengthened at the global or regional level? Was the effect on politics negligible because the third party in question was marginalized? Did the third party become hegemonic or potentially hegemonic because its adversaries were weakened by conflict? What role did the third party play in the postconflict period in ensuring regional or global security? Answers to these questions offer insight into the nature and direction of the political-security dynamics in which the third party assumes significance. And answering these questions requires that attention be given to the third party over a long period of time.

5. After identifying the impact of conflict on the third party, it is possible to ask more penetrating questions about what this means and implies. In the fifth part of the approach, the goal is to identify the policy- and theory-oriented implications of changes in the security and power of the third party. How can knowledge of the impact of conflict on the third party improve policymaking and evaluation and contribute to theory on statecraft, conflict, and world politics?

6. Finally, the third-party framework employs a particular method that helps identify and evaluate the relationship between conflict, its consequences,

and the security and welfare of the third party. This method is discussed at the end of this chapter and in the appendix. But in brief, the methodology operationalizes the strength of the security of the third party. It then uses the comparative method to compare the strength of the security of the third party before and after various events under study. In this book, these events are the Iranian revolution and wars in and near the Middle Eastern region. The methodology illuminates how conflict affected the third party in the short and longer run.

Sometimes it is easy to see how conflict has affected the third party. For instance, Syria benefited significantly from Iraq's invasion of Kuwait. Iraq, Syria's arch rival in the Arab world, was weakened, and Syria's image in the West improved thanks to its participation in the U.S.-led alliance against Saddam Hussein. In addition, Syria's participation also resulted in a handsome payment from the Saudis to the tune of $2 billion with which Syria went on a shopping spree for arms.

At other times, however, the impact of conflict on the third party is less clear and must be determined through a closer look at the short- and long-term effects of conflict. This is necessary because numerous interrelated political, military, and economic developments affect the power and security of the third party in the short and long terms. Identifying and interpreting these developments is a challenging task.

The manner by which conflict affects the third party can have great significance. In certain cases, third-party states rise in influence not because they achieve economic greatness or have a particularly astute foreign policy, but rather because conflicts between others thrust them into a position of greater responsibility and power. Thus, in the case of the Peloponnesian War, the conflict between Sparta and Athens made it possible for Macedonia to triumph over the Greeks.[6]

In this book, the United States represents the third party to conflicts between the Soviet Union and Afghanistan, Iran and Iraq, and Iraq and Kuwait. In each case, the United States was not initially involved in the conflicts but was greatly affected by them. In part, this is because the United States eventually became directly or indirectly involved, but also because these wars elevated the United States to a position of greater regional influence. Indeed, one of the more significant features of the history of the Persian Gulf in the last decade has been the substantial rise of U.S. power and standing.

While one can choose to focus on the United States in the conflictual Middle Eastern context, the third-party framework is of more general importance. As E. E. Schattschneider noted, the universal language of conflict lies at the root of all politics.[7] Conflicts, be they economic, political, or military in nature almost always affect the welfare and strength of third parties because many states, as David Singer, a distinguished professor of international relations, remarks, share "the same spatial, temporal, and socio-political environment."[8] States are much more likely to play the role of third party to a conflict than to be central actors in it. In this sense, their foreign and domestic successes and failures become as much a function of their own actions as of the foreign policy behavior of other actors, particularly if they are weaker actors. By creating conflicts, other actors initiate processes that the third party cannot easily control but that nonetheless often affect it significantly over time.

The impact of conflict on the third party can fundamentally change the interaction in and even the nature of the context itself. This is because the third party does not act in isolation. Rather, it plays an important role in the political-security context of which it is a part. If the third party is weakened or strengthened over time, this has broader implications. It can define how active and vital a role the third party plays in the post-conflict period. In this sense, the third-party framework is not just about the third party. It is about the entire context in which the third party plays a role.

If the third party under question is a major global actor such as the United States, then studying how conflict affects it is also likely to provide insight into broader contexts and issue areas. By affecting an important third party, conflict also affects the contexts and issue areas in which the third party is involved. Therefore, examining the third party can also illumine issues such as nationalism, transnationalism, international regimes in which the third party plays a role, arms races, the balance of power, the nature of relations between key global actors, the economic power and interaction of states, and the stability of governments. Hence, when we observe changes in any of these contexts or issue areas, we might attribute it to the altered role, security, and power of a key third party. Desert Storm is a case in point. As shown in chapter 5, previous conflicts in the Middle East altered the power and security of the United States in the 1980s and prepared it to check Saddam in 1990.

Awareness of the long-term impact of conflict on the third party also can help in decreasing misunderstanding in world politics. Thus, we might argue that Athens's attempt to improve its security by doing such things as imposing its will on smaller actors like Megara and Potidaea decreased the security of Sparta and pushed it over time toward war with Athens. Athens not only failed to foresee that its actions would seriously decrease the security of Sparta as the third party, but also failed to realize that this occurred after the fact.[9] In part, this is because Athens was so fixated on Megara and Potidaea. Had Athens been more attuned to how its actions against Megara and Potidaea were producing longer-term effects that threatened Sparta as the third party, it might have taken more effective steps to avoid war with Sparta. But this would have required a different perspective toward conflict, one based on an expanded scope of analysis.

Although the third-party question is relevant in any political context and time period, the rising complexity of world politics makes it increasingly more important. This is because in a more interconnected world in which the interests of diverse actors are linked, conflicts between two actors are more likely to have major effects on a third party. It is harder for any third party to be isolated from the effects of conflict between others.

Imagine, for instance, an Iraqi invasion of Kuwait in the eighteenth, nineteenth, or early twentieth century. The impact of the invasion on the United States would have been minimal in the eighteenth and nineteenth centuries and marginally significant in the early twentieth. By 1990, however, the Persian Gulf had become linked fundamentally to security in the broader Middle East and to world economic growth. As a result, the invasion not only challenged U.S. interests directly, but also those of numerous actors on which the United States depended economically such as the European Union, Japan, and third-world debtors. It was, therefore, inescapable that the United States even in its third-party role would be greatly affected by the invasion.

Despite the importance of the third-party question in modern world politics, remarkably little attention is devoted to it. When conflicts erupt in world politics, we usually ask questions such as these: Why are these actors in a conflict? Who is right or has the moral edge? Which side will win? And, *a posteriori*, who did win or did they both really lose? Our attention is often so riveted on the two principal actors in the conflict that we sometimes lose sight of the fact that conflicts take place in a larger setting where the interests of third parties are greatly affected in the short and longer term.

The third-party question is underexplored in political analysis chiefly for three reasons. First, analysts focus substantially more on the causes of conflict than on its effects. The lion's share of attention in the study of conflict is devoted to establishing a link between some independent variable such as regime type, arms races, balance of power or hegemonic decline on the one hand and conflict on the other. Scant attention is paid to examining and explaining the outcomes or results of conflict, let alone how conflicts produced by various foreign policy actions affect the foreign and domestic interests of third parties.

Second, as suggested at the outset, the third-party question does not fit into the traditional analysis of third parties as diplomatic intermediaries who contribute to conflict avoidance or resolution, or as actors that respond to conflict through alliances or balance-of-power policies. Indeed, in contrast to these two predominant approaches, the third-party framework examines how conflict affects the power of the third party in the short and long terms.

Third, when the third party is invoked in theory, it is usually more to explain why war occurred or how actors responded to war than to explain how war affected the power of the third party in the short or longer term. For instance, as suggested earlier in the chapter, the most prominent approach in which the third party is featured is balance-of-power theory. This theory explains how the use of force might affect the interests of the actor that initiates it. It predicts in particular that aggressors will suffer losses because actors in world politics are more likely to align together to prevent any one state from achieving dominance or hegemony than to support major aggressors. But, while balance-of-power theory demonstrates how third parties can be expected to react if one state becomes too powerful, it tells us little about whether the third party will be strengthened or weakened by conflict. Indeed, some third parties might emerge strengthened by balancing action, while others might emerge weaker.

MIDDLE EAST CONFLICT IN REVIEW

The Middle East is an appropriate case study for the application of the third-party perspective. It has probably seen more conflict in the second half of the twentieth century than any other region in the world. These conflicts have resulted from a number of factors, such as bitter historical rivalries, hegemonic ambitions, dictatorial leadership, ethnic and religious divisions, ill-defined territorial boundaries, and the politics of oil.

Regional conflicts have generated significant change in the Middle East, particularly in regard to U.S. interests. The Iranian revolution and the subsequent fall of the Shah of Iran, which is conveniently associated with his departure from Iran in January 1979, jeopardized U.S. regional security. The December 1979 Afghanistan intervention appeared to add an even more ominous threat to Gulf security, a threat that was compounded eight months later by the outbreak of the Iran-Iraq war.

Iraq's brutal invasion of oil-rich Kuwait in August 1990 was the culmination of a tortuous decade in the region. As is well known, Iraq used massive military force to invade Kuwait. The invasion had two major implications for U.S. regional interests. First, it suggested that if left unopposed, Iraq might use the example of Kuwait to intimidate other oil-rich Gulf states into supporting its inflated foreign policy agenda. Second, and even more ominously, it created the possibility that Iraq would not stop in Kuwait, but would also invade neighboring Saudi Arabia and gain direct or indirect control over more than half the world's oil resources. Indeed, the United States and Saudi Arabia considered seriously such a scenario, particularly a strong Iraqi push down the Saudi coast road that runs through Al-Mish'ab, Al-Jubayl, and Ad-Dammam toward Saudi port areas and coastal facilities.[10]

Against this backdrop, the United States decided to deploy massive forces and equipment to the Gulf, spearhead a multinational military alliance to defend Saudi Arabia, and organize a number of U.N. resolutions. The most consequential resolution provided for the removal of Iraq from Kuwait by use of military force. Ultimately, Iraq's refusal to withdraw from Kuwait after more than five months of occupation motivated the U.S.-led alliance to use military means. In the process, Iraq was forced to leave Kuwait in one of the biggest military defeats in strategic history. Its military capability was reduced substantially, its country was devastated, and its regime faced an unprecedented challenge to its rule.

The Kuwait invasion had a major impact on U.S. regional security and set numerous historical precedents. For the first time, one Arab state forcibly annexed another one, an economic embargo of substantial magnitude was enforced, and the Arab League was seriously divided over the offensive actions of one of its members. It was also the first time that U.S. forces were used en masse against an Arab state, that the Saudis allowed a massive U.S. presence on their land, and that military forces of several Arab states confronted a brother Arab state. Furthermore, it was the first time that the Soviet Union co-operated with the United States against a former regional ally and that the United Nations provisioned the use of military force by individual states against another sovereign state, the case of Korea perhaps notwithstanding.

The Kuwait invasion, however, was just one of a string of major conflicts that had affected U.S. regional security between 1978 and 1993. The 1978–79 Iranian revolution, the Afghanistan intervention, and the Iran-Iraq war were also highly significant and must be understood in order to put contemporary regional politics in perspective. While it is clear that the Iranian revolution undermined U.S. regional security, it is important to know how and why this occurred so as to understand the role of the revolution in the broader sweep of regional history and to distinguish more effectively the effects of the revolution from those of overlapping developments.

Prior to the revolution, the United States counted on Iran to help it maintain regional stability. After the revolution, however, Iran became the primary threat to U.S. regional security. At a general level, the United States and most Gulf states feared that Iran's revolutionary fervor might spread throughout the Gulf and undermine moderate Arab Gulf states.

The Iran-Iraq war, which began the year after the Iranian revolution, also affected U.S. security in numerous ways. The war threatened at times to leave Iran or Iraq in a dominant position in the Persian Gulf. By creating political instability and by increasing the importance of Moscow's role in attempting to resolve the conflict, the war also gave the Soviet Union a chance to increase its regional influence. In addition, it put in motion numerous political, economic, and military developments that would have an enduring effect on regional dynamics.

While it is clear that the Iran-Iraq war had a great effect on regional politics, what is perhaps less clear is how the Afghanistan intervention affected U.S. regional security. A brief look into history can serve us here. Long before the United States gained superpower status, Britain and tsarist Russia had vied for influence in Asia in the nineteenth century in what Rudyard Kipling famously dubbed the "Great Game." In the post-Napoleonic era, the British feared that tsarist armies, which had already overrun central Asia, would use Afghanistan to threaten Persia and Britain's lifeline to its primary overseas possession, India. For its part, Russia was concerned primarily with British expansion in Afghanistan and in other parts of Asia.[11]

With time, the "Great Game" evolved. The Soviet Union assumed tsarist Russia's role as the counterweight to perceived Western ambitions, and the United States replaced Britain in a trend that began in 1947 and culminated in full British withdrawal from the Gulf in 1971. After British withdrawal, the United States became more concerned with and responsible for the security of the Gulf.

The Afghanistan invasion translated this concern into near panic[12] and spearheaded another round of jockeying in the great game of global rivalry in Asia. The Soviet Union might well have invaded Afghanistan only to ensure the stability and the pro-Soviet orientation of the Marxist Afghan government that it had propped up by coup in 1978. However, at the same time, the invasion brought Soviet troops about 320 miles closer to the Gulf and placed them on Pakistan's doorstep. This generated fear in the United States, Pakistan, China, and, to a lesser extent, in the Persian Gulf that the Soviet Union's ambitions stretched beyond Afghanistan to Pakistan, Iran, and the Gulf. Like nineteenth-century Britain in its rivalry with tsarist Russia, the United States tended to assume the worst in Soviet intentions.

The Iranian revolution, Afghanistan intervention, and Iran-Iraq war produced consequences that shook regional security at its foundations. The invasion of Kuwait in 1990 came at the end of a war-torn decade and set in motion major consequences for the Persian Gulf, the Middle East, and world politics. The U.S. response to the invasion represented one of its more important foreign policy actions in the twentieth century. Had the United States not spearheaded Operations Desert Shield and Storm, it is highly unlikely that they would have been mounted. Both these operations had an enormous impact on the domestic, regional, and international politics of the Middle East and on the United States.

EXAMINING THE POWER OF THE THIRD PARTY

While the third-party approach is useful for deriving insights about politics, the following question arises: Can we really know how conflict affects the third party? A systematic approach to this question underlies this book's examination of Middle Eastern conflict and U.S. regional security.

Owing to the strategic importance of the Persian Gulf, and given the controversial nature of the politics of oil, defining U.S. security in the Persian Gulf could occupy volumes. In this book, I define U.S. regional security as the U.S. ability to meet its three basic, officially stated objectives in the Persian Gulf region during the period under examination here, 1978 to 1993. These three objectives were to ensure the unimpeded flow of oil to the United States and its Western allies at reasonable prices, to ensure the stability of pro-U.S. Gulf states, and to limit anti-U.S. influences.[13] The greater is the United States' ability to meet these goals, the more secure is its position.

To measure indirectly the strength of U.S. security, six variables are examined. When considered together, they present an accurate picture of the overall strength of U.S. regional security. Hence, they offer a reasonable guide in the effort to understand how the United States, as a third party, was affected by conflict in the short and long term. While these variables are useful in the Middle Eastern context, other variables will help operationalize the strength and power of third parties in other contexts. But the logic of the method will be the same. Establish variables to examine the security and power of the third party and then trace them through time as a function of conflict.

For the sake of brevity, variables of U.S. security in the Persian Gulf region and their subindicators are not examined explicitly in the text, but rather implicitly. The relevance and nature of the indicators are elaborated on in the

Appendix. The following discussion, however, should suffice for a basic understanding of the approach.

The first variable used in this book is the *level of Saudi domestic stability*. Conflicts can increase, decrease, or fail to affect the domestic stability of states. Since Saudi Arabia has been the linchpin of U.S. regional security, its domestic stability is vital to U.S. security. The stability of other regional states (such as Iran, Iraq, or Qatar) is far less important because they either challenged U.S. regional security or were not in a position to affect it greatly. The more stable Saudi Arabia is, the more secure are U.S. regional interests.

The second variable is *U.S. military capability for Persian Gulf contingencies*. Conflicts can enhance, damage, or fail to affect the military capability of states. U.S. ability to protect its three main goals in the Persian Gulf region is related to the effectiveness of U.S. military capability for Middle Eastern contingencies. The more effective U.S. capability is, the more secure are U.S. regional interests. Thus, if Washington cannot deploy its forces to the region in a timely and effective manner, this weakens its regional security or, in other words, the U.S. ability to protect its three principal objectives in the Persian Gulf region.

The strength of U.S. relations with key regional states is the third variable. The nature of U.S. relations with regional states is critical to U.S. security. U.S. regional interests are more secure when its relations with regional states such as Saudi Arabia, Bahrain, and Oman are stronger. These states can offer the United States facilities that make operations such as Desert Shield and Storm possible.

The fourth variable is the *strength of Soviet relations with key states in the Middle East*. While Russia is less relevant in the Middle Eastern context in the post-Soviet era, Moscow played a key role in affecting U.S. regional security from 1978 to 1989. Thus, it is impossible to understand U.S. security without understanding the regional role of the Soviet Union. U.S. security was weaker when Soviet relations with regional states were stronger. This is due to Soviet efforts to challenge U.S. regional influence in part by jockeying for political influence over U.S. allies and adversaries.

The fifth variable of U.S. regional security is the *strength of relations between pro-U.S. Arab Gulf states*. Conflict seriously affected relations among the eight Gulf states. U.S. security was served better by stronger relations among six of these states: Saudi Arabia, Qatar, Oman, Kuwait, the United Arab Emirates, and Bahrain. Strong relations between these states decreased the likelihood that they could be manipulated by Iran, Iraq, or Moscow and increased the probability that they could protect themselves from internal and external threats.

The final variable is the *regional balance of power*. Based on balance-of-power logic, the more closely balanced are regional superpowers Iran and Iraq, the less likely either state is to dominate the Persian Gulf either politically or militarily. A key point is that it is better for such a balance to exist at lower levels of capability on each side than at higher levels because then the relative military capability of more moderate states such as Saudi Arabia will be higher. The more balanced are Iraq and Iran, the more secure is U.S. security. This suggests, of course, that U.S. security is strongest when both Iran and Iraq are weak and balanced (*ceteris paribus*).

This study examines implicitly how these variables changed over time by comparing them before and after the Iranian revolution, the Afghanistan intervention, the Iran-Iraq war, and the 1990–91 Gulf crisis. By examining these variables, we can then see how U.S. security was affected by revolution and conflict.

THEORETICAL DEBATES IN INTERNATIONAL RELATIONS

In an effort to locate where this book falls on the broader intellectual landscape of the study of world politics, it is worthwhile discussing briefly international relations theory. Theory is often vital for how we understand the world. As Robert Jervis has pointed out,[14] our choices about what to study and how to interpret events is inevitably related to our *a priori* theoretical assumptions about the way the world works. Theory guides our perceptions of reality and thus affects how we choose to deal with it.

In the study of international politics, two basic theoretical constructs have vied for influence, which are often referred to as realism and liberalism.[15] Although the two schools share some beliefs about the nature of international relations, they differ in important ways.

While realists assume that states are the most important actors in world politics, those of the opposing school also place much emphasis on international organizations and non-state actors, such as multinational corporations, the United Nations, the European Union, and domestic-level actors such as bureaucracies and non-governmental elites. Thus, for instance, in examining a trade war, realists would focus on the power conflict between state actors, while liberalists might in addition examine such things as the role of the International Monetary Fund, domestic interest groups, and transnational businesses.

While the realists assume that military security imperatives dominate the foreign policy agenda of states, their detractors assume no particular hierarchy of issues. Rather, they argue that governments have become increasingly more concerned with numerous issues such as the environment, international political economy, and international health. Most realists accept that these issues are important, but by and large, they argue that a theory of international relations must focus on what is really critical in world politics and cannot consider too many variables as important. For realists, a theory that incorporates too many variables would resemble description more than theory.

Whereas the realist model assumes that the use of force is the critical instrument of foreign policy, the competing model downplays it relative to other tools. It assumes that the role of force in international politics has declined primarily because force cannot accomplish critical goals, such as economic advancement, goals that have become increasingly more important.

While both theoretical schools recognize that international relations takes place under anarchy, or in the absence of a government above states, realists tend to be more skeptical about the chances for inter-state co-operation under anarchy than their detractors. In part, this is because realist thinkers, from Thucydides to Hans Morgenthau and Robert Gilpin have held that the struggle for power as a means or as an end is an unchanging feature of world politics.[16] Realists are not particularly sanguine about the prospects of evolutionary learning in world politics. They dismiss the view that through learning from the past, states will slowly move away from war, the use of force, power seeking, and other modes of inter-state interaction. Rather, they see world politics as cyclical.

In recent times, realism has been adapted into something called neorealism. Neorealists are sometimes referred to as structural realists because they adopt the precepts of realism with the added assumption that state action is shaped by the larger system, an anarchic, self-help system in which the distribution of power capabilities is the crucial determinant of state behavior.[17] This last point is central in neorealism. Under anarchy, the distribution of power at the systemic level can explain state behavior in a simple and effective manner. If one knows where power lies in international relations, one can explain and predict important key developments in world politics.

Neorealists tend to ignore, or abstract from, domestic-level features of international relations such as the preferences of leaders or the nature of domestic politics. While they do realize that these variables affect state behavior, they ignore them in order to distinguish between domestic- and system-level variables, thus enabling the development of a theory of international politics. For a neorealist, the real stuff of world politics occurs at the system level, between influential state units that seek security and power in a dangerous world in which conflict is always possible and the resort to force the ultimate arbiter. If one wants a parsimonious and explanatory theory of international relations, the system level is where to look, according to neorealists.

Intellectual debates on matters of theory sometimes leave little room for compromise, but this need not be the case regarding whether realism/neorealism or liberalism makes more sense as a guide in the study of international relations. The relative usefulness of these models has much to do with the issue and context in question. When the issue is the evolution of U.S. security and the context is the Persian Gulf, then an approach anchored in the realist tradition makes more sense. If the question were about the evolution of the European Union and the context were Western Europe, then the liberal model would probably be a better guide to reality. While theory ideally should not by definition be region specific, the great variety of world politics across regions and time makes region-specific theories sensible. This does not mean that a grand theory of international relations, which explains and predicts phenomena across regions, is not possible. Rather, it suggests that some theories apply better in one region than another.

In the tradition of liberalism, this book pays heed to the impact of interdependence, to the complexity of world politics, and also to the importance that domestic-level factors such as the stability of Saudi Arabia play in U.S. regional security. But, on the whole, the book attempts to explain how conflict affected U.S. power and regional security primarily through an approach driven by the assumptions of realism.

PLAN OF THE BOOK

Chapter 2 develops the main argument of the book and presents some general insights derived from the third-party approach. Chapters 3 through 6 present case studies of the Iranian revolution, the Afghanistan intervention, the Iran-Iraq war, and the Gulf crisis (1990–91). Each case study identifies the principal regional and international implications of these four events and interprets what they mean for U.S. regional security and power. These four events were selected because they all produced dramatic effects on the political-security fabric of the Middle East-Persian Gulf region. Since they occurred in a similar temporal and geographic context and since they were connected, it is important to consider them together. This helps in understanding each of these events and their interrelationships.

Chapter 7 explains why and how regional conflict prevented Iran, Iraq, and the Soviet Union from seizing opportunities to advance their interests at U.S. expense. Conflict constrained these actors at a time when the United States was highly vulnerable, thereby giving the United States time to shore up its regional security before its adversaries could make serious political and military inroads.

The conclusion offers a brief summary of this book's findings, elaborates on the major implications of the book, and discusses the advantages of third-party status in general and, more specifically, with regard to the U.S. role in the Persian Gulf. The idea of the third-party actor is developed in theory and practice.

NOTES

1. Richard Ned Lebow, *Between Peace and War: The Nature of International Crisis* (Baltimore, MD: Johns Hopkins University Press, 1981), 2–3.

2. Notable books include Anthony H. Cordesman, *The Gulf and the Search for Strategic Stability: Saudi Arabia, the Military Balance in the Gulf, and Trends in the Arab-Israeli Military Balance* (Boulder, CO: Westview Press, 1984); Thomas McNaugher, *Arms and Oil: U.S. Military Strategy and the Persian Gulf* (Washington, D.C.: Brookings Institution, 1985); Shahram Chubin and Charles Tripp, *Iran and Iraq at War* (London: I. B. Tauris and Co., Ltd., 1988); and Lawrence Freedman and Efraim Karsh, *The Gulf Conflict 1990–1991: Diplomacy and War in the New World Order* (Princeton, NJ: Princeton University Press, 1993).

3. In probably the most comprehensive analysis of the consequences of the Iran-Iraq war to date, only one of the seventeen contributors, Thomas McNaugher, discusses in any

detail the war's effect on U.S. regional interests, and his analysis is not intended to be comprehensive. See McNaugher in *The Iran-Iraq War: Impact and Implications*, ed. Efraim Karsh (Tel Aviv: The Jaffe Center for Strategic Studies, 1989).

4. See, for instance, Jeffrey Record, *Hollow Victory: A Contrary View of the Gulf War* (Washington, D.C.: Brassey's, 1993); Mohamed Heikal, *Illusions of Triumph: An Arab View of the Gulf War* (London: Harper Collins, 1992); and U.S. News and World Report, *Triumph Without Victory: The Unreported History of the Persian Gulf War* (New York: Random House, 1992). Also, see John O'Loughlin, Tom Mayer, and Edward S. Greenberg, *War and Its Consequences: Lessons from the Persian Gulf Conflict* (New York: Harper Collins, 1994).

5. See Saadia Touval and I. William Zartman, eds., *International Mediation in Theory and Practice* (Boulder, CO: Westview Press, 1985).

6. Robert Gilpin, "The Theory of Hegemonic War," in *The Origin and Prevention of Major Wars*, ed. Robert I. Rotberg and Theodore K. Rabb (Cambridge: Cambridge University Press, 1989), 26.

7. E. E. Schattschneider, *The Semi-Sovereign People: A Realist's View of Democracy in America* (Hinsdale, IL: The Dryden Press, 1975), 2.

8. David J. Singer, "Inter-Nation Influence: A Formal Model," *American Political Science Review* 57 (1963): 421.

9. See Donald Kagan, *The Outbreak of the Peloponnesian War* (Ithaca, NY: Cornell University Press, 1969), 278, 281–82, 279–85, 288.

10. For details on such scenarios, see U.S. Department of Defense, *Conduct of the Persian Gulf War: Final Report to Congress* (Washington, D.C.: Government Printing Office [GPO], April 1992), 31–32 (hereafter referred to as U.S. DoD, *Conduct of the Persian Gulf War*).

11. On the great game, see George N. Curzon, *Russia in Central Asia in 1889, and the Anglo-Russian Question* (London: Frank Cass and Co., Ltd., 1967).

12. President Carter even considered using nuclear weapons to stop a potential invasion of the Gulf. See "Soviet Buildup Near Iran Tested Carter," *New York Times*, 27 August 1986, A3.

13. This book adopts the United States' official position on U.S. regional interests, a position which is plausible. These three interests were stated time and again. See, for example, Harold Brown, "Protecting U.S. Interests in the Persian Gulf Region," *Department of State Bulletin* (DSB) 80 (May 1980): 63; DSB 81 (June 1981): 43; DSB 85 (May 1985): 25; DSB 87 (July 1987): 64. Also, see U.S. Senate, General H. Norman Schwarzkopf, Commander of U.S. Central Command, "Witness Statement Before the Senate Armed Services Committee" (hereafter referred to as Schwarzkopf statement), 8 February 1990.

14. Robert Jervis, *Perception and Misperception in International Politics* (Princeton, NJ: Princeton University Press, 1976), especially chap. 5.

15. For a seminal discussion of complex interdependence, see Robert O. Keohane and Joseph S. Nye, *Power and Interdependence: World Politics in Transition* (Boston: Little, Brown, 1977). For the contemporary debate in international relations theory, see David A. Baldwin, ed., *Neorealism and Neoliberalism: The Contemporary Debate* (New York: Columbia University Press, 1993).

16. Sir Richard Livingstone, ed., *Thucydides* (London: Oxford University Press, 1982); Robert Gilpin, *War and Change in World Politics* (New York: Cambridge University Press, 1981). Waltz differs here in arguing that the ultimate concern of states

is not for power but for security. For the most recent statement, see Kenneth N. Waltz, "Realist Thought and Neorealist Theory," *Journal of International Affairs* 44 (Spring 1990): 36.

17. This approach is associated with Kenneth N. Waltz, *Theory of International Politics* (Reading, MA: Addison-Wesley, 1979). Gilpin has also applied it in combination with economic theory in *War and Change in World Politics*. For an authoritative account of how neorealism differs from realism, see Waltz, "Realist Thought," 21–37.

2

STATECRAFT, HISTORY, AND
THE THIRD PARTY

The primary goal of this book is to show how the Iranian revolution, and subsequent wars, affected the trajectory of U.S. security in a region that is critical to international security and to the functioning of the entire world economy. In this sense, the analysis in this book is useful in and of itself. The present work, however, is not solely devoted to understanding and analyzing the impact of revolution and war on U.S. regional standing. It also illustrates and applies an innovative approach to the study of conflict, deriving from this approach more general implications for policy and history. This chapter introduces these implications and, in the process, develops the principal argument of the book. These implications and others are elaborated on in the final chapter.

THE PRACTICE OF THE USE OF FORCE

The first implication concerns force in world politics. In comprehensively examining cases of the use of force in world politics, analysts have discovered repeatedly that force works; initiators of the use of force in world politics usually win their conflicts.[1] Their work suggests that states weigh the costs and benefits of the use of force and initiate it when the expected benefits exceed the expected costs. In other words, states are adept at anticipating the consequences of the use of force and, thus, are successful because they know when to use it.

This study, by contrast, presents cases where the actors using force met with entirely unexpected consequences. The least obvious, but one of the most important, was the rise of the third party or, in this case, of U.S. regional power.

The use of military force by the Soviet Union in Afghanistan, by Iran and Iraq during the Iran-Iraq war, and by Iraq in Kuwait in August 1990 was not intended specifically to undermine U.S. regional security. This was, however, a basic foreign policy aim of all three states for much of the period from 1978 to 1991. Indeed, this foreign policy aim significantly influenced Iran's post-revolutionary behavior. It also held sway in Baghdad even in the period when the United States tilted toward Iraq in its war effort against Iran. The goal of undermining the United States certainly was a basic feature of Soviet foreign policy, particularly prior to the end of the Cold War. In basic terms, each of these states wanted to weaken U.S. regional security.

The fact that war produced effects that enhanced U.S. regional power underscores how costly it was for the Soviet Union, Iraq, and Iran to pursue conflict in lieu of pacific means of protecting or advancing their national security. In the broader context, the conflicts these nations generated did precisely the opposite of what they might have expected or wanted: Conflicts strengthened in the long term the one actor that they all wished to weaken—the United States.

Conflicts pushed the United States to strengthen its relations with regional states, enhance its military capability for regional contingencies, and push for access to key regional facilities. Conflicts also produced effects that bolstered the position of generally pro-U.S. states such as Saudi Arabia and Egypt, enhanced transatlantic co-operation in the protection of regional security, and contributed to an improvement of relations between pro-U.S. regional actors.

Meanwhile, conflict weakened Iran, Iraq, and the Soviet Union, and decreased their ability to seize political and strategic opportunities at a time of unprecedented U.S. vulnerability. Conflicts also created consequences that allowed the United States to develop its regional security framework before its adversaries could make serious political, and perhaps military, inroads.

The consequences discussed above, and others like them that are examined in the following chapters, enabled the United States to deal more effectively with Iran, Iraq, and the Soviet Union during conflict, and also left the United States relatively stronger in the postwar period. That the United States and some of its allies had been strengthened by the pressures of conflict was an outcome that came back to haunt not only Iran during the latter period of the Iran-Iraq war but, more importantly, Iraq after its invasion of Kuwait.

Indeed, Iraq's use of force against Iran, which triggered the eight-year Iran-Iraq war, resulted in some obvious costs for Iraq. The war, for instance, took a brutal human and economic toll on Iraq. But one major cost to Iraq of its attack on Iran was not recognized. The ensuing war produced consequences that prepared the U.S.-led coalition to contain and reverse Iraq's invasion of Kuwait in 1990–91 and contributed to Iraq's demise. Iraq's debacle against U.S.-led forces in 1990–91, thus, should be viewed as perhaps the greatest cost for Iraq of its invasion of Iran in 1980. Indeed, Iraq's invasion of Iran and the war it produced are linked here to the serious diminution of Iraqi power in 1990–91.

Had Iraq never invaded Kuwait, some observers might have argued that Iraq's 1980 attack on Iran produced some benefits for Iraq and should not be viewed as a failure. They might have pointed to the fact that Iraq's attack on Iran impeded Iran's efforts to spread its revolution throughout the Gulf, enhanced Iraq's image in the Arab world, and helped Saddam build a major military capability, thereby offering him the means for subtle forms of influence building. This argument, however, is undermined if one links Iraq's attack on Iran and the ensuing Iran-Iraq war to Iraq's demise in 1990–91 at the hands of U.S.-led forces.

CAUSES, PATHWAYS, AND OUTCOMES

The second implication deals with the broader issue of causal analysis. That Iraq's invasion of Kuwait was contained and reversed makes it seem as if no other outcome could have resulted in the historical process. This is hardly the case. Under different historical circumstances, the world might have responded to Iraq's invasion by adopting a policy that leaned more toward accommodating Saddam than opposing him. Thus, Saddam might have withdrawn from most or all of Kuwait in exchange for political or territorial concessions.

Or, in another scenario, the United States might not have had the regional military capability and support to mount Operation Desert Storm or might have failed to muster international support, thus leaving Iraq in Kuwait for a much longer period of time. The continuation of economic sanctions against Iraq in lieu of the use of allied force might have created the potential for a peaceful withdrawal from Kuwait by Iraq or the basis for the eventual disintegration of the U.S.-led alliance against Iraq.

These alternate scenarios, which probably would have produced a different regional outcome, were not unlikely. It is not as if the entire history of the region would have had to have been different to produce a different outcome in 1990–91. It might have been enough, for instance, for the domestic forces in Saudi Arabia pushing for accommodation of Saddam to have had more influence than those pushing for a hard line against him. Numerous prior events could have created the conditions under which such domestic pressure would have prevailed.

The potential for different outcomes in history raises the interesting question of how we can explain particular outcomes. Why do certain outcomes occur and not others? What factors drive history down one path as opposed to another? These questions are not merely academic. They have significant policy and perhaps theoretical implications because they alert us to the link between observed outcomes and the events that precede them.

The term "outcome" can refer to many things in world politics. Almost any event can be called an outcome of something else. We might even refer to the outbreak of a conflict as an outcome. Here, however, the term "outcome" is used more strictly to refer to the consequence of conflict for the actors involved in it or affected by it. This is more than semantics. It emphasizes that one of the book's primary goals is to explain the results rather than the causes of conflict. Or, in other words, to deal with this question: What causes conflict outcomes?

At one level, we can conceptualize conflict outcomes as the result of two types of basic causes: proximate and antecedent. While some readers are probably familiar with these concepts, we can say that proximate causes are not removed in time from the conflict. Thus, for instance, we might explain Britain's defeat of Argentina in the Falklands war by observing that Britain had superior military capability. By contrast, an antecedent cause can be viewed as one which is put in motion well before the beginning of the development that it affects. Hence, at the extreme, we might argue that conciliatory U.S. foreign policy toward Japan after World War II could help explain Japan's international economic competitiveness today.

Analysts have debated the relative importance of the proximate and antecedent causes of war. They have argued over whether long-term causes of war are more important than the actual events that trigger war. But they have done little to argue the relative merits of the proximate versus antecedent causes of the outcomes of conflict. In particular, they have tended to neglect how events that occur long before a conflict begins can shape its outcome.

Chapter 4 shows how the effects of the Iran-Iraq war, such as the strengthening of U.S. military capability, the improvement of U.S.-Saudi relations, and the development of regional facilities for U.S. rapid deployment forces, became the antecedent causes of the U.S.-led successful containment and reversal of Iraq's August 1990 invasion of Kuwait. These Iran-Iraq war effects became the political-security foundation for Operations Desert Shield and Storm and enhanced its likelihood for success. Had the Iran-Iraq war not taken place and had Iraq invaded Kuwait in 1990, possible scenario given the nature of Iraqi-Kuwait relations and of regional politics, the U.S.-led coalition could not have counted on this critical political-security foundation against Saddam. Thus, it is quite reasonable to believe that the United States would have had much greater trouble dealing with Saddam.

POLICY EVALUATION AND THE THIRD PARTY

While the first implication dealt with the use of force, the third implication concerns evaluating when the use of force succeeds or fails. As observed earlier in this chapter, analysts have discovered repeatedly that force works—states that initiate the use of force have a disproportionately high chance of meeting their objectives. While interesting and valuable, this finding, however, has much to do with the definition of successful force. The use of force is generally viewed as successful if its user accomplishes short-term goals against its target.[2] But this definition does not account for the long-term effects of force. This is problematic because short-term outcomes are sometimes transformed over time.[3] That is, the success of an action might pale over time due to long-term effects.

Nor does the conventional approach account for the unintended effects of statecraft. This is problematic because the unintended effects of the use of force are seldom beneficial and can often be quite costly to the user of force. Ignoring them does not cause their negative effects to disappear for the foreign policy actor. Understanding them, however, can yield insights into the impact of the use of force. The implication then is that it would be useful to consider the long-term, unintended implications of the use of force (or of other instruments of foreign policy) before proclaiming it a success.

POLICYMAKING AND THE THIRD-PARTY PERSPECTIVE

While policy evaluation is important in the effort to determine the success of statecraft, leaders also want to know whether or not force should be used in the first place in lieu of other instruments of statecraft. Indeed, leaders often have to choose which of several foreign policy instruments to use in any given conflictual situation.

As suggested in the foregoing discussion, one major cost of the use of force can be the strengthening of a third-party competitor. Actors that use force certainly do not intend to produce this outcome. The fourth implication is to alert policymakers to the importance of considering how statecraft against a particular target will affect third-party competitors. For instance, if a third-party competitor is expected to gain from the use of force, actors might choose to pursue another form of statecraft in order to meet their goals. In other instances, such expectations might be irrelevant in affecting decision making either because the actors might believe that they have no choice but to use force, or that the payoffs of using force will far exceed the costs. In any case, focusing more attention on the third party is likely to provide leaders with a more complete assessment of the implications of their statecraft.

The fifth implication has to do with how the third party to conflict formulates policy. Should it intervene in the conflict or remain neutral? Is it sensible to use force or economic sanctions against one of the parties to conflict? Are diplomatic sanctions preferable to a policy of disengagement? Such questions will probably gain in importance in the postwar world as the nature of conflict moves from the global to the regional arena.

Answers to these questions depend on a number of factors. They are, however, related to the third party's expectations of how the conflict will affect national and international welfare. Before expending national treasure and risking lives, the third party must have some idea of whether the benefits of intervention will exceed the costs. If it believes that remaining neutral will cause it to emerge from the conflict a weakened actor, then the third party will be more inclined to intervene in order to bring about a more desirable outcome. If, by contrast, the third party believes that it will emerge from conflict a strengthened actor if it does not intervene, then it will be less likely to choose direct, costly, and potentially counterproductive intervention. But in order to choose the right course of action, the third party must ask how conflict affects its interests and conjecture as to whether it will emerge from conflict stronger or weaker.

Such a guess is very hard to make. No formula can predict whether the third party will emerge weaker or stronger from conflict or whether the actor that uses force will strengthen or weaken a third-party competitor. Policymakers must explore the questions raised above on a case-by-case basis, pending an accumulation of case studies that offer a better basis for theory building. Greater awareness of the third-party framework, however, should be beneficial to the policymaking process.

THE RESILIENT STATUS QUO

The sixth implication deals with the nature of the Persian Gulf region. While the history of the region shows that it is obviously conflict-ridden, it also shows that the Gulf is able to absorb major shocks and to maintain itself. The use of force by Moscow, Baghdad, and Teheran, while producing changes within the status quo system, did not overturn it. Quite the contrary, the use of force put in motion numerous effects that made it substantially more difficult for revisionist states to achieve their long-term objectives.

Thus, if there is a broader lesson to be learned from the perspective of regional states such as Iran and Iraq (and one uses the word *lesson* with caution), it is that the large-scale use of force in the Persian Gulf region is unlikely to succeed. Nor is it probable that active political subversion will bring about an alteration of the status quo. In the past, opportunities existed for revisionist states to overturn or alter significantly the status quo, had they adopted the right strategy. This was much less the case in the early 1990s. Conflict in the 1980s, while generating great instability in the short term, produced important stabilizing factors over the long term that mitigate against such revisionism. Thus, even if Saddam or another potential hegemon were to launch a major effort to dominate the region and were to apply a more effective strategy than Saddam applied in 1979 or in 1990, success would still be highly unlikely.

This is not to say that stabilizing factors will now predominate over elements of regional disorder and instability. The latter could again assume significant dimensions in the historical process, which, in any event, cannot be predicted *a fortiori*. However, the segment of history analyzed in this book suggests that conflict produced significant stabilizing factors that did not exist to such an extent before conflict and that could not have easily arisen in its absence. Regional actors that fail to recognize these developments do so at their own risk.

MANAGING INTERVENTION

The final implication concerns fashioning U.S. foreign policy toward the Persian Gulf. As discussed in greater detail in the concluding chapter, conflicts strengthened U.S. security in part because the United States' third-party status conferred upon it several strategic and political benefits. However, U.S. foreign policy since the 1980s has increasingly threatened to undermine its third-party status by pitting it directly against Iraq and Iran. While this served an important goal at times from 1980 to 1991 when these actors posed a clear, immediate, and serious threat to regional security, the United States should be cautious about becoming a primary antagonist in the postwar Persian Gulf region and should consider how to maintain its third-party status. This is a key to success in protecting regional security for the United States and other actors as well.

NOTES

1. For probably the best example of this approach, see Zeev Maoz, "Resolve, Capabilities, and the Outcomes of Interstate Disputes, 1816–1976," *Journal of Conflict Resolutions* 27 (June 1983): 195–229.

2. See ibid. Also, see Barry M. Blechman and Stephen S. Kaplan, *Force Without War: U.S. Armed Forces as a Political Instrument* (Washington, D.C.: Brookings Institution, 1978).

3. Maoz, "Resolve, Capabilities," 226.

3

THE UNITED STATES AND THE IRANIAN REVOLUTION

Revolutions are critical and defining events in the domestic history of the revolutionary state. They reject key elements of internal society, reconstitute the structure of domestic politics, and chart a tortuous, uncertain path for the new regime.

Observers of world politics are keenly interested in determining why revolutions occur. Indeed much of the vast literature on revolution focuses either on the causes of revolution or on the domestic consequences of revolutionary change.[1] By comparison, less attention is devoted to the question of how revolutions affect relations between states. This is surprising, considering that revolutions often have an immense impact not only on the domestic politics of revolutionary states, but also on the international politics of the regions in which they take place. Changes in the internal dynamics of revolutionary states produce significant changes in their foreign policy, which, in turn, often dramatically alter the nature of relations between the revolutionary state and its political-security environment. Indeed, history reveals that revolutionary states often fight wars soon after assuming power. Witness, for example, the revolutionary regimes of France (1789), Russia (1917), Turkey (1919), China (1949), and Iran (1978).[2]

The case of Iran is of obvious importance to this book. The 1978–79 Iranian revolution was a watershed event in Iranian history. Spearheaded by the Muslim cleric Ayatollah Khomeini, the revolution had a significant impact on regional politics and represented one of the few genuine grass-roots efforts to overthrow a regime. In the case of Iran, the regime was led by Muhammad Reza Pahlevi, the Shah of Iran, a man who was increasingly viewed as out of touch with his own people.

The revolution had many causes each of which was important in its own right. Scholars have debated the relative importance of these causes for over a decade and probably will continue to debate them for some time. The goal of this chapter is not to contribute to this rich debate. A brief background discussion of some key causes of the revolution, however, is worthwhile so as to put the revolution into some perspective. The balance of the chapter will focus on the impact of the revolution on regional politics and on U.S. security. This will pave the way for understanding how subsequent conflicts affected Middle Eastern politics and U.S. regional standing.

In general, the revolution was caused by a convergence of developments in the political, economic, cultural, and social spheres. At the political level, there was a reaction against autocratic rule under the Shah who was increasingly viewed as anachronistic. The Shah proved unwilling and/or unable to allow for the increased participation of Iran's increasingly more influential intellectuals, urbanized middle classes, and professional groups. Hence, there was no effective process by which the Iranian people could release political frustrations or translate political ideas into inputs in the political process. As with other revolutions in world history, such frustrations exploded and were directed at the regime that was thought to have caused and perpetuated them.

Economically, Iran was not at all in dire straits. Quite the contrary, despite the Shah's enormous and highly criticized expenditures on the military, the Pahlavis increased significantly Iran's national wealth, productive capacity, international financial standing, external trade, and other basic indicators of growth and welfare, and Iran showed good potential for long-term growth.[3] Perceived inequalities between rich and poor, however, created disdain for the regime and fueled revolutionary zeal, and the rigors of modernization created socioeconomic dislocation, which contributed to domestic discontent. Without an effective process through which such discontent could be decreased, resentment of the regime slowly mounted.

At the cultural level, antiregime sentiment was aimed at preserving Persian identity. Iranians believed that the Shah had become a corrupt despot, a stooge of the United States, which used him to protect its own regional interests without concern for Iran. They viewed him as a man who linked progress to Westernization and did not take sufficient stock in things Persian, a secular individual who showed little respect for Islam. Thus, in this sense, the overthrow of the Shah represented an attempt by Iranians to regain control of their nation's destiny and to recapture their national and religious heritage.

Socially, there was what one scholar has referred to as a "revolution against a growing stratification in outlook, values, interests, and lifestyles among traditional classes which, while going back to the turn of the century, seemed increasingly more pronounced and foreboding."[4] The people increasingly regarded the regime as elitist, alienated from the ways of the masses, and contemptuous of their values and preferences in the overall scheme of politics. This disconnect between the regime and the people made it difficult for the regime to communicate its goals and beliefs and to inspire the people behind its agenda and against the agenda of revolutionary forces. The real explanation for the Iranian revolution probably lies at the intersection of developments in these four arenas: the political, economic, cultural, and social.

While the revolution was a profound event in its own right at the domestic level, it also had a great impact on regional politics and on the U.S. role in the wider scheme of regional history. For several reasons, the revolution greatly undermined the security and power of the United States in the Gulf. At the regional level, the revolution severed the security link between Iran and the United States and threatened to spread a particular brand of anti-U.S. Islamic orthodoxy. At the global level, the revolution hurt U.S. credibility by creating the perception in some quarters that a superpower could not effectively save a key regional ally, the Shah, from ignominious defeat and prevent "Islamic fanatics" from seizing and holding fifty-one U.S. hostages for 444 days. Meanwhile, the revolution enhanced the perception that the Soviet Union had gained momentum in global rivalry. The fact that anti-U.S. states such as Iraq and Syria were increasing in influence only contributed to the perception of the decline of U.S. power at the regional and global level.

Paradoxically, the Soviet invasion of Afghanistan in December 1979, which is discussed in the next chapter, put in motion short- and long-term effects that would help the United States extricate itself from the security predicament created by the Iranian revolution. Such an outcome would have been predicted by few if any analysts at the time, given the weak state of U.S. security. Quite the contrary, the United States seemed particularly vulnerable to the exploits of anti-U.S. actors in and outside the Persian Gulf region.

SIGNS OF TROUBLE

Serious U.S. involvement in the Persian Gulf is of relatively recent vintage. Britain, not the United States, had military predominance in the Persian Gulf in the post-World War II period. This changed in 1968 when, to the United States' chagrin, Britain announced that it would withdraw from the Gulf "East of Suez." This withdrawal was motivated by Arab nationalist challenges, rising U.S. strength, and flagging British strategic and economic means. By 1971, Washington had assumed the responsibility for the defense of Western strategic interests in the Persian Gulf with Britain playing only a minor role.

For decades, Britain's hegemony over the Gulf had made the risks of opportunism by regional states and outside powers exceed the potential benefits. Britain enjoyed military predominance at sea and a monopoly of political control in the region. Others could not sensibly challenge the British position. British withdrawal, however, created a power vacuum. At the regional level, former powers such as Iran assumed new strategic responsibilities and smaller Gulf states became more vulnerable to the larger ones. As a harbinger of ensuing events, Iraq threatened to occupy parts of Kuwait one week after Britain withdrew its forces. At the superpower level, British departure set the stage for the intensification of global rivalry, which would fluctuate in intensity, alter the nature of regional interaction, and further complicate the international politics of the Gulf until the Soviet Union's demise.

British departure increased U.S. influence in the Gulf and heightened the Soviet Union's fears that Washington would either seize control of Gulf oil or use the Gulf to undermine Soviet security. These fears, coupled with Moscow's interests in advancing its own foreign policy agenda, motivated Soviet efforts to gain regional influence. Several regional developments, however, stymied these efforts.

Many territorial disputes between Gulf states were resolved successfully. In the 1975 Algiers Accord, for example, Iraq agreed to allow Iran joint control of the Shatt-al-Arab waterway (the confluence of the Tigris and Euphrates rivers) in exchange for Iranian assurances that it would cease supporting Kurdish rebels in Iraq. In addition, several subversive movements were suppressed. Most notably, the Dhofar rebellion against Sultan Qabus of Oman was quelled by 1975. To some extent, the rebellion had been supported by the Soviets and Soviet client states as a means of undermining Oman's pro-U.S. monarchy. The insurrection, however, was controlled with help from Iran, Britain, the United States, and Jordan. Furthermore, by 1975, Soviet relations with Iraq, Moscow's most solid Middle Eastern ally, had weakened, though they remained viable.

The 1975 Algiers Accord touched off a prolonged period of independent Iraqi foreign policy. Iraq began to diversify its arms suppliers, thus gaining leverage to defy Soviet wishes on issues where their interests diverged. A less vulnerable Iraq would also become less dependent on Soviet assistance and more inclined to assume foreign policy risks against Soviet wishes. Iraq's invasion of Kuwait over a decade later might be viewed as a partial manifestation of Iraq's slow and circuitous move out of the Soviet orbit.

THE IRANIAN REVOLUTION AND GLOBAL RIVALRY

There are two primary reasons why the United States began to lose the edge in global rivalry over regional influence from 1975 to 1979. First, Moscow established a political and military foothold in the Horn of Africa and in South Yemen from which it could more effectively project military power into the Gulf region.[5] Moscow's gains were militarily insignificant considering it probably never had the propensity to invade the Gulf region. They, however, created the impression that the Soviet Union, rather than the United States, had predominance in global and regional rivalry. The Saudis and Omanis even feared actual military action by the Cubans and Ethiopians, directed by the Soviets, against the strategically vital Strait of Bab el-Mandeb, which lies at the mouth of the Red Sea.[6] In a region where perceptions of power and strength are highly significant, Moscow's gains did not go unnoticed.

The second and much more important reason was the Iranian revolution. Emboldened by previous political and strategic gains and by U.S. failures, Moscow invoked the 1921 Soviet-Iranian Treaty, which allowed it to intervene in Iran if Soviet security were threatened, and in November 1978, warned the

United States against intervening in Iran.[7] Though this warning was motivated in part by Soviet fears of the increasing U.S. military profile in the area, it also suggested a shift in Soviet perceptions of the regional power balance. That Moscow could attempt in such a conspicuous manner to circumscribe U.S. policy toward its former ally indeed reflected a shift in the status quo. This action was also viewed by some U.S. officials as setting the stage for a more active Soviet campaign to influence Iran's revolutionary forces.[8]

The United States responded to the Soviet threat by declaring that it had neither the desire nor the ability to intervene in Iran. Although this response was not unreasonable given Washington's adherence at the time to the pacific principle of noninterference, it was perceived as weak by many regional and some U.S. officials.[9] The Saudis were particularly disappointed and reportedly considered re-establishing diplomatic relations with the Soviet Union.[10] While this must have been partly a political ploy, it did reflect serious annoyance with the United States in Riyadh.

After the Soviets determined the anti-U.S. nature of the Islamic revolution, they began an assiduous courtship of Iran, assuming that if Iran were anti-U.S., it might be pro-Soviet.[11] These efforts failed until the November 1979 Iranian hostage crisis, which temporarily changed Iran's view toward the Soviet Union. In the month after the seizure of the U.S. embassy in Tehran, M. Mokri, Iran's ambassador to the Soviet Union, initiated a visit to the Soviet Union, during which he described prospects for Soviet-Iranian relations as "the very best."[12] For his part, Soviet Foreign Minister Andrei Gromyko assured the Iranian ambassador that Moscow "would not remain neutral" if the United States attempted "armed aggression" against Iran.[13]

The Soviet Union did not succeed in making serious inroads with Iran. This was due in part to revolutionary Iran's preference to tilt "neither East nor West." As discussed in the next chapter, however, Moscow's invasion of Muslim Afghanistan in December 1979 also seriously strained Soviet relations with Iran. Iran, which viewed itself as leader of the Muslim world, opposed the invasion to the extent reasonable, considering that it did not wish to alienate Moscow after the eruption of the Iran-Iraq war in September 1980. With Iraq on the march, the Soviet Union became more important to Iran for potential pressure against Iraq.

THE FALL OF THE SHAH AND REGIONAL POLITICS

The fall of the Shah of Iran greatly affected Gulf security. It disrupted security interactions that for a decade had served as the foundation for relative stability. It also made the Gulf the focus of larger trends in the Middle East, such that Soviet influence on the Gulf's periphery gained a new meaning for the security of the Gulf. To understand how the Iranian revolution affected U.S. regional security, it is necessary to know to what extent and in what manner the Shah had supported U.S. regional security prior to his fall.

Following British withdrawal, U.S. regional security relied on Iran and, to a lesser extent, Saudi Arabia to play a policing role. The "twin pillar" policy as it was called appealed to U.S. policymakers because it obviated the need for Washington, in the post-Vietnam period, to intervene in the region. The United States could rely primarily on Iran to safeguard regional security in exchange for U.S. arms and technical support.

U.S. relations with Iran were not unproblematic. At times, the Shah appeared more willing to take U.S. arms than advice and based his security approach less on joint U.S.-Iranian goals than on Iran's goals alone. Nor was Washington particularly stingy in its arms transfers. Indeed, considerable concern existed in the U.S. Congress regarding the pace, scope, and implications of Iran's massive, U.S.-supported military build-up. The Shah's dismal human rights record also raised questions about the morality of supporting his regime. His disregard for basic U.S. values as reflected in the repressive, far-reaching, and shady nature of his secret police, SAVAK, were viewed as troublesome in some U.S. quarters.

However, given U.S. fears of Soviet power and of the ambitions of regional actors such as Iraq, morality took a back seat to U.S. strategic interests in the Persian Gulf as it did in most other regions around the globe. In retrospect, it did appear that U.S. support of the repressive Shah contributed to his downfall. The close U.S. connection helped paint him as a puppet of the United States, and, therefore, as a leader less likely to preserve the interests and integrity of Iran.

While U.S. support of the Shah was problematic, it also offered Washington numerous strategic benefits.[14] Between 1974 and 1979, the Shah established acceptable relations with all Gulf states and was, by and large, a mediating influence. Although the Arab Gulf states were made uneasy by the Shah's imperialist designs, found his arrogance annoying, and even feared that he might one day turn Iranian power on them, they also perceived Iran under the Shah to be a stabilizing force in the region.

On the Gulf's periphery, Iran served as a conduit for improved U.S.-Egyptian relations throughout the 1970s. Between 1971 and 1979, Iran helped lure North Yemen and Somalia away from the Soviet Union, and Iran's troops also played a role in defeating a communist-backed tribal revolt in Pakistan's Baluchistan province. In the Gulf, the Shah's troops were useful in helping Oman suppress the Dhofar rebellion in 1975 and maintain order thereafter. This was viewed by other Gulf states as important to their strategic interests, since Oman's stability was connected to that of the Gulf as a whole.

Iran also served as a check on Iraq and South Yemen, which, because of their links to Moscow and their own regional ambitions, were viewed as serious threats to regional security. Although Iran was more hawkish on oil prices than Saudi Arabia, Teheran also served as a reliable supplier of a high volume of oil. Indeed, the collapse of Iranian oil production in the postrevolutionary period led to a tripling of oil prices, which damaged U.S. interests and made a U.S. strategy for regional security vital.

The revolution initially did not lead to tensions between Iran and Arab Gulf states. Although radicals in Iran's government entertained a more ambitious foreign policy vis-à-vis the Arab Gulf states, Iran's overall threat was confined as long as the Gulf states appeared not to challenge the fundamental bases of the revolution. Iran even sought to maintain relations with Arab states.[15] The underlying incompatibility of Iran's foreign policy with the policies of the more moderate Arab Gulf states, however, eventually manifested itself and would be widened by the Iran-Iraq war. As with the Chinese, French, and even Russian revolutions, Iran's revolution transformed a moderate, monarchical, and basically agrarian state into one mobilized for conflict and ultimately war.[16]

Although the revolution affected Gulf politics in many ways, two are particularly important to this book. First, the revolution undermined Teheran's relations with regional actors, which, in most cases, had been correct. Prior to the revolution, the Saudis had been concerned about the Shah's increasing military strength and regional ambition, but they shared with Iran an interest in checking Soviet influence and in ensuring regional stability. Consequently, they engaged in a large degree of tacit co-operation.[17] The revolution put Saudi-Iranian relations on a path toward increased tensions and, in the 1980s, open conflict.

Saudi legitimacy rested on Riyadh's role as the guardian of the two most holy sites of Islam: Mecca, the birthplace of Islam, and Medina, where the prophet Muhammad launched his mission in God's service. Unlike Pahlevi Iran, revolutionary Iran challenged Riyadh's claim as the champion of Islam by offering an alternative Islamic model that rejected the monarchical, Islamic state and offered a theocratic one in its place. The clash between these two approaches to Islamic governance created frictions in Saudi-Iranian relations, which were dramatized by the Iran-Iraq war and, as discussed in chapter 5, erupted in earnest in July 1987 over the annual pilgrimage to Mecca.

In the postrevolutionary period, Iran's relations with Oman, Bahrain, and Iraq also deteriorated. Iran withdrew its forces from Oman, where they had played an important security role, and threatened to revive its historical claims to Bahrain, which the Shah had renounced. More importantly, the revolution eventually produced effects that undermined Iran's relations with Iraq, relations which had been relatively stable.

Iraq had followed a cautious policy toward Iran and expressed some interest in co-operation after the revolution, but was rebuffed. At some point, Iraq's fear of the revolution, its interest in exploiting the chaos in Teheran, and its desire to dominate Gulf politics pushed it to attack Iran. By late September 1980, both states were locked in what would become an almost decade-long war, a war that Saddam had thought would be relatively short.

The weakening of relations between Iran and other regional actors assumed particular importance because it coincided with the perception that Moscow was on the move and that Washington was weak. The Iranian revolution heightened considerably fears of Soviet intentions. Leaders in the Gulf and observers outside the Gulf felt that Soviet moves in the Horn, Southern Arabia, and Afghanistan were part of a long-term effort to encircle and subvert the Gulf.[18] For their part, the Saudis publicly expressed their hope for regional stability but privately were concerned that the chaos in Iran would create greater leftist influence and lead over time to Soviet domination.[19]

The disruption caused by the revolution was also exacerbated by the residual effects of the Camp David peace process. Camp David isolated Egypt, the only Arab state willing to make peace with Israel, from the Arab world and from Persian Gulf actors in particular. On April 7, 1979, Egypt announced the recall of its ambassadors to Bahrain, Kuwait, Qatar, Saudi Arabia, and the United Arab Emirates (UAE).[20] Later in the month, Saudi Arabia and Kuwait broke diplomatic relations with Egypt, an action that Egypt reciprocated.

Political and security relations between Egypt and Arab Gulf states would be restored in the late 1980s in response to the imperatives of the Iran-Iraq war. For almost a decade, however, Egypt, which had become more important to Washington as a result of its peace with Israel, would remain isolated from most of the Arab world and unable to play an effective moderating role.

The second major impact of the Iranian revolution on the politics of the Persian Gulf was the presence of a new political threat to moderate Arab regimes. While the Shah had been secular in outlook, Khomeini was dominated by a manichean, absolutist world view anchored in a particular brand of conservative, Shiite Islamic belief. In contrast to Sunni Muslims, Shiites are more likely to follow independent clerical leaders and to intertwine religion and state. Sunnis, whose lineage followed a different path after the founding of Islam in the seventh century, tended to view Shiites as heretical and did not believe in rule by religious figures. The significant differences that developed between Sunni and Shiite Islam were re-ignited by Khomeini, who often invoked the motif of Sunni repression of Shiites in history.

Whereas Iran was predominantly Shiite, the more secular Arab Gulf states in the region were under Sunni leadership. In the cases of Iraq and Bahrain, Sunni leaders ruled over a predominantly Shiite population. This presented Khomeini with the opportunity to subvert Sunni leaders by appealing directly to their people.

Khomeini, who was affected by an almost Marxist belief that the masses would prevail over their oppressors and that governments per se would diminish in importance, actively encouraged the overthrow of the Gulf monarchies, whose secular, Westernized rule he viewed as shameful. He promised to vouchsafe Islam not only to the Middle East but also to the world. While he appealed to some sectarian and fundamentalist impulses in many Muslim states and to Gulf states in particular,[21] his appeal did not assume significant dimensions.

Khomeini's radical foreign policy outlook, however, did create a potential threat to moderate Arab regimes and to U.S. interests. The United States, otherwise known as the "great satan," had no role in Khomeini's world. It was the leader of the camp of the oppressors and its influence was excessive and unjust. Consequently, Iran's foreign policy under Khomeini targeted the United States as the root of global evil.

SAUDI INFLUENCE COMPROMISED

The fall of the Shah pushed Washington to seek alternate means of protecting its interests in the Gulf. Saudi Arabia, the remaining pillar of the Nixon administration's security policy, became more important in this strategy. Although Riyadh lacked Iran's military capability and considerable manpower, it did have anticommunist credentials, strategic location, and relative clout in the Arab world, which made it an attractive replacement for the fallen Iran.

The Saudis, however, had always been wary of a close association with Washington, and political developments in 1978 and 1979 made Riyadh even less willing and able to align itself with the United States. Saudi wariness further undermined U.S. regional security by decreasing the chance that Saudi Arabia could even modestly replace Iran as a strategic pillar or play an effective moderating role in the region.

From late 1978 through 1979, Saudi influence declined significantly. This decline was the result of several internal and external factors. Internally, the Saudis were faced with two attempts to undermine the royal family's authority. The first attempt was the November 20, 1979 seizure of the Grand Mosque of Mecca, Islam's holiest shrine, by several hundred armed Muslim zealots. Eight days after this event, while the Saudi National Guard was still battling the zealots at Mecca, disturbances erupted in Saudi Arabia's oil-rich eastern province in a second attempt to undermine the country internally. These disturbances constituted the first political challenge posed by the Shiites to the Saudi regime and were viewed as serious enough by the royal family to prompt the dispatch of 20,000 troops to the area.[22] The Mecca incident further cast Saudi stability into question and raised some doubts as to whether the Saudi government would last even a few months.[23] Though, in retrospect, it appeared that the threat to Saudi stability had been much exaggerated, Saudi self-confidence and its reputation as a regional security asset came under question.

To be sure, there had always been the potential for instability in the Gulf. The ongoing modernization process, the clashes between different Islamic sects and between conservatives and radicals, the territorial struggles, the large influx of foreign workers, economic dislocation and transformation, and the difficult process of state building caused underlying tensions. But the Iranian revolution was the catalyst for more intense manifestations of instability and represented perhaps for the first time since the independence of most Gulf states in the early 1970s the potential for serious internal instability.

A link, then, can be drawn between the Iranian revolution and Saudi instability. The armed men who seized the Grand Mosque in Mecca criticized the Saudi royal family for corruption and not adhering to the tenets of Islam.[24] It was not coincidental that similar criticisms emanated from Iran. In addition, in the period after the Shiite uprising in the eastern Saudi oil province, Radio Teheran attempted to foment discontent among Saudi oil workers, even calling for the overthrow of the monarchy on December 11, 1979. In a demonstration on

February 1, 1980, in Saudi Arabia, Saudi Shiites carried pictures of Khomeini, a scene that was repeated in Bahrain.[25]

Another reason for the decrease in Saudi influence was the rise of the Arab rejectionist front. This front, composed of hard-line Arab states such as Syria and Libya, had pressured the more moderate Saudis to distance themselves from the United States. Given the perception of Soviet momentum in global rivalry, the precarious situation in Iran, anti-U.S. sentiment generated by the Camp David peace process, and the fear of the entrenchment of Soviet influence on their southern borders, the Saudis were inclined to appease hard-line Arab states rather than to tilt toward the United States. This propensity was reinforced by Saudi questions about U.S. credibility and by U.S. doubts about Saudi stability.

Saudi influence also decreased because the Shah's fall created an opportunity for Iraqi president Saddam Hussein to assume the mantle of Gulf leadership. Iraq's influence vis-à-vis Saudi Arabia increased substantially from 1978 to mid-late 1979, which further limited Saudi action. Though the Saudis feared Iraq less than they did revolutionary Iran, Iraq was still viewed by the Saudis as a military and political threat. This threat would eventually become reality in August 1990 with Iraq's invasion of Kuwait.

The Iranian revolution not only threatened Saudi Arabia, but also decreased Riyadh's leverage by making it more dependent on Iraq for security purposes. Despite fears of Iraq, the Saudis needed Iraq against Iran, and despite fears of Iran, they needed Iran to balance Iraq. In this sense, Saudi Arabia had no reliable security policy because it could not trust its would-be protectors and constantly had to adjust its balancing act. Given the prevailing political and security climate, the Saudis even had serious doubts about whether the United States, on which they had relied for outside support, could play an effective security role.

The combination of these factors placed Riyadh in a position of weakness domestically and regionally. This affected U.S. regional security negatively because the Saudis were more likely to support U.S. regional interests than other Gulf states and assumed a much more important role after the fall of the Shah of Iran.

A "POWERLESS" UNITED STATES

Saudi regional weakness was matched by that of the United States. The Nixon administration's twin pillar policy in the 1970s was designed to absolve Washington of the need to develop its own military capability in the Gulf. Consequently, when U.S. regional security deteriorated in 1979, Washington realized how unable it was to affect developments militarily.

The Iranian revolution, along with perceptions of a growing Soviet threat, created high-level interest in the prospect of increasing U.S. military presence, which consisted of only a noncombatant flagship and three destroyers. This prospect translated into some concrete actions.

In January 1979, Washington sent twelve unarmed F-15 fighter planes to Saudi Arabia. This military display reassured the Saudis at a time when the government of moderate Iranian prime minister Shahpur Bakhtiar faced significant popular opposition.[26] Two months later, in response to the outbreak of the war between Saudi-backed North and Soviet-supported South Yemen, Washington again took action. The aircraft carrier *Constellation* was dispatched to the entrance of the Indian Ocean, air-warfare control planes were sent to Saudi Arabia, tactical air force jets were offered, and North Yemen was given $400 million in military aid. These actions were aimed at reassuring "jittery allies" that the United States was ready to "go up in flames with the Shah."[27] But, more specifically, they were designed to discourage foreign intervention in Yemen and to appease the Saudis. Riyadh feared a Soviet-backed invasion of such territory by South Yemen seriously enough to cancel all military leaves and to request urgently U.S. support.[28]

To be sure, these efforts reflected U.S. concern for and commitment to Gulf security. They, however, were not sufficient to shore up U.S. credibility because they were viewed as temporary demonstrations of U.S. force rather than legitimate strategic actions.[29]

The Iranian revolution, however, helped convince Pentagon analysts to push for the development of a Rapid Deployment Force (RDF). This move represented a more significant demonstration of U.S. resolve than previous U.S. actions. The National Security Council met on February 28, 1979, in part to propose the RDF's formation, and by April, the Department of Defense was preparing plans.[30] This policy would become cemented during the following eight months. While there was clearly increased concern for U.S. regional security, however, no consensus developed on a long-term policy to improve it and no specific programs for expanding the U.S. military presence were approved.

Several factors could explain this lack of real urgency in U.S. foreign policy. At the domestic level, there was deep disagreement over how to proceed, which continued until the Afghanistan invasion. Indeed, even two weeks before the Soviet invasion of Afghanistan, Washington was unable to achieve a consensus on plans for improving the U.S. position.[31]

This lack of urgency might also have resulted from Washington's view that the Iranian revolution, although a major setback, was not necessarily irreversible and dangerous. Indeed, shortly after the Shah left Iran, President Jimmy Carter downplayed the threat that the Shah's fall posed to Western interests, noted that Iran could still be a factor for stability, and asserted that the Soviet Union shared the U.S. desire for a stable Iran.[32] The view of high-level officials was that the United States and Iran shared a strong interest in a noncommunist Iran, which could serve as a basis for wary co-operation.[33]

Furthermore, Washington believed that it had another potential alternative to a direct U.S. presence. The offices of another pillar could have been secured, be it Saudi Arabia, Iraq, Pakistan, or even Israel. Thus, while the revolution dealt a blow to the 1970s U.S. foreign policy of relying primarily on proxy powers to protect U.S. interests, it did not totally undermine it. This would come in stages, culminating in the 1990 Iraqi invasion of Kuwait, which made abundantly clear the importance of the U.S. role in protecting Gulf security.

Finally, despite the revolution, the United States still hoped for a favorable turn in Iran's domestic struggle. In February, President Carter asserted that the Khomeini government desired "close working and friendly relations with the United States."[34] Washington also continued to believe that the Iranian military would support pro-U.S. forces in Iran. Throughout 1979, U.S. policymakers tried to rebuild friendly relations with Iran in the hope that conciliation would elicit future Iranian co-operation,[35] a strategy that would later contribute to the Iran-Contra scandal in which the United States sought to exchange arms for U.S. hostages. As late as October 1979, the Defense Department announced that it had resumed the delivery of spare parts to Iran for U.S.-built military aircraft.[36]

From February to November 1979, Washington tolerated Iran's massive human rights violations, pursued a military-training relationship, and cultivated the Iranian "moderates" whom it expected would gain power. The seizure of the U.S. embassy in Teheran on November 4, 1979, altered Washington's approach to the revolutionary regime.[37] In the throes of revolutionary fervor, and angered by U.S. acceptance of the Shah into the United States for medical treatment, Iranian militants stormed the embassy, captured fifty-one U.S. citizens, and held them for 444 days in what would become a national and international drama.

The hostage crisis renewed U.S. interest in formulating a new strategic framework for Gulf security and seriously altered the climate of U.S.-Iranian relations. While in October, President Carter saw no prospects for U.S. military intervention anywhere in the world,[38] the hostage crisis altered his views. It became clear that U.S. interests abroad could be threatened enough to warrant military intervention. Indeed, President Carter would later launch the ill-fated hostage rescue mission and issue statements indicating U.S. will to use major force to protect the Persian Gulf region.

In an attempt to bolster diplomatic efforts to free the hostages, the United States built a twenty-one-ship naval force around the Gulf. President Carter also asked the Joint Chiefs of Staff for a list of military force options against Iran. The president recognized the inadequate state of U.S. military capability when, on November 24, 1979, the Joint Chiefs of Staff informed him that the United States was virtually powerless to release the hostages.[39] While it is highly doubtful that the United States could have freed the hostages even with a more developed military capability, the hostage crisis,[40] as well as concern about the broader Soviet threat, motivated stepped-up efforts to secure U.S. access to forward basing facilities in Southwest Asia. By November 1979, Carter's fiscal year 1981 defense request would push legislators to decide about funding an RDF force for the first time.[41]

THE EBB IN U.S. FOREIGN POLICY

Despite the measures taken in response to the Iranian revolution to bolster U.S. regional security, the United States was, as one official noted, "starting from scratch in building Carter's security framework."[42] It could no longer count on its allies in the Middle East to protect its interests, to facilitate U.S. military movements, or to defend even their own interests.

Tensions in U.S.-Saudi relations following the Shah's departure were not offset by improvements in U.S. relations with other states. Although it might have been reasonable to assume that the deterioration of U.S.-Iranian relations would have brought Iraq and Washington closer, this would not be the case. Washington tried unsuccessfully to improve relations with Baghdad throughout 1979. Although Iraq feared a resurgent and implacable Iran, it also viewed the chaos created by the Iranian revolution as an opportunity to heighten its influence in the Gulf. This challenge to U.S. regional security exacerbated U.S.-Iraqi relations.

Perceptions of Soviet vigor and of U.S. ineffectiveness seriously damaged U.S. credibility.[43] The Carter administration's foreign policy in the Horn of Africa was widely viewed as leading to the increase of Soviet influence in the Middle East, particularly between 1977 and 1978. Washington's failure to support Somalia with adequate force during the 1977 Somalia-Ethiopia war prompted widespread doubts about U.S. credibility as a stabilizing force in the region. Several Arab countries, including Saudi Arabia, had urged the Carter administration to provide arms aid to Somalia in order to offset Soviet support of Ethiopia, but the administration, which was committed to diplomacy and accommodation in superpower relations, chose to keep a low profile.

The Iranian revolution was a significant blow to U.S. credibility because it created the perception that Washington was incapable of protecting a vital ally. Had Washington's ineptitude been expected by regional states and around the world, the repercussions for U.S. interests might have been less severe. On many quarters in the Middle East, however, it was believed that the United States would take the necessary steps to save the Shah.[44]

The leaders of Gulf states were particularly distraught by the replacement of the conservative Shah with radical Khomeini. Although the Shah's imperialist stand in the Gulf was not appreciated by the Gulf states, he at least was a devil they knew. Khomeini, on the other hand, was an unpredictable political threat at the outset of the revolution and later a more direct military threat. The Saudis in particular feared that the Iranian revolution would create a "military vacuum" that Moscow could exploit.[45]

Whether Washington could have saved the Shah had it taken swift action is very doubtful. What is more clear is that inadequate U.S. intelligence hindered U.S. efforts to understand the gravity of the situation. Despite important indications to the contrary, U.S. intelligence repeatedly stated from August 1977 through late 1978 that Iran was stable.[46] Speculation concerning U.S. intelligence failure was confirmed in an official report that concluded that intelligence collection and analyses were weak and that policymakers and the intelligence community were overconfident of the Shah's longevity.[47]

The U.S. inability to resolve the hostage crisis quickly was yet another blow to U.S. prestige. The prime minister of Bahrain, reflecting the general sentiment in the Gulf, was baffled that the United States could be "brought down to its knees" by a religious fanatic, and he questioned U.S. reliability.[48] At a general level, the events in 1979 led the Saudis[49] and other states to conclude that Washington could not effectively translate armed strength into military influence. This perception would change slowly in the 1980s in response to strong U.S. military actions during the Iran-Iraq war and, then, more dramatically in response to the U.S.-led Operations Desert Shield and Storm in 1990 and 1991.

CONCLUSION

U.S. standing in the Persian Gulf region was clearly in tatters in 1979. For nearly a decade, Iran and, to a lesser extent, Saudi Arabia, had helped safeguard U.S. interests in the Gulf under the Nixon administration's "twin pillar" policy.

The 1978–79 Iranian revolution transformed U.S.-Iranian relations from cooperation to confrontation and undermined Iran's relations with other Gulf states. Tensions in U.S.-Saudi relations and the decrease in Saudi influence further undermined U.S. regional security at precisely the time when it was most vulnerable to the exploits of anti-U.S. actors.

In addition, a string of perceived Soviet gains in Angola, Ethiopia, South Yemen, and finally in Afghanistan, combined with U.S. inability to prevent the downfall of the Shah of Iran and to resolve the ensuing Iranian hostage crisis, weakened U.S. credibility with pro-U.S. Gulf states. These states reconsidered the merits of close association with Washington.

The fact that the United States lacked the military capability to deal with major threats to regional security compounded its security predicament by accentuating its loss of regional support. Neither the United States nor its regional allies had the capability to protect regional security after the Iranian revolution. On the eve of Moscow's December 1979 invasion of Afghanistan, there appeared to be ample opportunity for states in and outside the region to improve their position at cost to the United States. Ironically, the Afghanistan intervention, which is discussed in the next chapter, would reverse this negative trend rather than intensify it.

NOTES

1. Stephen M. Walt, "Revolution and War," *World Politics* 44 (April 1992): 322.

2. For more details on the link between revolution and war, see ibid., 324–25.

3. See Jahangir Amuzegar, *The Dynamics of the Iranian Revolution: The Pahlavis' Triumph and Tragedy* (New York: State University of New York Press, 1991), 305.

4. The discussion of the causes of the revolution is based in part on ibid., 5.

5. Omani officials in particular took this Soviet threat seriously. See *Salalah Domestic Service*, 27 August 1981 in *Foreign Broadcast Information Service* (hereafter FBIS): Middle East and Africa (MEA), 27 August 1981, C1.

6. Drew Middleton, "Arabian Anxieties: What Soviets Might Do and What U.S. Might Not," *New York Times*, 16 June 1979, A2.

7. For details, see Shahram Chubin, "Soviet Policy Toward Iran and the Gulf," *Adelphi Papers* 157 (Spring 1980): 11.

8. Gary Sick, *All Fall Down: America's Tragic Encounter with Iran* (Boulder, CO: Westview Press, 1985), 95–97.

9. See U.S. Congress, House of Representatives, *U.S. Policy Toward Iran*, Hearings Before the Subcommittee on Europe and the Middle East of the Committee on Foreign Affairs, 17 January 1979 (Washington, D.C.: GPO, 1979), 34.

10. See U.S. Congress, House of Representatives, *Saudi Arabia and the United States*, Report Prepared for the Subcommittee on Europe and the Middle East of the Committee on Foreign Affairs (Washington, D.C.: Congressional Research Service [CRS], August 1981), 12.

11. On this effort, see testimony before Congress by Harold Saunders, U.S. Congress, House, *U.S. Policy Toward Iran*, 43.

12. Iran's ambassador cited in *Pravda*, 27 November 1979, in *Current Digest of the Soviet Press* (CDSP) 31, no. 48 (26 December 1979): 21.

13. Gromyko cited in Jack Anderson, "Double-Dealing on Iran Laid to Soviets," *Washington Post*, 31 December 1979, D12.

14. For the views of key U.S. officials on the role of Iran in U.S. security, see Cyrus Vance, *Hard Choices: Critical Years in America's Foreign Policy* (New York: Simon and Schuster, 1983), chaps. 14, 15.

15. See *Middle East Economic Survey* (MEES) 22, no. 42 (6 August 1979): 3. Iran praised the Gulf states for rejecting the Omani plan that called for increased co-operation with Washington. See *AL-RAY'Y AL-'AMM*, in *Joint Publications Research Service* (JPRS): Near East and North Africa (NENA) 74695, 23 September 1979, 23.

16. Theda Skoçpol, *States and Social Revolutions: A Comparative Analysis of France, Russia, and China* (New York: Cambridge University Press, 1979).

17. For a good discussion of the twin pillars, see Richard Haass, "Saudi Arabia and Iran: The Twin Pillars in Revolutionary Times," in *The Security of the Persian Gulf*, ed. Hossein Amirsadeghi (New York: St. Martin's Press, 1981), chap. 8.

18. See comments by Oman's Qabus, *Oslo Arbeiderbladet*, in FBIS: MEA, 16 February 1979, C2. Also, Middleton, "Arabian Anxieties," A2; "Saudi Arabia and the United States," House Foreign Affairs Committee, CRS Report, 8.

19. William B. Quandt, *Saudi Arabia in the 1980s: Foreign Policy, Security, and Oil* (Washington, D.C.: Brookings Institution, 1981), 40.

20. On the Egyptian response to attempts to isolate it, see MEES 22, no. 26 (16 April 1979): 3.

21. For a concise description of Khomeini's world view, see R. K. Ramazani, *Revolutionary Iran: Challenge and Response in the Middle East* (Baltimore, MD: The Johns Hopkins University Press, 1986), 19–31.

22. For a factual record of the Mecca crisis, see *Middle East Contemporary Survey* (MECS) 4 (1979–80): 682–88.

23. See U.S. Congress, Senate, *Security Interests and Policy in Southwest Asia*,

Hearings Before the Committee on Foreign Relations, 6 February 1980 (Washington, D.C.: GPO, 1980), 275–76.

24. For details, see *Middle East Economic Digest* (MEED) 23 (7 December 1979): 24.

25. A small rally supported Khomeini. See *Manama Gulf News Agency*, in FBIS: MENA, 23 February 1979, C1.

26. Charles Mohr, "F-15 'Fly-In' to Saudi Arabia Met Host of Problems," *New York Times*, 5 March 1979, A5.

27. Quoted in Richard Burt, "U.S. Reappraises Persian Gulf Policies," *New York Times*, 1 January 1979, A3.

28. On Saudi fears, see U.S. Congress, House of Representatives, Committee on Foreign Affairs, *Chronologies of Major Developments in Selected Areas of Foreign Affairs* (Washington, D.C.: GPO, 1979), 45. (Hereafter referred to as U.S. House, *Chronologies*, 1979.)

29. See MEED 23 (9 March 1979): 14.

30. See U.S. House, *Chronologies*, 1979, 170.

31. Richard Burt, "U.S. Studying Ways to Bolster Strength in Mideast," *New York Times*, 10 December 1979, A16.

32. Bernard Gwertzman, "U.S. Officials React Warily; Put Bakhtiar Odds at 50-50," *New York Times*, 17 January 1979, A10.

33. Vance, *Hard Choices*, 343.

34. Jimmy Carter, *Public Papers of the Presidents of the United States* (Washington, D.C.: GPO, 1979), 352.

35. On these U.S. efforts, see Barry Rubin, *Paved with Good Intentions: The American Experience and Iran* (New York: Oxford University Press, 1980), 295–96, 253, 260.

36. Chronology in ibid., 370.

37. See Sick, *All Fall Down*, 188, 215–16, 241. Also, for a discussion of the impact of the embassy seizure, see Shahram Chubin, *Security in the Gulf: The Role of Outside Powers* (Aldershot, England: Gower Publishing Co., 1982), 16–21.

38. U.S. House, *Chronologies*, 1979, 198.

39. Maxwell Orme Johnson, *The Military as an Instrument of U.S. Policy in Southwest Asia* (Boulder, CO: Westview Press, 1983), 9 (citing interview with Komer).

40. A defense department team was sent to the Gulf in December, prior to the Soviet invasion, for exploratory talks on access to facilities in the Middle East. U.S. House, *Chronologies*, 1979, 208.

41. George C. Wilson, "Carter Budget Envisions a Force for Quick, Long-Distance Reaction," *Washington Post*, 27 November 1979, A8.

42. David Newsome, "America Engulfed," *Foreign Policy* 43 (Summer 1981): 27.

43. See Jacob Goldberg in *The U.S.S.R. and the Muslim World*, ed. Yaacov Ro'i (London: Allen and Unwin, 1984), 264–70. The damage was not confined to the Middle East. See *West Europe Report* in JPRS: NENA (75777), 28 May 1980, 40.

44. *Aden Domestic Service*, in FBIS: MEA, 4 January 1979, C1–C2.

45. On the Saudi view, see *London AL-HAWADITH*, in JPRS: NENA (73101), 107.

46. See R. K. Ramazani, *The United States and Iran: The Patterns of Influence* (New York: Praeger, 1982), 126–28.

47. For details, see U.S. Congress, House of Representatives, *Iran: Evaluation of U.S. Intelligence Performance Prior to November 1978*, Staff Report—Subcommittee on Evaluation, Permanent Select Committee on Intelligence, January 1979 (Washington, D.C.: GPO, 1979), 7. For an inside view of the intelligence failure, see Sick, *All Fall*

Down, 89–93.

48. See comments by Sultan Qabus of Oman, *Oslo Arbeiderbladet*, in FBIS: MEA, 16 February 1979, C2.

49. MECS 3 (1978-79): 752.

4

MOSCOW PLAYS INTO U.S. HANDS

*We are the other superpower on Earth, and it became my
responsibility, representing our great nation, to take action that
would prevent the Soviets from this invasion with impunity.*[1]
—President Jimmy Carter

The Soviet invasion of Afghanistan in late December 1979 shook the world and
created an almost decade-long war between Moscow and anti-Soviet, Afghan
rebels. While the war was principally played out between these two actors, it also
affected numerous other parties at the regional and global level. Although no third
party became directly involved, many of them took military, economic, and
political actions that affected Moscow's prospects in Afghanistan and the long-
term security of the United States in the Middle Eastern context.

The Afghanistan case offers an interesting basis for applying and illustrating
the third-party approach. At a glance, one might wonder how the war in faraway
Afghanistan affected the security of the United States in its third-party role in the
Middle East. Indeed, the connection is not very intuitive and has not been
explored in much detail by analysts. While valuable work appeared on why the
Soviets invaded Afghanistan, on the intervention's effects on Afghanistan and on
South Asia,[2] on Soviet political relations with Muslim states of the Gulf in the
aftermath of the invasion,[3] on changes in U.S. foreign policy catalyzed by the
invasion,[4] and on how the Afghanistan intervention affected Moscow's strategic
reach into the Gulf,[5] little work examined how the position of the United States
in the Persian Gulf region was affected over time. The Afghanistan war produced
major effects at the global, regional, and inter-regional levels, which greatly
affected U.S. security in the Persian Gulf.

Although the Soviet Union no longer exists, the Afghanistan case is crucial to understanding the evolution of U.S. regional security. Despite the end of the Cold War and the fragmentation of the Soviet Union, Russia continues to play a regional role in the 1990s through arms transfers and political jockeying. If history is any indication, Russia is likely to renew in earnest its interest in the Persian Gulf region in the coming decades.

This chapter examines how the United States as a third party was affected by the Afghanistan war. In particular, it shows that while the Iranian revolution hurt U.S. relations with important regional actors, the Afghanistan intervention pushed the United States to improve these relations and to focus its effort on defending its regional interests. The Khomeini revolution left the United States looking weak and vulnerable; the Afghanistan intervention, however, pushed the United States to assert itself more effectively, thereby taking steps toward restoring U.S. credibility.

While the Iranian revolution left Moscow with an opportunity to capitalize on U.S. weakness by improving relations with regional actors such as Saudi Arabia, the Afghanistan intervention damaged Soviet relations with most Muslim states in the region and largely dashed whatever opportunities Moscow might have had to make regional inroads. It also wasted Soviet resources and sapped its will, which might have been used more effectively to challenge its third-party competitor, the United States, in the Persian Gulf region. The Iranian revolution left the overall regional security framework in shambles; the Afghanistan intervention, however, catalyzed some level of intra- and inter-regional defense co-operation among more or less pro-U.S. states.

WHY THE SOVIETS INVADED AFGHANISTAN

Two general schools of thought emerged to explain the invasion. The first school assumed that Moscow invaded Afghanistan out of fear that an anti-Soviet Muslim state in Afghanistan could easily have fomented discontent among the Soviet Union's approximately sixty million Central Asian Muslims. Not insignificantly, the loss of nearby Afghanistan to anti-Soviet Afghan forces would have undermined the Soviet Union's prestige. Therefore, Moscow's attempt to secure Afghanistan under a pro-Soviet regime could be viewed as limited and generally defensive,[6] and not as a great threat to U.S. security.

The second school generally subscribed to the notion that the intervention was part of an age-old grand Russian design to gain influence over the Gulf's oil and warm waters, that it was the continuation of a decade-long expansionist policy that had been played out in the Horn and in the Yemens and now was being exercised through Afghanistan as well. This school held that the invasion was motivated by more than just an interest in dominating Afghan politics. As a consequence, it was necessary for Washington to demonstrate resolve lest the Soviets try to parlay their newly acquired strategic position in Afghanistan into increased influence in South Asia, the Gulf, and beyond.[7] While most observers combined aspects of both schools of thought in their interpretations of the invasion, the latter view gained prominence at official levels in the United States in the postinvasion period.

The invasion had a particularly significant effect on U.S. foreign policy because it was seen as a dramatic departure from what might loosely be termed a "regime" in U.S.-Soviet relations. U.S. officials had repeatedly asserted that a tacit agreement had existed between the superpowers that Afghanistan would remain neutral territory.[8] The use of large contingents of Soviet troops outside the Warsaw Pact area seemed to sweep away, as the Soviets recognized,[9] the tacit rules that had modestly governed aspects of superpower rivalry. Moscow appeared to be extending itself beyond its traditional and generally accepted sphere of domination in Eastern Europe.

IMPERIALISM: THE SEEDS OF ITS OWN DEMISE

The Soviet withdrawal from Afghanistan in 1988 represented a rather peculiar litmus test for Soviet moderation in a period of detente. It was less a concession to the United States than a necessity for the Soviets. Indeed, the Afghanistan intervention was a classic case of the failure of the use of force in international relations and, among other things, improved U.S. security in the Persian Gulf. This confirms what may be developing into an historical truism: Imperialism sows the seeds of its own demise.

While the Iranian revolution undermined U.S. security from within the Gulf, the Afghanistan intervention threatened to capitalize on U.S. vulnerabilities from outside the Gulf. The Soviets, many observers believed, could have exploited both their proximity to the Gulf from Afghanistan and U.S. vulnerability to make political and military advances in the Gulf. But this never transpired. The Soviet intervention at once created and dashed Soviet opportunities and played into U.S. hands. It had a profound effect at the inter-country, inter-regional, superpower, and regional levels; each of these levels will be discussed in this chapter.

THE POLITICAL DAMAGE OF THE INVASION

Opinions varied as to whether the Soviet invasion truly damaged Moscow's political relations with Gulf states. It can be argued that prior to the invasion the Soviets lacked influence in the region, that criticisms of the invasion from Gulf states were more rhetoric than substance, and that "any loss of good will among weak Third World countries would be more than offset by respect for its [Soviet] power and willingness to use it."[10] While there is reason in these arguments, evidence suggests the opposite.

Iran

The Soviet Union had gained its limited influence with nations of the generally anticommunist world in part by portraying itself as a protector of liberation struggles while underscoring U.S. "imperialist" exploits. These efforts were undermined by the Soviet invasion and subsequent efforts to "crush the brave resistance" of the Afghan rebels,[11] despite Soviet attempts to paint Afghanistan in a positive light.[12]

The anti-U.S. Iranian revolution created opportunities for the Soviets to capitalize on U.S. misfortunes. The Soviets tried arduously to befriend Iran,[13] perhaps on the assumption that if Iran loathed the United States it would embrace the Soviets. To Moscow's disappointment, Iran spurned such efforts despite its need for Soviet assistance and its fear of Soviet military power. In part, this was related to Iran's negative reaction to the Soviet invasion.

In the postinvasion period, Iran reduced the Soviet diplomatic staff in Teheran, closed down its consulate in Leningrad, and even rejected Soviet arms offers in October 1980. Iran also committed itself to supporting the anti-Soviet Afghan rebels, providing them with economic and military support, permitting them to operate from its territory, firing on Soviet helicopters in pursuit of Afghan rebels,[14] uniting and providing headquarters for five Afghan resistance groups, and insisting, to the Soviets' disappointment, on rebel representation at various meetings aimed to resolve facets of the Afghan crisis. Iran's aid to the Baluch rebels in Afghanistan, as well as the Iranian refusal to terminate the Gulf war, exacerbated Soviet-Iranian relations through 1987.

Khomeini benefited from his stand against Soviet oppression in Muslim Afghanistan because it legitimized his Muslim and anti-imperialist credentials. Washington also gained from Khomeini's anti-Soviet actions. Soviet successes with Iran at a time of U.S. vulnerability would have clearly endangered U.S. regional interests; Moscow *inter alia* could have used improved relations with Iran to co-opt other Gulf states. In addition, Khomeini's continued support of the Afghan rebels put constant pressure on Moscow in Afghanistan, only adding to the Soviet Union's strategic problems.

Iran's interest in improving relations remained partly contingent on Soviet withdrawal from Afghanistan[15] until perhaps late 1980 to early 1981. In July, a three-year Soviet-Iranian military agreement was signed, which provided for the "sending of Soviet military experts" to Iran[16] and the transfer of Soviet arms to Iran.[17] Iran subordinated its anti-Soviet sentiment to its strategic concerns during this period because it was politically isolated, Iraq had the upper hand in the Gulf war, and Khomeini needed Soviet support against internal challenges to his control.

Soviet-Iranian relations, however, took a turn for the worse in 1982. This had little to do with the invasion of Afghanistan and much to do with the resumption of Soviet arms sales to Iraq in 1982 as well as with Iran's resentment of infiltration by the Soviet-controlled communist Tudeh Party, both of which motivated the Iranian expulsion of eighteen Soviet diplomats in 1983. Iran's need for military spare parts and its fear of combined U.S. and Soviet support for Iraq, coupled with potential Soviet leverage over separatist movements in Iran, compelled Iran to seek closer ties to the Soviets in 1984. The Afghanistan occupation, however, remained a contentious issue, which arose at almost every official Soviet-Iranian meeting through 1989.

Despite the fact that Iran's republic vested its authority more in Khomeini than in popular consensus, the domestic climate in Iran, which was not insignificant in affecting Iranian foreign policy,[18] was adversely affected by the Afghanistan intervention. This was evident when Iran's leaders in an apparent demonstration of anti-Soviet resolve allowed Afghan refugees to storm the Soviet embassy in Iran on the first anniversary of the Soviet invasion. It could also be seen when Iranian leaders again condemned the occupation of Afghanistan on the invasion's anniversary in 1985, and when widespread mass rallies in Iran against the Soviet occupation marked the departure from Iran of a Soviet economic delegation in February 1986. The Soviet paper *Pravda* noted that Iran used the Afghan issue "more often than any other pretext to justify hostile attacks on the USSR's interests."[19]

Soviet-Iranian relations improved in early 1987 when it became more evident that Moscow would withdraw from Afghanistan. Iran's ambassador to Moscow made it clear that the Soviet Union's actions in Afghanistan had "deadlocked their policies in Muslim countries" and had provided the United States with "an excuse to increase its influence in their region."[20] Despite temporarily improved relations, the Soviet Union continued to aid Khomeini's opponents, and Iran increased its support of the Afghan rebels in 1987.

It is worth noting that Iran's displeasure over the Afghanistan intervention did not push it toward the United States. Washington gained only to the extent that Soviet involvement in Afghanistan at certain times decreased Iran's interest in better relations with the Soviets. This can be termed a negative U.S. gain. By contrast, in the case of Saudi Arabia, the United States made positive gains.

Saudi Arabia

The anti-U.S. reaction in the Arab world to the Camp David accords spurred Saudi leaders to intimate that diplomatic relations with the Soviets were possible.[21] To be sure, this may have been staged to gain leverage with Washington, but it did seem to reflect some genuine Saudi interest in relations with the Soviets. The invasion foiled this significant opportunity for the Soviets.

With respect to Saudi Arabia, Soviet military force in Afghanistan ultimately created resistance to rather than influence for Moscow. In the wake of the invasion, the Saudis questioned U.S. resolve and were wary of the Soviet Union's growing shadow to the north; appeasing the Soviets instead of co-operating with the seemingly vacillating United States was viewed by the Saudis as a plausible security alternative.[22] When Washington demonstrated increased anti-Soviet resolve, however, the Saudis became more inclined to seek U.S. protection against the Soviet threat. The Soviet Union's ability to translate the threat from Afghanistan into real influence, therefore, was in part a function of U.S. resolve. Had the Afghanistan intervention not undermined Soviet opportunities with Saudi Arabia in 1979, Washington may have lost considerable influence in the Gulf. Indeed, credible relations with Saudi Arabia were a prerequisite for broader regional influence because, in this time period, most of the smaller Gulf states, except perhaps for Kuwait, followed Riyadh's foreign policy lead.

The Saudis also joined Iran and other Gulf states in rejecting the December 1980 proposal of Soviet leader Leonid Brezhnev, which called for the removal of superpower influence from the Gulf. This proposal probably reflected Soviet fears of the increasing U.S. regional presence. In general, the Gulf states found it absurd for the Soviet Union to propose Gulf neutralization while firmly entrenched in Muslim Afghanistan.

The Gulf states' rejection of the Brezhnev proposal was not insignificant. Compared to the United States, the Soviets had a minor presence in the Gulf. Consequently, regional acceptance of the Brezhnev proposal would have constituted a Soviet strategic gain and decreased the U.S. ability to respond legitimately and effectively to the Gulf war. The U.S. response to the Gulf war undoubtedly had its costs, but also improved U.S. credibility and led to more solid security relations with the Gulf states. Hence, one can see a linkage between Soviet actions in Afghanistan and the Iran-Iraq war: The Afghanistan intervention created repercussions that helped Washington pursue its interests during the Iran-Iraq war.

In July 1980 and in April 1981, the Soviets attempted to woo the Saudis again[23] and to discredit U.S. efforts to portray Afghanistan as a threat to Saudi Arabia. The Saudis rejected these overtures and stressed once more that they would not pursue relations with the Soviet Union while it occupied Afghanistan. This sentiment continued through 1982,[24] despite Saudi interest in using the Soviet card to encourage U.S. support for Saudi King Fahd's 1981 Middle East peace plan.[25] Favorable Saudi references toward the Soviet Union were made in 1983 but were again qualified by Saudi assertions that the future of relations with the Soviet Union depended on "the extent of the Soviet leadership's responsiveness to Islamic causes, in Afghanistan and elsewhere."[26] It is safe to say that the Soviet occupation of Afghanistan, at certain junctures, affected the domestic policymaking debate in Saudi Arabia[27] (and in other countries) in a manner favorable to the United States: Internal elements that promoted closer ties to Washington were probably strengthened. It is no coincidence that Soviet withdrawal "paved the way" for the Saudis in 1989 to allow the Soviet Union to open a trade office in their country.[28]

Saudi support of the Afghan rebels, which like that of Iran was notable, posed an additional problem of relations with the Soviet Union. The Saudis helped organize Afghan political opposition to the Soviets and also gave the rebels military support through Saudi branches of the Islamic brotherhood. Under the Reagan administration, Saudi arms lifts to the rebels increased to estimated value of $1.5 billion.[29]

Iraq

While the Afghanistan intervention damaged Iranian and Saudi relations with the Soviets for a prolonged period, Soviet-Iraqi relations were, for two basic reasons, only temporarily affected. First, the regimes of Saudi Arabia and Iran, unlike that of secular Iraq, gained legitimacy through unquestioned support of Islamic causes. Consequently, they were more disturbed by and compelled to challenge the Soviet intervention, as suggested by their considerable aid to the Muslim resistance in Afghanistan. Second, Iraq, unlike Saudi Arabia or Iran, was dependent on the Soviet Union for arms and could not take as hard a line on Afghanistan over the long term.

Nonetheless, despite these constraints, Iraq did help spearhead the Muslim world's condemnation of the invasion and increased its harassment of Iraq's Communist Party through which the Soviets had gained influence in Iraq. Moreover, the invasion, and the Gulf war to a much larger extent, helped shift Iraq's alignment from pro-Soviet Syria and Libya to the more pro-U.S. Saudi Arabia and Jordan. Iraq's increasing moderation helped ensure that, at least for some time, it would be less inclined to challenge U.S. interests. By late 1980, Soviet neutrality in the Iran-Iraq war had replaced Afghanistan as the primary cause of deteriorating Soviet-Iraqi relations, and the Afghanistan issue thereafter had little influence on Iraqi foreign policy.

Smaller Gulf States

Unlike Saudi Arabia and Iran, the United Arab Emirates (UAE), Bahrain, and Kuwait provided economic rather than military aid to the rebels. Moreover, the invasion pushed Kuwait, the only "pro-Soviet" Gulf state at the time other than perhaps Iraq, to distance itself from the Soviets. Prior to the invasion, Kuwait had acted as a conduit for the Soviets to the other Gulf states and was used by them to demonstrate the benefits of a pro-Soviet stance, while after the invasion, Kuwait increasingly promoted superpower noninterference in the region. However, Kuwait, unlike Oman, continued to stress that the Soviets were not the main threat to the Gulf. It is possible that Kuwait still hoped to capitalize on perceived Soviet influence with Iran, which threatened Kuwait throughout the Gulf war.

As to be expected, the invasion worsened already strained Soviet-Omani political relations. Like Saudi Arabia and Iran, Oman handily rejected Brezhnev's 1980 Gulf proposal, in part because of the Soviet presence in Afghanistan, and called for a Soviet withdrawal. This call was reiterated in 1981 and again in 1982; the Omani view was that if the Soviet Union withdrew its troops from Afghanistan, the Gulf nations would be able "to consider future relations with Moscow in the interests of peace and stability."[30] The Afghanistan occupation remained of concern to Oman. But the escalating Gulf war, and some signs of Soviet moderation toward the Gulf, played a role in pushing Oman to join Bahrain and the UAE in taking out an extra insurance policy against Iran by establishing diplomatic relations with the Soviets in 1985.

THE INTER-REGIONAL RESPONSE TO THE INVASION

The invasion not only had repercussions at the superpower and regional level, but also motivated countries outside the Persian Gulf region, namely Egypt, China, and Pakistan, to take actions that limited Soviet regional influence. Egypt's President Anwar Sadat called for closer U.S.-Egyptian military ties to confront the Soviet threat. He also sent military personnel to Oman within "the framework of a joint U.S.-as-Sadat scheme" and claimed that after the invasion, he would be willing to give the United States "every facility to reach the Gulf whenever any state of the Gulf is threatened."[31] For a high price, Washington was also given qualified use of Egypt's base at Ras Banas. This helped improve U.S. force projection and reconnaissance capabilities. In addition, Egypt reportedly sold the United States Soviet-made weapons for transfer to the Afghan rebels[32] and established military camps on its territory to train the rebels.

China joined Egypt in urging a stronger U.S. response to the Afghanistan intervention, which had exacerbated Sino-Soviet tensions. China repeatedly condemned the invasion, refused to recognize Afghanistan's Soviet-controlled Karmal regime, and viewed Soviet presence in Afghanistan as a stepping stone to the encirclement of China and to control of the Gulf.[33] This led to strengthened Chinese-Pakistani political and military relations.

China's firm commitment to Pakistan's defense intensified the Chinese response to the Soviet intervention, which had considerably compromised Pakistan's security. This commitment improved Pakistan's stability in the face of the Soviet threat. Since the defense of the Gulf depended in part on Pakistan's stability, China's commitment to Pakistan indirectly contributed to U.S. security interests in the Gulf; the Carter administration consulted China on how to co-operate in assisting Pakistan to contain the Soviets.[34]

For its part, China sold Pakistan submarines, patrol boats, modern tanks, Mig-19s, Tu-2 and Tu-16 bombers.[35] Chinese military instructors assisted Pakistan with internal instability and external intrusions by Soviet aircraft. China also reportedly massed troops[36] in the small strip of land facing Afghanistan's Wakhan corridor, which was seized by the Soviets in the invasion. In addition, China aided the Afghan resistance; by 1984, Chinese arms lifts to the rebels were expanded and reports suggested that the United States and China were co-operating to support the Afghan resistance.[37]

China's strategic and political response to the Soviet intervention placed added costs on potential Soviet adventurism and probably decreased Soviet flexibility in the postinvasion period in South Asia and the Persian Gulf. Although China was generally interested in reducing both superpowers' influence in the Gulf as a means of enhancing its own regional status, the invasion inclined it to challenge Soviet interests more than those of the United States. This can be said despite increased Chinese arms sales to Iran after 1985, which Washington condemned; China's focus remained the containment of Soviet influence. Overall, Chinese third-world policy, at least for some time, was boosted by the Soviet invasion.[38]

In some ways, the Soviet invasion created a growing link of anti-Soviet defense efforts that had varying levels of relevance to U.S. regional security. For example, the Chinese strategic response to the invasion improved both Chinese and Pakistani defense, and Pakistan also expanded its role in Gulf security.

In the invasion's aftermath, relations between Saudi Arabia and Pakistan improved as "diplomatic visits took place at a high level and in rapid succession."[39] Indeed, Afghanistan may have been the clinching argument for Pakistan to send troops to Saudi Arabia. In February 1980, Pakistan's President Zia-ul-Haq encouraged Washington to forge improved Saudi-Pakistani military cooperation,[40] which led the Saudis to agree to an exchange of arms for Pakistani security assistance. This deal was related to joint attempts to contain Soviet regional influence.[41]

By early 1981, 1,200 Pakistani noncombat forces and advisers were in Saudi Arabia, with as many as 10,000 more expected.[42] These forces also could have helped protect Saudi Arabia against internal or external threats. Since the United States was committed to Gulf stability, Pakistani assistance to Saudi Arabia indirectly served U.S. strategic interests in the region as did Chinese assistance to Pakistan.

GLOBAL POLITICS: THE U.S. RESPONSE TO AFGHANISTAN

Dire predictions were made in the aftermath of the Soviet invasion. Even though in retrospect it appears that the Soviet threat was greatly exaggerated, at the time presidents Carter and Reagan and numerous analysts contemplated the gamut of Soviet opportunism including an invasion of the oil fields of Iran. The Soviets heightened such suspicions by conducting exercises simulating an invasion of Iran. Irrespective of true Soviet regional designs, the invasion heavily contributed to a major shift in U.S. foreign policy. It added several unique elements to an already unstable region, which had their impact on U.S. foreign policy and standing in the Gulf.

First, while the U.S. strategic position had crumbled prior to Afghanistan, this did not necessarily imply automatic Soviet gains. Moscow did gain to the extent that U.S. standing was undermined. In this sense, it scored negative gains or benefited from U.S. failures. It had not yet, however, enjoyed the positive gains or benefits accruing from its own opportunism. The Afghanistan intervention presented the West with the possibility that Moscow would exploit negative gains to maximize positive gains by perhaps invading the Gulf.[43] Consequently, a specter of threat was created that the Iranian revolution alone could never have created.

Second, unlike the Iranian revolution, which was primarily a regional threat, Afghanistan was an external threat and therefore had different implications. After the Shah fell, many analysts believed that internal instability was the greatest threat to Gulf security. Therefore, it was important to reduce arms sales to the region and to limit the U.S. military profile. The Afghanistan invasion complicated this view and made it clear that threats to regional stability were varied. While the November 1979 Iranian hostage crisis suggested that military force could not be the sole solution to a deteriorating strategic position, the Afghanistan invasion was evidence of the need to shore up U.S. defense. It changed the focus of U.S. policy from the debacle in Iran to the Soviet threat to the Gulf, albeit the former goal certainly did remain important in U.S. foreign policy.

Third, by posing a threat to the Gulf, Afghanistan fueled superpower rivalry. It represented one more link in a chain of events that had begun in earnest with British withdrawal and paved the way for the more direct linkage of interaction between the regional and superpower levels. Whereas before the invasion the United States was more concerned with regional than with superpower threats, after 1979, Washington aimed to secure the Gulf more against Soviet than regional threats. Subsequent strategic events would reverse this trend. Indeed, the Iran-Iraq war would raise the status of regional threats to a level paralleling that of the Soviet threat. The end of the Cold War, coupled with the Iraqi invasion of Kuwait, would shift U.S. concern almost totally toward regional threats and almost de-link the global and regional levels.

The invasion seemed to be viewed in Washington as the last straw in a trend that saw the regional power balance shifting to the Soviet Union. Prior to the invasion, the U.S. public, moderates in the U.S. government, and even the president were not sufficiently impressed by Soviet gains in Angola, Ethiopia, and South Yemen to promote a noticeable shift in what was widely viewed as a policy of accommodating Moscow. After the invasion, the domestic milieu shifted significantly; U.S. hardliners, who espoused geopolitical resolve against the Soviet Union, gained precedence over moderates,[44] and the U.S. public and Congress were sufficiently persuaded by the Soviet threat to increase their support of U.S. strategic efforts significantly. This should be contrasted with the political mood following the fall of the Shah, which discouraged activism; in a poll conducted in February 1979,[45] approximately 29 percent of the respondents favored cuts in defense spending in order to balance the federal budget (see Table 4.1).

Increased public support for defense spending, as suggested by Table 4.1, was related to Afghanistan and was at the highest point recorded in Gallup polls in

Table 4.1. Public Support of Defense Spending

	Too Little	Too Much	About Right	Don't Know
Before Invasion	34	21	33	
After Invasion	49	14	24	13

Source: Adapted from *The Gallup Poll: Public Opinion 1980* (Wilmington, Del.: Scholarly Resources, Inc., 1981), 47.

more than a decade.[46] In January 1980, a surprising 9 percent of Americans polled even favored sending U.S. troops to Afghanistan;[47] in a February poll, Americans supported the use of U.S. troops to defend other countries against a Soviet invasion by a significant 75 percent to 18 percent. The number of Americans who wanted to get tough with Moscow rose from 53 percent in late 1979 to 67 percent by January 1980.[48] In addition, whereas in an October 1978 survey only 6 percent of Americans named an international problem as the most important problem facing the nation, 44 percent did in a January poll.[49] By January 1981, 51 percent of Americans, the highest number in over a decade, supported higher defense spending.[50] Writing in the aftermath of the invasion, U.S. ambassador to Moscow, George Kennan, stated that there had not been since World War II, "as far-reaching a militarization of thought and discourse in the capital."[51]

As a result of polls and other factors, the widely held perception in Congress and in the president's cabinet was that Americans would support defense increases. This resulted in even higher spending. Immediately prior to Afghanistan, the Carter administration was committed to a 3 percent real increase in fiscal year 1981 defense spending. This budget request was withdrawn in direct response to Afghanistan; on January 28 and March 26, 1980, a substantially revised budget was submitted that called for significantly higher spending. Confronted by the Soviet threat, Carter asked for $157 billion for military expenditures in fiscal year 1981, nearly $20 billion more than in 1980.[52] Congress insisted on even higher spending; the budget that resulted in the final fiscal year 1981 budget appears below in Table 4.2.

In particular, President Carter's view of Soviet motives changed abruptly. He had asserted prior to the invasion that the United States needed to stand firm against the Soviet Union and to have better forces and means for rapid deployment.[53] He was not, however, disturbed enough by Soviet advances at the global level to translate his concern into action, preliminary plans for the RDF notwithstanding. This reflected an absence of suspicion in his interpretation of

Table 4.2. National Defense Budget Function for FY 1980–81 (in billions of dollars)

	FY 1980 2nd Conc. Resolution	Request January 28 1980	Request March 26 1980	FY 1981 2nd Conc. Resolution
Budget Authority	143.7	161.8	164.5	172.7
Outlays	135.7	146.2	150.5	159.05

Source: U.S. House, Committee on Foreign Affairs, *Congress and Foreign Policy—1980* (Washington, D.C.: GPO, 1980), 18–19.

Soviet intentions, which was underscored by his claim after the Shah's fall that the Soviets shared a desire for a stable Iran.[54]

The invasion, however, shocked the president, who described it as "an unprecedented act," a "radical departure from the policies or actions that the Soviets have pursued since the Second World War,"[55] and "the most serious threat to the peace since the second World War."[56] Carter asserted that his opinion of the Soviets had "changed more drastically in the last week than in the previous two-and-a-half years,"[57] and sent Brezhnev a message on the presidential hot line that claimed that the invasion "could mark a fundamental and long-lasting turning point" in superpower relations.[58] Brezhnev's claim that Moscow aimed only to prevent Afghanistan from becoming "an imperialist military bridgehead" was condemned as false by the president.[59] Carter also emphasized to U.S. adversaries and allies that they should not have "the slightest doubt about U.S. resolve," as if he knew that this were in serious question,[60] and claimed that the invasion taught him more about the Soviets than any other event.

Three weeks after the invasion, the president issued the Carter Doctrine:

> Let our position be absolutely clear: An attempt by any outside force to gain control of the Persian Gulf region will be regarded as an assault on the vital interests of the United States of America, and such an assault will be repelled by any means necessary, including military force.[61]

Although events prior to the Soviet invasion made the Persian Gulf more important in U.S. foreign policy, the Carter Doctrine, as Brzezinski would subsequently note, virtually tied Gulf stability to U.S. global security.[62] Unlike Carter's approach to the Iranian crisis, which downplayed the use of military options,[63] his response to Afghanistan was more forceful and direct.

The Carter Doctrine was reminiscent of the Eisenhower Doctrine, which promised U.S. military resolve against international communism. Unlike the

Eisenhower Doctrine, however, it was not extensively debated by the American people, by Congress, or by the press. Rather, as former Secretary for Political Affairs David Newsome remarked, it was "uncritically accepted,"[64] despite the fact that it gave the president broad discretion to use force in a region where instability and high stakes could have combined to spark superpower confrontation. This was yet another indication of how the Afghanistan intervention had shifted U.S. public opinion.

Over time, however, aspects of the Carter Doctrine were criticized. Some observers, not the least of whom was Carter's own secretary of state Cyrus Vance, viewed the doctrine as too dramatic.[65] Other analysts and officials believed that Washington could not back it up and that it did not address the fundamental problems of political instability in the Gulf region. Although these were valid criticisms, it was not lost on the administration that the threat to U.S. interests was political as well as military. Although the potential for a Soviet invasion of Iran was played up at both government and academic levels, political instability in the Gulf was seen as the major short-term threat rather than the threat of Soviet military intervention in the region.[66]

The Carter Doctrine was novel in that unlike the Nixon Doctrine of the 1970s, it clearly and formally committed the United States to a direct military role in regional defense. Its message of containment was somewhat reminiscent of the 1947 Truman Doctrine—the Cold War seemed to be on again in earnest. Although the United States had some form of commitment to Gulf security since the 1940s, the Carter Doctrine clearly raised the commitment a couple of notches.

While the shift in U.S. policies had definite costs in terms of increased military expenditures, opportunity costs, and the constraints implied by the resort to militarism, it can be said with some reservation that the United States gained more from this policy shift than it lost. The invasion alerted Washington to the importance of ensuring that U.S. inaction in the world theater not be misperceived as timidity. Even after the Soviets consolidated ties with South Yemen and the Shah of Iran fell to Islamic fundamentalists in 1979, the United States had not yet taken major steps to protect its own interests. To be sure, numerous plans and proposals existed for such action, including planning for the U.S. RDF. But the feeling in Washington may have been that although the Iranian revolution was a major setback, it was not an irrevocable one. Washington still hoped for a favorable turn in Iran's domestic struggle or for an alternate means of protecting U.S. interests.

The Soviet invasion, however, changed this view. U.S. vulnerability in the Gulf became coupled with potential Soviet opportunism from Afghanistan. This combination created perceptions in the United States of a threat that the Iranian revolution alone could not have created.

The increased U.S. resolve at the superpower level translated into U.S. defense efforts that improved U.S. regional security. Hundreds of strategic studies emerged that intelligently helped guide U.S. regional defense efforts. Improvements in U.S. intelligence capabilities, in force projection, and in flexible response contributed to the U.S. deterrent. After the invasion, U.S. radar planes began operating from Egyptian airfields and providing the United States with valuable information. Diego Garcia, the closest permanent U.S. base to the Gulf was significantly upgraded, and access agreements for U.S. forces were reached with Oman, Kenya, and Somalia. In addition, in the period after the Carter Doctrine was issued, the RDF's development was intensified. In January 1983, the RDF would be transformed into the unified central command called CENTCOM.

Some observers have argued that the Iranian revolution and other regional crises spurred the Carter Doctrine and the RDF irrespective of Afghanistan.[67] This view has merit insofar as plans for the RDF were in motion before the Soviet invasion. Significant features of the RDF, however, were developed in earnest after the Soviet invasion. The invasion thus played an important role in the incremental process that led to the development of the RDF.

The RDF, a concept coined in 1958 and revived by a 1977 Presidential Directive, faced opposition, and was correctly viewed by many observers[68] as a reality only on paper, until the Afghanistan intervention. After the invasion, military hardliners prevailed in Washington, and substantial monies were allocated for RDF expansion. Most of the 4.5 percent increase in defense spending for the 1980s proposed by President Carter was earmarked for the RDF.[69]

The establishment of RDF headquarters and the issuance of the Carter Doctrine in the post-invasion period caused Congress to "reverse its niggardly attitude towards Pentagon budgetary requests."[70] As the tenor of congressional hearings suggested, administration requests for defense funds and congressional accommodation of them were directly related to Afghanistan.[71]

Beyond playing a role in the funding of the RDF, the Afghanistan invasion motivated its size and configuration and gave the RDF an anti-Soviet role, particularly with respect to Gulf defense.[72] The size and planning of the RDF was based on an actual, albeit unlikely, Soviet invasion of the Gulf. As Secretary of Defense Harold Brown stressed, the RDF as it developed was not a response to internal matters in the Gulf, but rather was intended "to offset Soviet forces."[73]

In the post-invasion period, the Pentagon requested funding authority to develop the capability to project force by air and sea.[74] The fiscal year 1981 budget shifted the emphasis from conventional forces configured to fight a short intensive war on the central front of Europe to a new emphasis on flexible forces for areas such as the Persian Gulf.[75] The largest comparative increase in the budget was in airlift and sealift, which reflected the commitment to the RDF.[76] (See Table 4.3.)

Initiatives on sealift mobility enhancement in the post-invasion period were taken in a threefold approach. The Near Term Prepositioning Ships Program (NTPS), a direct response to Afghanistan, was designed to increase U.S. force projection capability by decreasing deployment time and accelerating the prepositioning of combat materials. It represented a significant addition to the RDF posture.

Table 4.3. Defense Authority by Program, FY 1980–85 (in billions of current dollars)

Program	1980	1981	1982	1983	1984	1985	1980–85
Airlift & Sealift							
1/79	1.9	2.1	2.2	2.4	2.5	2.6	13.7
1/80	2.0	2.3	2.7	3.1	3.6	4.2	17.9

The overall difference between 1/79 and 1/80 projections was 30.6 percent.

Source: Adapted from U.S. Senate, Hearings before the Committee on the Budget, *First Concurrent Resolution on the Budget—Fiscal Year 1981*, February-March 1980 (Washington, D.C.: GPO), 381.

By early June 1980, the seven ships assigned to NTPS were anchored at Diego Garcia, and by October 1981, six more ships had joined them. In addition, a U.S. aircraft carrier, battle group, and marine detachments were diverted from Europe and Asia. These efforts led to a tripling of the U.S. naval presence in the region. Accompanying this naval increase was an 1,800-man marine force, which was sent to the Gulf with enough materials to support approximately 10,000 more men.

The second program aimed at improving sealift capability was the Maritime Prepositioning Program (MPS), which differed from the NTPS program primarily in its depth and ambition. The MPS combined airlift and sealift, to include thirteen Maritime Prepositioning Ships. These ships would provide the supplies and equipment for three U.S. Marine Corps amphibious brigades. Although this program was announced in August 1979, funds for it were approved only after extensive analysis and discussions. Funding for the SL-7 (Sea Land Container Ship) for high-speed military sealift also came well after the Soviet invasion. Indeed, Congress appropriated $18 million for urgent sealift capability. Interestingly, significant support for the first deployed units in Operation Desert Shield a decade later came from the Marine Corps Maritime Prepositioning Squadron.[77]

Initiatives for improving U.S. airlift capability were also put in motion before the invasion. Studies on this issue had been conducted since 1974, but only in the post-invasion environment was significant action on funding taken.[78] Purchases for KC-10 aerial tankers and for high-speed civilian ships were accelerated, and a long-term program for the procurement of a new "CX" transport aircraft for long distance deployment was begun.[79] Although the CX airlifter was in the administration's proposed budget prior to the invasion, funding for it was denied by the Senate Armed Services Committee.[80] Only after considerable debate following the Afghanistan invasion did Congress appropriate $5 million for it.[81]

The Carter Doctrine and the RDF were directed primarily at the Soviet Union, at the containment of "outside forces," and only secondarily at Iran. Despite its shortcomings and costs, the RDF served an important role; it underscored U.S. resolve at the global and regional level, which was heavily in doubt at the time. Washington's response to the Afghanistan invasion was, to some extent, welcomed in the Gulf, and may have served to convince regional leaders that Washington was committed to their security.[82] More importantly, the development of the RDF, which would be accelerated and altered by the Iran-Iraq war in the 1980s, would later play a role in stopping Saddam Hussein's aggression against Kuwait in 1990.

The Afghanistan intervention also pushed the United States to give precedence to its strategic concerns and to take actions outside the immediate Gulf region that were designed to protect U.S. interests in the Gulf. To cite one notable case, all U.S. aid to Pakistan had been cut in April 1979 in response to Pakistan's pursuit of nuclear capability. After the December invasion, Pakistan's strategic importance to Washington superseded the nuclear issue. While it can be argued that U.S. interests were well served by linking aid to the nuclear issue, it may also be said that U.S. influence over Pakistan's nuclear future was probably decreased by such a policy; without U.S. aid and support, Pakistan would have been more inclined to develop the nuclear option for protection.

AFGHANISTAN: THE VIEW FROM THE PERSIAN GULF

The intervention's effect on the perceptions of Gulf leaders was varied and somewhat ambiguous. For the most part it was overshadowed by the reverberations of the Iranian revolution and the Iran-Iraq war, which erupted in September 1980 and presented an immediate threat to Gulf stability. Although most Gulf states welcomed a firm U.S. response to the Soviet invasion, U.S. attempts over time to convince Gulf leaders that the Soviets posed a major and calculated threat from Afghanistan met with as much success as had Britain's attempt a century before to convince Persia of czarist Russia's imperialistic intent. In general, Britain and the United States, to a lesser extent, were viewed as over-reacting.

To be sure, Saudi Arabia and other Arab states initially viewed the Soviet invasion as a strategic threat. Partly in response to this perceived threat, the Saudis agreed to act as a conduit for U.S. aid to Pakistan. Saudi interest in formal cooperation with the United States, however, flagged thanks to fear of Syria and Iraq, both of which were vying for Gulf political supremacy; doubts over U.S. intentions; and concerns about appearing too pro-U.S.

U.S. efforts to form a "strategic consensus," which aimed to enlist formal support for U.S. interests by demonstrating a firm U.S. commitment to regional security, also met firm regional opposition. At the time, the Saudis were interested in mediating a settlement of the Iran-Iraq war, and both Iran and Iraq held U.S.-Saudi ties suspect.[83] Moreover, the other Gulf countries, such as Saudi Arabia, wanted to avoid the political costs of allowing U.S. bases on their territory.

It is difficult, therefore, to argue that the Afghanistan intervention made the Gulf states more interested in offering the level of co-operation that Washington desired. It might even be fair to say that the Gulf states manipulated their security relations with the United States to accommodate what one observer aptly called "immediate fluctuations in the security situation" of the Gulf.[84] The invasion, however, benefited the United States in a significant manner; it justified informal U.S.-Gulf state co-operation in the United States and in the Gulf region. This could be seen in several ways.

First, the Arab world's condemnation of the invasion "[turned] the tables on countries such as Syria and Libya, which cooperated with Moscow while chiding the Saudis for their association with the United States."[85] Pressure on Riyadh for its ties to the "imperialist" United States became less sensible and more ineffective because their patron was now firmly entrenched in Muslim Afghanistan. Second, prior to the invasion the chasm between the West and the Gulf states had been growing. After the invasion, however, the concurrence of security perceptions between the Gulf states and the United States increased, and the common goals of Pan-Islamism and the United States were reinforced. This helped further justify U.S.-Gulf state co-operation.

Finally, efforts to improve U.S. regional security required a basic recognition in the United States that such an improvement was needed and a regional willingness to co-operate. The Afghanistan occupation largely provided the former; the Iran-Iraq war increased the latter. For example, although the Saudis requested Airborne Warning and Air Control System (AWACS) in February 1980 in response to the Iran-Iraq war, Washington agreed to sell AWACS in 1981 partly in order to strengthen Saudi Arabia against the communist threat. Without the Soviets in Afghanistan, U.S. domestic and institutional support for such a sale might not have existed thanks to inadequate justification.

Hence, a dichotomy of security perceptions and interests developed with the Afghanistan interaction, driving the United States at the superpower level and the Gulf war motivating the Gulf states at the regional level. To be sure, Washington was also concerned with the Iranian threat. Meanwhile, the threat from Afghanistan served to remind the leaders of Gulf states that Moscow could invade a Muslim country despite the potentially high human, political, and military costs.

The Soviets had feared that the Afghanistan intervention would push Gulf states to seek U.S. protection and to support the U.S.-RDF. Thus, Moscow's aim through 1987 was to limit U.S.-Gulf state co-operation. Ironically, the Afghanistan invasion helped defeat this longstanding Soviet aim.

As in the case of Saudi Arabia, Oman's efforts to improve its security position were intensified by Soviet actions in Afghanistan. On February 13, 1980, Oman agreed to allow Washington use of its military facilities to meet the Soviet threat and signed a military agreement with the United States in response to the Soviet invasion.[86] In February 1982, Oman and Saudi Arabia signed a security co-operation agreement five days after Oman reiterated its fear of Soviet intentions.[87] This agreement also reflected Omani fears of Iran and of increased Soviet influence with South Yemen and Ethiopia in addition to Omani concerns over the Soviet presence in Afghanistan.

THE IMPACT ON SOUTH ASIA

In the wake of the invasion, fears existed that the Soviets would invade Pakistan's province of Baluchistan, where they had stirred nationalist sentiment for decades. By mid-1981, some observers were noting that Baluchi leaders actually desired Moscow's intervention in their affairs. As time passed, however, Soviet use of discontented Baluchi groups as proxies became a more likely threat than military action; the latter would have generated a new wave of negative repercussions for the Soviet Union because many countries were primed by the Afghanistan invasion to respond politically and militarily to further Soviet adventurism.

Influence over Baluchistan and its 900 miles of Gulf coastline may have offered the Soviets bases of immense strategic value for influencing the politics of the Persian Gulf. Moscow, however, was unable to translate its military gains in Afghanistan into notable influence over Pakistan or Baluchistan. The invasion created negative effects for the Soviet Union, which more than cancelled out the positive ones.

For example, as has been noted, U.S.-Pakistani relations had deteriorated throughout the 1970s. The Soviets could have capitalized on this; however, the invasion revived U.S.-Pakistani security co-operation. President Carter phoned Pakistan's President Zia the day after the invasion to assure him of U.S. support against the Soviet threat. At first, Pakistan was reluctant to pursue close relations with the United States because it feared Soviet reprisals and doubted U.S. credibility. President Zia described President Carter's proposed aid plan of $400 million as "peanuts," and his reluctance to associate with Washington in the absence of a firm strategic commitment was underscored by his overly courteous welcome in late 1981 of the high Soviet official, Nikolai Firyubin. But, like Saudi Arabia, Pakistan responded more positively when the United States displayed a substantial commitment against the Soviet threat.

In March 1981, the United States offered Pakistan $3.2 billion in aid to be spread over a five-year period and pledged to protect Pakistan against unprovoked aggression in exchange for Pakistani consideration for U.S. Middle East interests. This plan was a direct response to the Soviet invasion and was aimed at containing Soviet influence over Pakistan and, indirectly, over the Gulf.

The Soviet Union's defeats in Afghanistan were detrimental not only militarily but also in terms of overall Soviet morale. Moreover, the invasion and the successful Muslim resistance to it to some extent created an Islamic resurgence in Soviet Central Asia, and Moscow was certainly averse to fanning the fires of Islam. These concerns reduced the Soviet will and ability to assume added risks, which could have jeopardized U.S. interests in the Gulf.

Several additional obstacles created partly by the Soviet invasion, militated against Soviet influence over Baluchistan. First, Baluchi leaders disliked superpower imperialism; the Soviet invasion, according to one observer, made people in Baluchistan see the Soviet Union's true colors.[88] Baluchis were hesitant to risk an exchange of Pakistani domination for that of the Soviets. Also, Baluchi frustration with Punjabi oppression was tempered by fear of Moscow's intentions. Second, as a result of the Soviet threat from Afghanistan, Pakistan received immense aid from the United States, Japan, China, and Gulf states, which helped stabilize it economically and militarily and which decreased the Soviet interest in and capability of manipulating Pakistani weakness for strategic gain. U.S. Sidewinders, Stingers, and other air defense equipment helped protect Pakistani air space from violations by communist aircraft, and foreign economic aid helped quiet dissident elements within Pakistan.

Third, events in Afghanistan enabled Zia's regime to further suppress political opposition by invoking the Soviet threat to Pakistan's national security. While revived U.S.-Pakistani security co-operation, a product of the Soviet invasion, served both countries, it also presented them with potential and real costs. Though Washington viewed its arms assistance to Pakistan primarily in anti-Soviet terms, India believed, not without reason, that Pakistan wanted U.S. arms primarily for use against it; India was particularly concerned with the sale of U.S. F-16s to Pakistan.

To be sure, Washington did not ignore the consequences for U.S.-Indian relations of stepped-up U.S. military aid to Pakistan. But the Afghanistan intervention made the importance of the U.S. strategic connection to Pakistan overshadow U.S. interests with India. This posed the interrelated costs of moving India closer to the Soviet Union and of exacerbating Indo-Pakistani relations, thus potentially compromising U.S. strategic interests. Several important factors, however, tempered these costs and benefited Washington.

First, although India viewed renewed U.S.-Pakistani strategic ties apprehensively, it probably recognized that these ties were less than opportunistic. Indeed, the Soviet invasion presented both Pakistan and the United States with legitimate security concerns. Consequently, India could construe U.S.-Pakistan strategic efforts as less threatening than otherwise would have been the case; by contrast, it was more difficult for the United States and Pakistan to view the Afghanistan intervention as justified and defensive in nature. This may help explain why the Soviets suffered more negative repercussions for their military actions in Afghanistan than the United States did for its strategic response to these Soviet actions. It also suggests that the costs of the use of force rise when it is viewed as illegitimate.

Second, though India benefited from its relations with the Soviet Union as a means of deterring China and gaining leverage over Pakistan, India was less than enthusiastic about the Soviet invasion. In part, this was because the invasion threatened to increase superpower rivalry in South Asia, where India had predominance; nor did India want Pakistan's stability to be so undermined that the Soviet Union could substantially enhance its influence in South Asia.[89] By threatening Pakistan's stability, the Soviet invasion disrupted links both within and between South Asia and the Persian Gulf. While India refrained from condemning the invasion, it privately expressed its displeasure with it and also let the Soviets know "bluntly and publicly" that their troops "had to leave Afghanistan."[90]

Third, the U.S.-Pakistan-Chinese axis that developed in response to the invasion also gave India reason to be more cautious. The potential for an escalation of tensions in South Asia threatened not only to increase India's reliance on the Soviet Union but also to invite even more superpower intervention in the region. While India's dependence on the Soviet Union was, to some extent, increased by the heightened U.S.-Pakistani military profile, the invasion also persuaded Indira Ghandi to pursue a more balanced foreign policy in relations with the superpowers.[91] In this sense, the Soviets both gained and lost from the invasion.

Fourth, if India had some incentive to improve its relations with Pakistan, Pakistan had even more reason in the aftermath of the invasion to calm India's fears. This is true not only because the invasion increased the threat to Pakistan's security, but also because Pakistan wanted to avoid antagonizing India. The possibility did exist that India and the Soviet Union would collude to undermine Pakistan. Pakistan's numerous peace efforts probably decreased tensions in Indo-Pakistani relations. In October 1982, the leaders of both countries met for the first time since 1972 in what was described as an improving climate of relations,[92] and by February 1984, Zia even described Pakistan's peace efforts as a "peace offensive." Washington also tried to allay India's fears in the wake of the invasion. For instance, President Carter decided to sell uranium fuel to India in 1980, in part, to maintain good relations with India because of the Soviet invasion.[93]

CONCLUSION

When Moscow invaded Afghanistan, the last thing it expected was that its intervention would benefit its primary global adversary, the United States. But this was precisely what occurred in the Persian Gulf context. While we might have predicted in 1979 that Moscow's actions in Afghanistan would prove ominous for the United States given U.S. vulnerability in the Middle East, we would have been wrong. The Afghanistan intervention helped pave the way for the U.S. rise to power in the conflictual Middle East. Although Moscow's struggle with the Afghan rebels was initially unrelated to Washington, it created numerous unexpected consequences at the regional and global level, which over the long run strengthened the United States as the third party.

In brief, the Afghanistan intervention spurred the United States to improve its deterrent in the Gulf, revive foundering defense alliances, and focus intelligent attention on defending its regional interests. To some extent, it damaged Soviet relations with important Muslim states and catalyzed a level of intra- and inter-regional defense co-operation. Finally, the invasion exhausted Soviet resources, which otherwise may have been exploited to challenge U.S. regional security.

In the case of Afghanistan, the use of force backfired in part because the Afghanistan invasion coincided with Western weakness, the Soviet Union's intentions were unclear, and Washington was willing to assume an activist role in protecting the Gulf against perceived threats. These factors, in addition to the ones discussed below, combined to motivate major countermeasures against the Soviet Union that benefited Washington.

Paradoxically, if the invasion had coincided with Western stability, and had the Soviet Union's intentions been more clear, its repercussions may have been less severe. The West would have been less pressed to take serious steps to protect its interests and to undermine Soviet efforts, and the invasion may have been viewed in regional rather than global terms. This suggests, contrary to conventional wisdom, that security enhancement can be more risky in an unstable environment, where it is often tempting and sometimes needed than in a stable one where limited goals could be accomplished without superfluously creating perceptions of as great a threat.

This chapter further suggests that the long-term risks of security enhancement can increase if the actor increasing its security is feared and if there is a plausible security alternative to capitulation for threatened states. The Soviet Union, particularly in light of its perceived advances on the Gulf's periphery and of Iran's anti-U.S. swing, was especially feared in 1979–80. However, threatened states had the primary choices of either accommodating the Soviets or moving closer to the West as a means of ensuring their security. They leaned more toward the latter, particularly after Washington showed increased resolve in response to Afghanistan. Pakistan and Saudi Arabia became more willing to co-operate with Washington. Hence, U.S. strategic efforts, irrespective of their true value in defense terms, communicated a positive message that was not insignificant in affecting the perceptions of important actors.

NOTES

1. Text of President Carter's remarks at a White House briefing, "Hostages in Iran, Invasion of Afghanistan," 8 January 1980, in DSB 80 (March 1980): 34.
2. See Henry S. Bradsher, *Afghanistan and the Soviet Union* (Durham, NC: Duke University Press, 1985), 162, 200–204; also, Anthony Arnold, *Afghanistan: The Soviet*

Invasion in Perspective (Stanford, CA: Hoover Institution Press, 1985). See Zalmay Khalilzad, "Soviet-Occupied Afghanistan," *Problems of Communism* 29 (November–December 1980). For an analysis of South Asian security in the years prior to and after the invasion, see G. S. Bhargava, *South Asian Security After Afghanistan* (Lexington, MA: Lexington Books, 1983).

3. Mina Graur, "The Soviet Union Versus Muslim Solidarity Following the Soviet Invasion of Afghanistan," *Slavic and Soviet Studies* 4 (1979): 79–80, 82, 89. Also, for a brief discussion of the Muslim response, see Robert O. Freedman, "Soviet Policy Toward the Middle East Since the Invasion of Afghanistan," *Journal of International Affairs* 34 (Fall/Winter 1980–1981): 289–90.

4. See Bradsher, *Afghanistan*, 189–99.

5. For an instructive discussion of increased Soviet opportunities in the Gulf in 1979, and for an assessment of the Rapid Deployment Forces (RDF) ability to ensure U.S. interests in the region, see Maxwell Orme Johnson, *The Military as an Instrument of U.S. Policy in Southwest Asia: The Rapid Deployment Joint Task Force 1979–1982* (Boulder, CO: Westview Press, 1983), 7–9; also, Dennis Ross, "Considering Soviet Threats to the Persian Gulf," *International Security* 6 (Fall 1981): 159–80.

6. Bradsher, *Afghanistan*, 155–57; also, Raju G. C. Thomas, "The Afghanistan Crisis and South Asian Security," *Journal of Strategic Studies* 4 (December 1981): 415–34.

7. For the opposing view, see Richard Pipes, "Soviet Global Strategy," *Commentary* 69 (April 1980): 31–39.

8. See Thomas E. Gouttierre, "The Role of Perceptions Concerning U.S. Interests in the Afghanistan Resistance," in *Afghan Alternatives: Issues, Options, and Policies*, ed. Ralph H. Magnus (New Brunswick, NJ: Transaction Books, 1985), 154.

9. U.S. Congress, Senate, *First Concurrent Resolution on the Budget—Fiscal Year 1981*, Hearings Before the Committee on the Budget, February–March 1980 (Washington, D.C.: GPO), 178–82. (Hereafter cited as U.S. Senate, *First Concurrent Resolution*.) See statement by Robert Levgold, which is based on his discussions with Soviet officials.

10. See Bradsher, *Afghanistan*, 162.

11. See the text of Foreign Minister Qotbzadeh's message to Andrei Gromyko in *Tehran Domestic Service*, in FBIS: South Asia, 15 August 1980, I5–I6.

12. See Graur, "The Soviet Union Versus Muslim Solidarity," 79–80, 82, 89.

13. See Shahram Chubin, "Gains for Soviet Policy in the Middle East," *International Security* (Spring 1982): 140–41.

14. Also, Iran reportedly launched sixty-three acts of armed aggression in support of the rebels. See CDSP 19 (11 June 1986): 18.

15. See the text of Foreign Minister Qatzbadeh, *Tehran Domestic Services*, in FBIS: South Asia, 15 August 1980, I5–I6.

16. For excerpts of the agreement, see Paris *IRAN-E AZAD*, in FBIS: South Asia, 16 December 1982, I6–I8.

17. *Radio Iran*, in FBIS: South Asia, 27 October 1981, I5.

18. On the effects of domestic determinants on Iranian foreign policy, see Gary Sick, "Iran's Quest for Superpower Status," *Foreign Affairs* (Spring 1987): 697–715.

19. Commentary in *Pravda*, in CDSP (3 April 1985): 9.

20. Interview with Iran's ambassador to the USSR, in *Tehran Keyhan*, in FBIS: South Asia, 15 April 1987, I3.

21. See Jacob Goldberg in Yaacov Ro'i, ed., *The U.S.S.R. and the Muslim World* (London: Allen & Unwin, 1984), 266–68. Igor Belayev, the author of the study in which

this assertion was made, strongly confirmed the assertion in a discussion with this author.

22. Goldberg in Ro'i, *The U.S.S.R. and the Muslim World*, 266–70.

23. See *Ash Shariqah*, in FBIS: MEA, 3 April 1981, C1.

24. See *Paris AFP*, in FBIS: MEA, 22 July 1980, C3; also *Paris AFP*, in FBIS: MEA, 14 December 1982, C6. In addition, for a view from the Saudi press, see *UKAZ*, in FBIS: MEA, 23 December 1982, C3.

25. See MECS 7 (1982/83): 760.

26. Defense Minister Prince Sultan, quoted in *Riyadh SPA*, in FBIS: MEA, 18 December 1985, C3.

27. On the Saudi domestic debate, see MECS (1984/85): 596–97.

28. Saudi sources cited in *Baghdad Al-Thawrah*, in FBIS: USSR, 6 March 1989, 16.

29. Stephanie G. Neuman, "Arms, Aid, and the Superpowers," *Foreign Affairs* (Summer 1988): 1049.

30. Omani minister quoted in *Paris AFP*, in FBIS: MEA, 27 December 1982, C2.

31. Interview with *Tokyo NHK*, in FBIS: MEA, 10 July 1980, D1.

32. *Far Eastern Economic Review*, 2 October 1981, 9.

33. On China's view of and response to the Soviet invasion, see Yaacov Vertzberger, "Afghanistan in China's Policy," *Problems of Communism* (May–June 1982): 6–14.

34. Christopher Van Hollen, "Leaning on Pakistan," *Foreign Policy* (Spring 1980): 35.

35. *Tehran Ettela*, in FBIS: South Asia, 21 July 1983, F2.

36. *Hong Kong AFP*, citing "knowledgeable sources" in *Press Trust of India News Agency*, in FBIS: MEA, 18 January 1980, S12.

37. See *Bakhtar*, in FBIS: South Asia, 4 June 1984, C3.

38. On this, see Vertzberger, "Afghanistan in China's Policy," 17–19.

39. See Dieter Braun, "The Afghanistan Conflict as a Regional Problem," *Journal of South Asian and Middle Eastern Studies* (Summer 1983): 36.

40. Zbigniew Brzezinski, *Power and Principle: Memoirs of the National Security Advisor, 1977–1981* (New York: Farrar, Straus, and Giroux, 1985), 449.

41. S. P. Seth, "Afghanistan in Global Politics," *Institute for Defense Studies and Analyses* (New Delhi, October/December 1980), 190.

42. William B. Quandt, *Saudi Arabia in the 1980s: Foreign Policy, Security, and Oil* (Washington, D.C.: Brookings Institution, c. 1981), 41.

43. See statement by Matthew Nimitz, former under secretary of state for security assistance, "U.S. Security Framework," *Current Policy* 221 (16 September 1980): 1–4.

44. Even *Izvestia*, the official Soviet government newspaper, recognized that the invasion gave U.S. hardliners a boost. Bradsher, *Afghanistan*, 191.

45. This figure is based on an average of all separate sampling groups in this poll. *The Gallup Poll: Public Opinion 1980* (Wilmington, DE: Scholarly Resources, Inc., 1979), 83–84.

46. Ibid., 47.

47. Ibid., 17.

48. U.S. Congress, House of Representatives, Committee on Foreign Affairs, *Congress and Foreign Policy—1980* (Washington, D.C.: GPO, 1980), 2.

49. *The Gallup Poll—1980*, 47.

50. *The Gallup Poll: Public Opinion 1981* (Wilmington, DE: Scholarly Resources, Inc. 1980), 98.

51. Quoted in Fred Halliday, *Soviet Policy in the Arc of Crisis* (Amsterdam: The Netherlands Institute for Policy Studies, 1981), 9.

52. *The Gallup Poll—1980*, 47.

53. For example, see President Carter, "U.S. Defense Policy," remarks at the White House, DSB 80 (February 1980): 58–60.

54. Gwertzman, "U.S. Officials React Warily," A10.

55. See President Carter, "Meet the Press," interview in DSB 80 (March 1980): 30.

56. "Transcript of President's State of the Union Address to Joint Session of Congress," *New York Times*, 24 January 1980, A12.

57. In excerpts from his interview on NBC's "Meet the Press," Carter explains this comment in *New York Times*, 21 January 1980, A4.

58. Jimmy Carter, *Keeping Faith: Memoirs of a President* (New York: Bantam Books, 1982), 472.

59. "Excerpts from Brezhnev Statement Answering a Question on World Situation," *New York Times*, 13 January 1980, A16.

60. "Transcript of President's Speech on Soviet Military Intervention in Afghanistan," *New York Times*, 5 January 1980, A6.

61. *Public Papers of the Presidents of the United States* (Washington, D.C.: U.S. Government Printing Office, 1981), 197.

62. Brzezinski, *Power and Principle*, 430.

63. See Gary Sick, *All Fall Down: America's Tragic Encounter with Iran*, (Boulder, CO: Westview Press, 1985), 173–74.

64. See David B. Newsome, "America Engulfed," *Foreign Policy* (Summer 1981): 17; also, see Michael Getler, "Persian Gulf: Little Debate on Buildup," *Washington Post*, 10 August 1980, A1.

65. Testimony by Secretary of State Vance in U.S. Congress, House of Representatives, Hearings before the Committee on Foreign Affairs, *Foreign Assistance Legislation for Fiscal Year 1981* (Part I) (Washington, D.C.: GPO, 1980), 22.

66. Testimony by Secretary Brown, ibid., 244.

67. Elaboration on this view in R. K. Ramazani, "America and the Gulf: Beyond Peace and Security," *Middle East Insight* (January/February 1982): 7–8.

68. For example, see comment by John C. West, former ambassador to Saudi Arabia, in Jack R. Perry, ed., *Proceedings of a Conference on Gulf Security* (Charleston, SC: The Citadel, 1983), 2.

69. See tables and discussion in U.S. Senate, *First Concurrent Resolution*, 381–93.

70. Johnson, *The Military as an Instrument*, 65.

71. See statement by Secretary Brown, and by Jones, former chairman of the Joint Chiefs of Staff, in U.S. House, *Foreign Assistance Legislation for Fiscal Year 1981*, 202–203, 221.

72. See U.S. Congress, *Rapid Deployment Forces: Policy and Budgetary Implications* (Washington, D.C.: Congressional Budget Office [CBO], 1983), XIV, 4, 8, 11.

73. Interview with Brown, *Wall Street Journal*, 1 July 1980, 22.

74. Jeffrey Record, "The RDF: Is the Pentagon Kidding?" *Washington Quarterly* 4, no. 3 (Summer 1981): 49.

75. See U.S. Senate, *First Concurrent Resolution*, 361.

76. Ibid., 384.

77. U.S. DoD, *Conduct of the Persian Gulf War*, 396.

78. The immediate text on the RDF is based largely the analysis in Johnson, *The Military*, 68–73.

79. Address by Secretary Brown, DSB 80 (May 1980): 66.

80. U.S. Congress, House of Representatives, *U.S. Interests in, and Policies Toward the Persian Gulf*, Hearings Before the Subcommittee on Europe and the Middle East, Committee on Foreign Affairs, 24 March, 12 April, 5 May, 1 and 28 July, and 3 September 1980 (Washington, D.C.: GPO, 1980), 85.

81. On the CX program, see U.S. Senate, *First Concurrent Resolution*, 165.

82. Brzezinski, *Power and Principle*, 445.

83. Nadav Safran, *Saudi Arabia: The Ceaseless Quest for Security* (Cambridge, MA: Belknap Press of Harvard University, 1985), 415.

84. Ibid., 412.

85. Ibid., 359.

86. See *Stockholm Dagens Nyheter*, in FBIS: MEA, 21 May 1980, C3.

87. On this agreement, see *Riyadh Domestic Service*, in FBIS: MEA, 24 February 1982, C5-6.

88. A veteran newsman in Baluchistan quoted in *Beijing XINHUA*, in FBIS: China, 6 November 1980, F2.

89. See Stephen P. Cohen, "South Asia After Afghanistan," *Problems of Communism* (January–February 1985): 30-31.

90. Paul H. Kreisberg, "India After Indira," *Foreign Affairs* (Spring 1985): 884.

91. Rodney W. Jones and Brad Roberts, "Pakistan and Regional Security," *Journal of South Asian and Middle Eastern Studies* (Spring 1983): 8.

92. See William K. Stevens, "Pakistan's Leader to Confer in India," *New York Times*, 31 October 1982, A11.

93. See Richard Burt, "U.S. Decides to Send Atom Fuel to India," *New York Times*, 8 May 1980, A1, A11.

5

THE CHAIN OF HISTORY: LINKING REGIONAL WARS

The impact of conflict on the third party can have critical short-term implications in the historical process. This is because the third party often plays a key role during conflict either by taking or failing to take actions that can contain or prolong it. While the role of the third party is often important in conflict, it also has profound consequences in the long term. This is because the third party not only affects the course of conflict, but also plays a role in affecting ensuing historical events. Conflict, then, can alter history by influencing the third party in a manner that makes it either more or less able and willing to deal with events occurring long after the end of the conflict. Such was the nature of conflict in the Middle East in the 1980s. The United States and its allies were unknowingly being prepared by the Iran-Iraq war for Operations Desert Shield and Storm.

The Iran-Iraq war (1980–88) was a shattering event in regional politics. The horrible human suffering it wreaked, the tremendous economic damage, and the political upheaval were on a scale not easily matched in the recent annals of interstate war. While significant in its own right, the war also put in motion developments that played a critical role in regional and world history. Saddam Hussein's use of force in September 1980, which triggered the Iran-Iraq war, would generate unintended consequences that would come back to haunt him after Iraq's dramatic invasion of Kuwait in August 1990.

The principal goal of this chapter is to show how the successful U.S.-led containment and reversal of Iraq's invasion of Kuwait was related to developments put in motion by the Iran-Iraq war long before Iraq invaded Kuwait. These developments laid part of the security-political foundation for the U.S.-led Operations Desert Shield and Storm, which devastated Iraqi power. While the United States was a third party to conflict in that it was not initially involved in Iraq's dispute with Kuwait, it would, of course, become a heavily involved third party over time and a direct antagonist when it spearheaded the military attack on Iraq.

We cannot understand fully why the U.S.-led alliance was so successful in the 1990–91 Persian Gulf war unless we understand the role of the Iran-Iraq war in the regional historical process. A crucial, unforeseen effect of the Iran-Iraq war was that it prepared the United States to deal with Saddam Hussein in 1990–91. This becomes clear only in focusing over time on the United States as the third party to regional conflict.

This chapter briefly discusses the causes of the Iran-Iraq war and then examines how the Iran-Iraq war was related to Iraq's decision to invade Kuwait. The body of the chapter is then devoted to an assessment of how the Iran-Iraq war was related to the successful containment and reversal of Iraq's invasion of Kuwait or, in more general terms, to the outcome or result of the second Persian Gulf war. In this sense, it shows how the effects of the Iran-Iraq war, such as the strengthening of Saudi power and the development of U.S. relations with regional states, became antecedent causes of the outcome of the second Persian Gulf war. That is, they became causes of the successful U.S.-led containment of Iraq in 1990–91.

THE ORIGINS OF THE IRAN-IRAQ WAR

Like the Afghanistan intervention, Iraq's September 1980 invasion of Iran had the trappings of both a defensive and offensive act, although it was probably more the latter than the former, despite the failure of the U.N. Security Council to identify Iraq as the aggressor. Although the reasons for Iraq's decision to invade were multifaceted, the decision can be viewed as a function of three factors: Iraqi fear, opportunism, and miscalculation.

Iraq feared Iran because unlike Iran under the Shah, Khomeini's revolutionary Iran sought to subvert Iraq's predominantly Shiite population and to spread Islamic fundamentalism throughout the Arab Gulf, thereby undermining Iraq's influence. In addition, as the other major power in the Persian Gulf, Iran posed a moderate short-term military threat to Iraq and possibly a more significant long-term threat in the event that Iran emerged intact from its revolutionary chaos.

Long-standing territorial disagreements between Iran and Iraq over control of the Shatt-al-Arab waterway (confluence of Tigris and Euphrates rivers), personal hatred between Saddam and Khomeini, Iran's theocratic rule as opposed to Iraq's more secular regime, Iraq's Sunni tradition versus Iran's Shiite legacy, and Iraq's Arab heritage versus Iran's Persian background also created serious points of friction, which made intense and prolonged conflict between the two antagonists more probable and reconciliation less likely.

These situational factors led Iraq to believe that war would come sooner or later, a belief that greatly enhanced its interest in attacking Iran. As history suggests, states are more inclined to attack others if they feel that war is inevitable and that the balance of power is shifting against them.[1] Saudi King Fahd asserted that prior to Iraq's attack on Iran in 1980, Saddam told him that "it is more useful to hit them [the Iranians] now because they are weak. If we leave them until they become strong, they will overrun us."[2]

But while Iraq viewed the revolutionary chaos in Iran as an opportunity to reduce the long-term Iranian threat, it also aimed to advance its own inflated foreign policy agenda. Saddam's attack was intended to deal Iran a decisive blow so that Iraq could chart the future of the region unencumbered by Iran and realize Saddam's long-standing ambitions of regional hegemony. Saddam, however, grossly miscalculated. When Iraq attacked Iran in September 1980, it appeared that Iran, caught in the throes of revolution, would swiftly or eventually capitulate. Saddam believed that the war would be over in a matter of weeks, thus leaving Iraq dominant over Iran, or with substantially increased influence.[3]

But from the perspective of Iran's theocracy, Iraq's attack was a vicious attempt by an inferior Arab side to neutralize the glorious Iranian revolution and could not go unpunished. Iran would muster soul and limb to fight off the Iraqi attack. By November 1980, Iraq's war effort was stymied and Iran turned the conflict into a stalemate. Thereafter, Iran sporadically threatened the Arab Gulf states not only because they aided Iraq in the war, but also because Khomeini's world view predisposed Iran to undermine them.

HOW WAS THE IRAN-IRAQ WAR LINKED TO IRAQ'S KUWAIT INVASION?

The Iran-Iraq war contributed to Iraq's decision to invade Kuwait in five basic ways. First, U.S. support of Iraq during the Iran-Iraq war made Iraq more self-assured and thus more likely to invade Kuwait than it otherwise would have been. Iran's threat to the region, particularly after its significant military victory at the Faw Peninsula in early 1986, left Washington with few good options but to tilt toward Iraq in order to prevent an Iranian victory in the war. Indeed, it appeared possible at the time that Iran could defeat Iraq and dominate the region politically and even militarily. A *Pax Irani* in 1986–87 probably would have been as threatening to U.S. and regional interests as a *Pax Iraqi* in 1990 after Iraq's invasion of Kuwait.

Regardless, Washington should have taken a stronger stance against Iraq after the 1988 cease fire in the Iran-Iraq war when the threat from Iran had diminished and Iraq began flexing its regional muscles. In this period, Saddam sent sufficient signals that Iraq was back in the opportunistic mode that had characterized its pre-war foreign policy. Instead of moving closer to the West for purposes of obtaining monies and technology with which to rebuild Iraq's war-ravaged country, Saddam chose a strategy based on force, power, and brinkmanship.

In a number of speeches, beginning with the famous one of February 24, 1990, Saddam spearheaded a new offensive against the United States and Israel.

Describing the United States as the dominant force in the region, Saddam called on Arab states to offset U.S. power and on the United States to withdraw its naval forces from the region and to decrease its overall political role in Arab affairs. In addition, Iraq did not noticeably demobilize its army, used chemical weapons on its own people, and stayed on a war footing.

In foreign relations, Saddam appeared perfectly willing to provoke Western powers. In March, Iraq hanged an Iranian-born British journalist for apparent espionage. Not much later, U.S. and British officials seized high-tech devices and machinery destined for use in Iraq's multi-billion dollar effort to develop nuclear weapons and a long-range supergun.

In April, Saddam claimed provocatively that Iraq's new Al-Abbas Scud-B missile, loaded with binary chemical weapons, could hit Israel and that Iraq had the power to burn half of Israel if it attacked any Arab state. At the Arab League summit meeting in the following month, Saddam again attacked the United States and challenged Israel. More importantly, he assailed Gulf states, particularly Kuwait, for waging economic war against Iraq, ignoring oil production quotas, keeping oil prices down, refusing to forgive Iraq's war debts from the Iran-Iraq war, and failing to extend post-war reconstruction credits. From February through late August, Saddam issued various threats, backed at times by military maneuvers, that implied potential military action against Kuwait.[4]

Despite these actions, however, U.S. policy toward Iraq continued to be conciliatory up to the invasion of Kuwait. Even after it became clear that Saddam sought to develop nuclear capability, the Bush administration provided Iraq with agricultural products, military intelligence, and financial access; it also shielded Iraq from potential congressional sanctions for Iraq's use of chemical weapons against its Kurds and for its threat on April 1 to "burn half of Israel" should it attack any Arab state.

Rather than focusing its efforts solely on much-needed postwar economic reconstruction, Iraq used U.S. economic support for military purposes, a fact known to at least some U.S. officials. Although it is not fully clear to what extent U.S. support of Iraq was consequential in Iraq's attempt to develop nuclear weapons, at the least the United States was much more co-operative with Iraq than Iraq's behavior warranted.

The now famous meeting between Saddam and U.S. Ambassador April Glaspie on July 25, 1990, further reflected the United States' conciliatory approach toward Saddam.[5] According to Iraqi transcripts of the meeting, Glaspie asserted that the United States had "no opinion on the Arab-Arab conflicts, like your border disagreement with Kuwait." To what extent Saddam took this as a "green light" to invade Kuwait is unclear. Intuition suggests, however, that Glaspie gave Saddam less reason to fear a strong U.S. response in the event that he invaded Kuwait. Indeed, at the time, Saddam was massing troops in southern Iraq near the Kuwaiti border. From his perspective, it could not have been lost on the United States that he intended, at a minimum, to flex his muscles against Kuwait. Glaspie's message might very well have looked like either weakness or indifference in the face of such action.[6]

Table 5.1. Trends in Iranian Military Forces*

Force Category	1980/81	1987/88
Major Combat Equipment		
Main Battle Tanks	1,740	900–1,150
Fighting Vehicles	1,075	1,190–2,000
Major Artillery	1,000+	750–1,000
Air Forces		
Combat Aircraft	445	60–118
Combat Helicopters	500	45
Total Helicopters	750	120–370

*Regular army and air force manpower increased significantly. Iranian naval power was not greatly affected.

Source: Adapted from Anthony H. Cordesman, *The Gulf and the West: Strategic Relations and Military Realities* (Boulder, CO: Westview Press, 1988), 82–83. See Cordesman for more details on each weapon category and for an analysis of trends in Iraqi military forces.

The second connection between the Iran-Iraq war and Iraq's invasion of Kuwait was that Iraq emerged from the war with a considerably more developed military capability. For instance, its regular army quadrupled in size to 955,000 men and the number of aircraft under its control increased by well over one-third.[7] That Iraq's huge standing army could not be effectively reintegrated into the shaky Iraqi economy also made a military adventure more attractive to Saddam.

Third, as shown in Table 5.1, the war significantly weakened Iran militarily. For instance, the war, coupled with the near cut off of Western supplies of major equipment and spare parts, decreased Iran's air power by about 90 percent by 1982 when a cease fire was declared. That Iraq did not have to contend with a powerful Iran on its border also made an invasion of Kuwait more plausible.

Fourth, the Iran-Iraq war devastated Iraq's economy and left it heavily indebted to Kuwait and Saudi Arabia, both of which had loaned Saddam monies for the war against Iran. Estimates suggest that Iraq began the Gulf war with US $35 billion in reserve and ended the war $80–$100 billion in debt.[8] Adding Iran-Iraq war reconstruction and debt repayment costs and basic yearly expenditures, it would have taken Iraq nearly two decades to recover under optimal conditions.[9]

Thus, in theory, by invading Kuwait Iraq would erase its war debt, control Kuwait's oil wealth, and increase world oil prices. In reality, Iraq did attempt to justify the invasion partly in economic terms. Iraq's foreign minister, Tariq 'Aziz, claimed shortly after the invasion that Baghdad had to "resort to this method" because its economic situation had deteriorated and it had no alternative.[10]

Fifth, despite the fact that Iraq attacked Iran in 1980, Iraq believed (or at least argued) that it had sacrificed its treasure to stave off the Iranian threat to the entire Arab Gulf, to regain respect for all Arabs, and to advance the Arab cause. And like Athens, which had contained the Persian threat to all of Greece in ancient times, Baghdad believed, albeit with much less justification than Athens, that it deserved the allegiance and support of the states that benefited from its military action.

Iraq's argument was that Kuwait not only refused to renounce Baghdad's war debts and to loan Iraq more monies for economic reconstruction in the post–Iran-Iraq war period, but that it lowered oil prices by pumping too much oil, some from oil fields over which Iraq laid joint claim. Iraq accused the Kuwaitis of angle drilling into the Rumaila oil field. By starting oil wells on their side of the Iraqi-Kuwaiti border and angling their oil equipment under the border, the Kuwaitis could draw on oil from Iraqi sources.

Because the Kuwaitis and Saudis were not forthcoming with economic support and because Iraq's economy was devastated, Saddam sought to raise money for economic recovery by limiting OPEC production and thus increasing the price of oil. The Saudis and Kuwaitis opposed this approach. That Kuwait would do so after Iraq had staved off the Persian threat and had positioned itself to carry the pan-Arab torch against Israel and the resurgent United States was particularly annoying to Saddam.

These arguments suggest that part of the rationale for Iraq's invasion of Kuwait can be traced to the Iran-Iraq war. However, it is plausible to believe that Iraq might very well have invaded Kuwait even if the Iran-Iraq war never occurred. This is implied by Iraq's 1980 invasion of Iran, which triggered the Iran-Iraq war. More important, it is strongly suggested by the fact that Iraq attempted to annex Kuwait in the 1930s, laid claims to Kuwait until 1963 when it temporarily recognized Kuwait's independence, and invaded and occupied small ports of northern Kuwait in 1973. Thus, the absence of the Iran-Iraq war would not have necessarily resulted in the absence of the Kuwait invasion and thus of Operations Desert Shield and Storm.

LINKING THE IRAN-IRAQ WAR AND THE OUTCOME OF OPERATIONS DESERT SHIELD AND STORM

In order to show how the Iran-Iraq war was related to the successful containment and reversal of Iraq's Kuwait invasion, it is necessary to establish a plausible connection between the Iran-Iraq war and its effects (intervening variables) and between these effects and the short-run success of U.S.-led operations against Iraq. The following six sections of this chapter are devoted to this task; each section identifies one major effect of the Iran-Iraq war. Those effects of the war that were less important to U.S.-led operations are examined first, then the more important ones follow.

The Development of the Gulf Co-operation Council (GCC)

The Saudi-led GCC, composed of Saudi Arabia, Kuwait, Oman, Qatar, the United Arab Emirates (UAE), and Bahrain was founded in May 1981. The GCC served as a forum through which these states could co-ordinate military, economic, and social policy for purposes of common security and welfare. Although efforts to bring the GCC together preceded the Iran-Iraq war, it developed through the 1980s largely in response to the Iranian threat, which was dramatized by the Iran-Iraq war.

The GCC states perceived Iran to be behind the December 1981 coup attempt in Bahrain and interpreted this as an attack on their collective interests.[11] In the aftermath of the coup, several GCC states signed bilateral security agreements,[12] and Bahrain proposed the formation of a GCC rapid deployment force (RDF). This proposal gained currency in 1982 after Iran scored military gains, and by October 1983, the Peninsular Shield joint GCC military exercises commenced. These exercises, while militarily unimpressive, represented a novel attempt to co-ordinate GCC military maneuvers and to develop the Gulf RDF as a shock absorber[13] that could buy time for regional or "over the horizon" reinforcements. Finally, the eruption of the tanker war between Iran and Iraq in 1984 intensified efforts to integrate GCC air defenses. The Saudis agreed to share AWACS with geostrategically exposed Kuwait[14] and later with other Gulf states.

The GCC did not support Kuwait effectively against Iraqi intimidation in the period preceding the actual invasion of Kuwait. GCC states did not want to provoke Iraq and believed as did the United States, Egypt and even Kuwait, that Saddam would not invade Kuwait. Even after Iraq's invasion, GCC states managed only to hold innumerable emergency council meetings in order to support Kuwait politically and to reaffirm their pact, which in any event was overshadowed by the more prominent role of the Arab League.

At best, the GCC played only a questionable military role against Iraq, a role that was viewed with disdain in some quarters. Yet observers who implied that the GCC should have played a major military role missed the point. The GCC was not created to match Iraq or Iran militarily; it lacked the manpower and battlefield experience for such a task. Although it attempted without great success to increase its military capabilities in the post-Gulf-crisis period, it had since its creation depended on the United States to ensure its security.

The development of the GCC, however, was not irrelevant to Operations Desert Shield and Storm. On the one hand, the U.S.-led coalition did not need the

GCC to conduct its political-security operations against Iraq, provided the Saudis were willing to co-operate. On the other hand, throughout the 1980s the GCC helped increase the internal stability of pro-U.S. Gulf states and enhance their military co-ordination. It also gave them a political forum to co-ordinate their policies and improved their defense and strategic interaction with Washington.[15] This was manifested when the Saudis deterred a limited Iranian air attack in 1984 and an Iranian naval attack on their offshore oil fields in 1987. Both times they had U.S. support.

In addition, the GCC was the vehicle by which the otherwise reserved Saudis assumed a greater role in regional politics and security. Since the U.S.-led coalition benefited from quick and effective security-political co-operation with Arab Gulf states, particularly the Saudis, it is reasonable to believe that Operations Desert Shield and Storm would have proceeded less smoothly had the GCC never been formed.

Saudi Power and Stability Increased

The development of the Saudi-led GCC, as noted in the previous section, began a trend toward increased Saudi influence in the Gulf. This trend was accelerated by the war-related riot at Mecca in July 1987. Overall, the war, while posing significant short-term threats to Saudi interests, prepared the Saudis for the challenge Iraq posed in 1990-91.

The Mecca riot, in which over 400 Iranian pilgrims were killed by Saudi security units, was the most significant war-related political instability in the Gulf in the 1980s. The Saudis touched off the riot when they moved in to stop a forbidden political demonstration by Iranian pilgrims in front of the Grand Mosque in Mecca. Despite evidence to the contrary,[16] Iran denied that it instigated the subversion, blamed the Saudis, and called on Iranians as "the implementers of divine principles" to overthrow the Saudi royal family in revenge.[17] This caused alarm across the Gulf.

Reflecting royal family views, Saudi Prince Nayef asserted that Iran aimed to challenge Saudi rule over Islam's holy places,[18] thus damaging Saudi ties to other GCC states. This would have facilitated Iran's efforts to woo these states into supporting its war position against Iraq. Iran also wanted to use Mecca to challenge U.S. regional influence and to retaliate against Washington for reflagging Kuwaiti tankers.[19] Riyadh was a less risky target than the United States.

The riot, and Ayatollah Khomeini's ensuing invective in which he described Saudi King Fahd as an "infidel" unable to keep peace at the sacred heart of Islam, rendered the Saudis ready to sever relations and reportedly go to war.[20] While the latter never occurred, Riyadh did adopt an uncharacteristic activism against Iran and eventually broke diplomatic relations, citing Mecca and Iran's threat against Gulf navigation as the reasons. This was significant because Riyadh had attempted throughout most of the Iran-Iraq war to accommodate Iran.

Relations between the two countries remained tense. The Mecca riot was a primary cause of the launching of about sixty armed Iranian speedboats against a Saudi offshore oil field in October 1987. Riyadh responded with a full military mobilization, including land troops, and was reportedly ready to "make a stand" against Tehran.[21]

Oddly enough, the crisis at Mecca put in motion several developments that laid part of the security-political foundation of Operations Desert Shield and Storm. It pushed the Saudis to take major measures to improve their own security and moved them closer to Washington. In interviews, the Saudis expressed fear over how close to war with Iran they had come and, in the words of a Saudi official, wanted the United States to "insure our total security by ensuring Iran's total paralysis."[22] As a result, Riyadh provided Washington with more direct and comprehensive military co-operation.

In addition, the Mecca crisis motivated Riyadh to encourage Kuwait, Bahrain, and the UAE to improve their ties with Egypt, an effort that included a Saudi initiative to arrange an aid package for Egypt with help from Kuwait and the UAE.[23] As will be discussed, Egypt's increasing reintegration into the Arab world would later benefit U.S.-led operations against Iraq.

Overall, the Iran-Iraq war clearly helped prepare the Saudis for Iraq's invasion of Kuwait. It pushed them to assume a leadership role in the Gulf and to co-operate more meaningfully with U.S. forces. It also helped the Saudis develop and ready their forces for conflict. Saudi defense minister Prince Sultan even went so far as to say in September 1990 that Riyadh had "military technologies capable of destroying the Iraqi army" and that Iraq was aware that the Saudis had the "power, will and determination capable of deterring it."[24] While this statement was hyperbolic and made from behind the U.S. deterrent, and although changes in Saudi Arabia's military capability were not vital to the success of Desert Shield and Storm, these changes did benefit the U.S.-led operations.

Had the Iran-Iraq war not taken place, Riyadh would have been less confident and capable and, as will be shown in the next sections, less trusting of Egyptian and, much more significantly, of U.S. ability and determination. Certain implications follow from this analysis, particularly if it is considered in tandem with aspects of alliance theory.

Scholars studying alliances have shown that states are more likely to appease than to oppose the threatening state if they are weak and lack effective allies.[25] Thus, we have some reason to believe that had the Iran-Iraq war not taken place, Riyadh would have been more likely to appease Iraq. That is, Riyadh would have been more likely to agree to some compromise solution in which Iraq would withdraw from Kuwait either in exchange for movement on the Palestinian issue or for political-territorial compromise with Kuwait.

Of course, the Saudis would have been reluctant to accommodate Saddam given the threatening posture of Iraqi military forces on their border. Few states intentionally flirt with suicide when they have some hope of preserving their autonomy. Regardless of its initial position, Riyadh would have been more likely to choose an accommodating policy after U.S. forces arrived in Operation Desert Shield. At this point, the Saudis would have had to recalculate and, assuming the absence of the Iran-Iraq war, what they would have lacked as a point of reference was their own enhanced regional role, increasing assertiveness, and a developed political-security relationship with Washington. As will be shown, Saudi Arabia also would not have been able to count on as strong an Egyptian and European role, and on an the United States as militarily capable for Gulf contingencies.

If we add to this picture the fact that accommodation was a cornerstone of Saudi foreign policy prior to and even throughout most of the Iran-Iraq war until the Mecca crisis, and that several influential Saudi princes were strongly anti-U.S. and preferred Arab solutions to Arab-world problems, we can see that a policy of appeasement might very well have been adopted by the Saudis under less favorable conditions. Even with the benefit of strong allies and increased self-confidence, the Saudis considered appeasing Iraq in 1990. This was not surprising because the Saudi royal family had been split into two factions for some time. The pro-U.S. faction, led by King Fahd and his brother Sultan, were willing to consider a major U.S. role. The counter faction led by Crown Prince Abdullah, the King's half brother, viewed a potential large U.S. presence in the kingdom as threatening the traditional Islamic role of the kingdom and as introducing a destabilizing foreign presence.[26] For their part, Egypt and Iran strongly opposed the implication by Saudi defense minister Prince Sultan, one of the leaders of the pro-U.S. camp no less, that Iraq be given some territory in Kuwait in exchange for withdrawal from Kuwait.[27] And, at the outset of the conflict, Riyadh showed some hesitation in enlisting the United States against Saddam.

Less than two days after the Iraqi invasion, the pro-U.S. Saudi ambassador to the United States, Prince Bandar bin Sultan, paid a visit to U.S. national security adviser Brent Scowcroft. Bandar reminded Scowcroft of pre-Iran-Iraq war Saudi doubts about U.S. determination and expressed Saudi concern that the United States would lend a temporary hand against Saddam and then "pull it back," thus leaving Saddam on the Saudi border "twice as mad as he is now."[28] Had the Iran-Iraq war not strengthened U.S.-Saudi political-security relations, it is probable that such Saudi doubts would have been much greater. Indeed, the United States demonstrated during the Iran-Iraq war its commitment to regional security. The Saudis were particularly impressed by U.S. determination to carry through the policy of reflagging Kuwaiti tankers, despite Iraq's alleged accidental air attack on the U.S.S. *Stark*, which killed thirty-seven U.S. sailors. Such military efforts by the United States lent Washington credibility, which would make Riyadh more inclined to agree to Operation Desert Shield and to confront rather than accommodate Saddam in 1990–91.[29]

What would increased pressures for appeasement have meant for the U.S.-led operation against Iraq? First, the United States' ability to deal with the crisis as it wanted to would have been decreased, resulting in an outcome less favorable than the one that occurred. Second, and less likely, the United States might have been put from day one of the crisis on a path toward agreeing to some veiled form of back-door compromise with Saddam. In the first scenario, U.S.-led operations would have suffered. In the second scenario, Operation Desert Storm might have been either delayed or suspended. While this would have saved many lives, it would have also allowed Saddam's nuclear program, which was farther along than U.S. intelligence ever suspected, a greater chance to succeed. Saddam's army would also have been left intact with the attendant negative implications for long-term peace in the Gulf and broader Middle East.

U.S.-Regional Military and Political Preparation

The increase in Saudi influence and capability caused by the Iran-Iraq war was related to another effect of the war that would later benefit U.S.-led operations. The war significantly improved U.S. relations with Gulf states. Overall, the GCC states preferred to accommodate Iran as a security alternative to co-operating significantly with the United States. But as the Iranian threat and their confidence in the United States increased, so did their propensity to oppose instead of appease Iran.

To be sure, the Saudi-U.S. strategic connection did not develop overnight. Government documents dating back to 1947 show that Washington made a strong commitment to protect Saudi Arabia long before the Iran-Iraq war. The 1947 pact between President Harry S. Truman and King Ibn Saud was described in a 1947 State Department cable. In this cable, the United States pledged that if Saudi Arabia should "be attacked by another power or be under threat of attack, the U.S. through medium of [the] U[nited] N[ations] would take energetic measures to ward off such aggression." To back up this commitment, President John F. Kennedy sent U.S. air forces to Saudi Arabia in 1963 against threats from Nasser's Egypt.[30]

As early as 1945, the United States recognized formally the importance of Saudi oil not only for the purpose of supplementing and replacing the United States' own exhaustible resources, but also as a great potential leverage for any actor that gained control of it. This recognition pushed President Truman on September 28, 1945, to approve the completion of the air base at Dhahran, Saudi Arabia, which would play an important role in Desert Shield and Storm in 1990–91. The United States also established the Middle East Force in the period 1948 and 1949, which consisted of a flagship and two destroyers permanently stationed in the region, with access to stations in various countries in the region.[31]

Yet, while the U.S. commitment to Saudi Arabia existed for decades, it increased significantly as a result of the Iranian revolution, the Afghanistan intervention, and the Iran-Iraq war. The Saudi military infrastructure was well developed incrementally, beginning in earnest in the 1970s. However, the military infrastructure necessary for supporting a large-scale operation such as Desert Storm remained rudimentary until the 1980s.

Prior to the Iranian revolution and the Afghanistan intervention, no one in the

Saudi royal family was willing to discuss offering the United States even temporary access to Saudi bases. But these events and the Iran-Iraq war created consequences that altered Saudi perceptions considerably. In a secret oral undertaking between the United States and Saudi Arabia in February 1981, which was to be followed by a series of additional agreements, Washington agreed to sell the latter AWACs aircraft, and Riyadh agreed to build networks of command, naval and defense facilities large enough for a massive deployment of U.S. forces. The goal was to create the world's most advanced network of superbases.

Initial estimates placed the cost of this clandestine project at $50 billion, but the final price tag ended up closer to $200 billion. The project was so clandestine and the information about it so compartmentalized that even key high-level U.S. officials did not understand its scope and sophistication. By 1990, the command, control, communication, and intelligence facilities developed by the Saudis paralleled that of the NATO alliance.

 The improvements in the Saudi military infrastructure made Desert Shield and Storm much more possible. In 1980, there had only been two major non-oil docks in Saudi Arabia capable of unloading one ship at a time. By 1990, dozens of ships could be unloaded simultaneously at nine major ports. Saudi airfields became significantly more sophisticated and doubled in number, and the Saudis integrated their ground-based radar missile systems, fighter bases, fighters, and command-communication posts into a single network. Military roads, emergency fuel storage facilities, air conditioned bunkers, nuclear-proof command posts became part of this elaborate military infrastructure.

General H. Norman Schwarzkopf, commander of allied forces during Desert Shield and Storm, stated that had this infrastructure not existed, U.S. CENTCOM would not have recommended sending in such a substantial U.S. force. Had war been launched, in the absence of such a complex, supporting infrastructure, the outcome would have been different. At a minimum, the victory would not have been as quick and decisive.[32]

 While the United States' foreign policy during this period, as implied by several U.S. officials,[33] was primarily motivated by the Soviet threat, the Saudis were most concerned with the regional threat from Iran. Although Riyadh had historically feared Iraq's intentions, it probably did not suspect that the facilities it was planning to build would benefit it not against Iran but against Iraq, which, ironically enough, had appointed itself the protector of the Arab Gulf against the perceived Iranian threat.

As the Iran-Iraq war progressed, the Saudis agreed more publicly to U.S. access to these military facilities against the Soviets or in a major flare-up in the Persian Gulf. When Iraq invaded Kuwait, U.S.-led coalition forces used these facilities to support rapid deployment and other logistics for Operation Desert Shield and to conduct military attacks on Iraqi territory in Operation Desert Storm.

Iran's successful military offensive at the Faw Peninsula in February 1986 represented the most significant militarily related instability in the Gulf during the

Iran-Iraq war. Together with escalated attacks on Gulf shipping, it put in motion effects relevant to the outcome of Operations Desert Shield and Storm. In the post-1985 period, GCC states provided assistance for U.S. transit operations and forces. Bahrain provided support for port visits by the U.S. Navy and a logistics base facility for U.S. forces; the Saudis allowed the U.S. RDF enhanced access to their airfields and ports; Oman accepted a "quantum" increase in the use of its airspace for U.S. forces; UAE and Qatar allowed port visits, ship repairs, and refueling.[34] Saudi Arabia and Bahrain quietly gave U.S. forces prepositioning rights. Moreover, joint U.S. military maneuvers with GCC states increased in intensity and frequency. These maneuvers, such as the Bright Star exercises in 1987 and 1990, provided the means to project U.S. forces in conjunction with host nations.[35] They improved U.S.-GCC security co-operation and gave U.S. forces valuable experience. Finally, as indicated by Kuwait's request that the United States reflag its oil tankers, the war reversed GCC opposition to U.S. naval intervention in the region.[36]

Had the war not taken place, it is highly unlikely that the Gulf states would have co-operated with the United States to the extent that they did; they would have lacked a strong enough incentive to do so. Thus, this integral part of the political-security groundwork for Operations Desert Shield and Storm would not have existed.

U.S. Military Capability Strengthened

Just as the Iran-Iraq war improved U.S.-GCC relations, it also accelerated U.S. defense efforts for Gulf contingencies, which had been put in motion by the Iranian revolution and the Soviet invasion of Afghanistan.[37] Thus, the Iran-Iraq war played a role in preparing the United States militarily for Iraq's invasion of Kuwait.

The regional threat to U.S. interests created by the Iran-Iraq war compounded the perceived threat of Moscow's Afghanistan invasion at the global level. This had two major implications. First, and as already noted here, the Iran-Iraq war helped motivate the Saudis to develop major facilities for U.S. rapid deployment forces and for Arab states to engage in joint military exercises with Washington. Second, the war was added incentive for Washington to develop the rapid deployment capability that was crucial for Operations Desert Shield and Desert Storm.[38]

Concerned with global and regional threats to Gulf security, Washington was determined not only to improve its capability to deter "outside" pressure on the Gulf,[39] but also to deal with pressures arising within the Gulf. In that spirit, President Ronald Reagan stated in October 1981 that there was "no way" the United States could "stand by" and see Saudi Arabia threatened to the point that the flow of oil could be shut down.[40] This statement and others of a similar kind later became known as the Reagan Doctrine, which was widely perceived as a

U.S. commitment to protect Saudi Arabia against not only external threats but also internal ones. In this sense, it was a departure from the Carter Doctrine that aimed more toward the deterrence of "outside" as opposed to internal threats to Gulf security.

While the idea of the RDF was put in motion by the Iranian revolution, it was budgeted, developed, and implemented primarily after and as a result of the Afghanistan intervention and was configured to deter a Soviet invasion of Iran.[41] On the whole, however, it did not receive great support in the Gulf in part because most Gulf states viewed the Soviet Union as less of a threat than Washington portrayed it to be.

The Iran-Iraq war, however, altered regional perceptions of the value of an over-the-horizon U.S. military force. Partly in response to the war, the RDF's role was expanded after 1982 with the dual goals of deterring the Soviets at the global and regional levels. Washington sought the capability to deter an outside threat, to respond appropriately to friendly requests for assistance, and to make up for the significant weakness of physical distance from the Persian Gulf.

Although the RDF's development contributed to suspicions in the Gulf of U.S. strategic intentions, it represented one of many U.S. defense efforts that allayed some fears that Washington was incapable of protecting Gulf security.

The improvements in U.S. force projection in the 1980s were significant. While in 1980, U.S. projection to the Gulf of minimal forces would have taken many weeks,[42] by 1983, the United States could have had the first ground force to the Gulf in a few days. U.S. airlift, sealift, and prepositioning capabilities continued to improve substantially throughout the 1980s.[43]

From 1980 to 1987, U.S. airlift capabilities increased from 26.9 to 39.6 million-ton-miles per day (MTM/D). The United States also enhanced the Military Sealift Command active fleet from forty-four to fifty-seven ships and the Ready Reserve Force (RRF) from twenty-seven to eighty-two ships.[44] Overall, the Department of Defense spent over $7 billion to improve sealift capabilities in the 1980s. Key improvements included a prepositioned force of twenty-five ships, some of which provided the first supplies during the Persian Gulf crisis; eight fast sealift ships especially suited to transport heavy army unit equipment, and an additional increase in the ready reserve force to ninety-six ships.[45]

By 1988, the United States had reached 89 percent of the Department of Defense sealift goal,[46] although its capability in this area declined in the post-cease-fire period following the Iran-Iraq war.[47] In addition, the MPS program that had been put into effect in 1980 became a distinct capability, enabling forces to reach critical contingency areas within seven days.[48] This would prove critical in the first weeks of Operation Desert Shield.

RDF capability was also significantly enhanced by U.S. efforts to upgrade facilities to which it was allowed access. Improvements were made at Masirah Island in Oman, Diego Garcia, bases in Turkey, and negotiations were under way for improvements at Somalia.[49] These efforts were particularly important considering that Washington's only permanent facility in the Gulf had been a

Table 5.2. USCENTCOM Country Specific Military Construction Programs (MILCON) (in millions)

States	FY 80–82	FY 83	FY 84	FY 85	FY 86	FY 87	FY 88
Oman	$164.7	$60.4	$28.6	$2.3	$0.0	$0.0*	$14.3
Somalia	$24.4	$30.0	$0.0	$0.0	$0.0	$0.0	$0.0
Kenya	$49.6	$8.3	$0.0	$0.0	$0.0	$0.0	$0.0
Bahrain	$0.0	$0.0	$0.0	$0.0	$0.0	$0.0	$0.0
Subtotal	$238.7	$98.7	$28.6	$2.3	$0.0	$2.6	$14.3

*$7.0 million was obtained through emergency construction

En Route							
States							
Morocco	$0.0	$0.0	$25.0	$5.05	$3.1	$25.4	$0.0
Lajes	$66.6	$0.0	$0.0	$0.0	$0.0	$0.0	$0.0
Diego Garcia	$377.1	$57.9	$72.8	$15.3	$5.3	$0.0	$4.5

Source: U.S. Senate, Hearing before a Subcommittee of the Committee on Appropriations, *Department of Defense Appropriations for Fiscal Year 1989* (Washington, D.C.: GPO, 1988), 245.

Defense Fuel Supply Station in Bahrain. As Table 5.2 shows, monies devoted to these efforts were insignificant prior to 1980, increased greatly from 1980–82 partly in response to Afghanistan and to the Iran-Iraq war, and then decreased in 1985. This decrease suggests that the Afghanistan invasion, more than the Iran-Iraq war, motivated these particular efforts. Otherwise, we would expect that such efforts would have increased as the Iran-Iraq war dragged on, particularly after 1986 when Iran scored strategic gains at the Faw Peninsula. We, however, find a precipitous decline in expenditures during this period.

The U.S. military build-up for Gulf contingencies came at great cost[50] and was not without its inadequacies. If Iraq had invaded Kuwait instead of Iran in 1980, Washington would not have had an effective conventional response. The fact that President Carter considered the nuclear option against a possible Soviet invasion of the Gulf from Afghanistan in 1980 underscores this point.[51]

Egypt Reintegrated into Persian Gulf Security System

The improvement in U.S.-GCC relations, the development of Gulf-related U.S. military capabilities, and Egypt's reintegration into the Arab world benefited U.S.-led operations against Iraq. The GCC states alienated Egypt for its decision to make peace with Israel. They refused to co-operate with Egypt politically or militarily and even severed diplomatic relations. Their approach to Egypt, however, changed as a direct result of the Iran-Iraq war. Diplomatic ties to Egypt were restored primarily because of its potential anti-Iranian role. Saudi King Fahd's visit to Cairo in March 1989, the first trip by a Saudi monarch since the Camp David accords were signed, symbolized Egypt's reintegration into the Arab world.

The Iran-Iraq war slowly eased Egypt into the political-security system of the Persian Gulf. Egypt was even viewed as prepared to provide military advisors and instructors to GCC states. Although it was reluctant to involve itself in the Iran-Iraq war, Egypt probably provided added insurance for GCC states against the threat from Iran.[52] Had the Iran-Iraq war not occurred, it is much less likely that Egypt would have assumed a role in Gulf security and bridged its differences with Arab-Gulf states. These states would have lacked the incentive provided by the war to restore security and diplomatic ties to Egypt, and Egypt would have been deprived of an important catalyst for improving its relations with Gulf states. Thus, Egypt probably would not have been in the position to play a role in the U.S.-led coalition against Iraq as its most influential Arab member.

Transatlantic Security and Political Framework Laid

The Iran-Iraq war not only reintegrated Egypt into the Gulf security system, but also increased Europe's role. For the European allies, the Persian Gulf represented an out-of-area challenge, an issue area that fell outside the purview of the NATO charter. While NATO's concern with European security has decreased with the end of the Cold War, out-of-area issues have arisen on the security agenda of European states more in the last ten years than at any other time in the past. In no region has this been more the case than in the Persian Gulf, where the allies share the interest of ensuring the flow of oil at reasonable prices.

As discussed in chapter 3, the threat to Western interests in the Persian Gulf increased significantly in 1979 when the Shah of Iran was overthrown and the Soviets invaded Afghanistan. The United States tried to meet these challenges with numerous defense efforts, one of which was an unsuccessful attempt to forge a common allied defense strategy toward the Gulf.[53] In 1981, Washington once again requested European assistance in Gulf security,[54] but attempts to co-ordinate independent national efforts toward the goal of overall NATO security failed "for lack of implementation," despite the endorsement in 1981 of the NATO Council.[55] Little progress was made on this issue until the Iran-Iraq war pushed the allies into taking some action in 1987.

As is well known, the United States agreed to reflag eleven Kuwaiti tankers in June 1987. In doing so, it wished to improve its credibility with Arab Gulf states after the Iran-Contra debacle. Arab officials had been puzzled and disturbed by the Reagan administration's attempt to exchange arms for hostages. The secret U.S. arms sales to Khomeini's radical regime raised questions about U.S. strategy and commitment to Arab Gulf states. Although the arms were not militarily significant, they generated doubt that long-term U.S. policy might be aimed at accommodating Iran at the expense of closer U.S.-GCC relations. Interviews revealed that Gulf officials were initially ambivalent about the reflagging mission because it was high profile, threatened to increase superpower regional intervention, and challenged Iran openly.[56] But by deterring Iran's ability to prosecute the war through its attacks on shipping and on the interests of GCC states that supported Iraq, the U.S. reflagging mission clearly benefited GCC states. The reflagging policy also aimed to ensure Gulf stability and deny Moscow a more extensive protective role. Indeed, Kuwait had requested reflagging protection from both the Soviets and Americans.

Once in the Gulf, however, U.S. naval forces found themselves deficient in mine-sweeping capability and subsequently requested mine-sweeping support from Britain, France, Italy, Belgium, the Netherlands, and West Germany. The U.S. request was handily rejected.[57] While this was an embarrassment to Washington, it was not entirely unexpected. Although the British had been active in the Gulf since 1980 with the two-frigate Armilla Patrol and France had an Indian Ocean naval presence, the allies wanted to avoid the escalatory potential and the costs of additional naval deployment to the Gulf.[58] Also, they were reluctant to confront Iran.

By September 15, 1987, however, the allies, with the exception of West Germany, had reversed their decisions and agreed to support U.S. mine-sweeping efforts. Thereafter, the European naval presence in the Gulf increased to approximately thirty ships.[59]

The role of the Iran-Iraq war in preparing the European allies to meet the challenges of Operations Desert Shield and Storm was significant. The allied naval intervention during the Iran-Iraq war, while economically inefficient and politically shaky,[60] laid part of the political and military groundwork for transatlantic co-operation during these operations. In political terms, it accomplished three basic things.

First, it showed the states of the Western European Union (WEU), the nine-member group of European states that deals with out-of-areas problems,[61] that their military participation alongside U.S. naval forces could serve to contain Iran and protect Gulf shipping rather than exacerbate the political-security situation in the Gulf. As previously suggested, these states had initially rejected Washington's request for mine-sweeping support.

Second, it allayed European fears that the United States would be a trigger-happy superpower which would drag them unnecessarily into a regional conflict. The U.S. effort during the Iran-Iraq war seemed measured and effective. While

Iran was less than daunted at times by U.S. force, at other times, the opposite seemed to hold true. By the end of 1987, U.S. forces escorted twenty-three convoys without attack from either Iran or Iraq. The U.S. helicopter attack that crippled an Iranian mine-laying ship in September 1987 also seemed to deter Iran for several months.

Third, the allied intervention during the Iran-Iraq war undoubtedly provided experience in ironing out transatlantic political differences regarding Gulf security and helped in the difficult task of developing patterns of political co-operation for out-of-area operations.

It stands to reason that these factors made it more probable that the Europeans would support U.S.-led operations against Iraq in lieu of espousing a negotiated settlement with Iraq at one point or another in the crisis. Indeed, France and Germany were disposed to accommodate Iraq, despite the fact that the United States' credibility was tied to reversing Iraq's aggression. Co-operation between the allies showed visible signs of strain. Such differences probably would have been more significant had the allies not profited from their positive interaction in the previous Gulf crisis.

In military terms, the European allies clearly built on their experience during the Iran-Iraq war. U.S. and European navies did not co-ordinate their naval presence during this war. Among themselves, European forces did engage in some bilateral and multilateral naval co-operation. For instance, Dutch and Belgian mine sweepers received tactical support from British warships on a bilateral basis. Efforts were also made to co-ordinate a joint European naval force for the Gulf within the framework of the WEU. However, other than an agreement in early 1988 among Britain, the Netherlands, and Belgium for some mutual cooperation, European forces were generally unco-ordinated.

European naval participation during the second Gulf crisis was considerably more co-ordinated. Unlike during the Iran-Iraq war crisis, the WEU ministers agreed formally to co-ordinate their respective areas of operation in the Persian Gulf, to exchange intelligence, and engage in mutual protection of forces. They also provided mutual logistical and operational support.[62] This level of co-operation proved important in enforcing the economic embargo against Iraq and in conducting extensive mine-sweeping operations.

CONCLUSION

The manner by which the third party is affected by conflict can have critical consequences in the historical process. This chapter helped show how and why this is so. The Iran-Iraq war strengthened the United States in its third-party capacity and enabled it to play a key role in stopping Saddam Hussein in 1990–91 after Iraq invaded Kuwait. In this sense, history played a cruel joke on Saddam. Little did he expect that his use of force in 1980 would produce consequences that would help undo him a decade later.

At the broadest level, this chapter has sought to explain aspects of the policy choices, behavior, and performance of some of the key actors in the 1990–91 Gulf crisis. It has shown that their actions and the outcome of their actions were linked to the previous crisis of the Iran-Iraq war. Thus, it suggests that we cannot understand the second Gulf war without understanding the Iran-Iraq war. Beyond this, two major issues should be distinguished. The first deals with the link between the Iran-Iraq war and Iraq's decision to invade Kuwait. On this point, this chapter argues that while the Iran-Iraq war produced consequences (such as an imbalance of regional power) that made an Iraqi attack on Kuwait more likely in 1990, the Iran-Iraq war was not a necessary cause of Iraq's invasion. That is, given Iraq's historical claims to Kuwait, its invasion of Iran in 1980, and Saddam's demonstrated ambition, it is plausible to believe that Iraq might have invaded Kuwait even if the Iran-Iraq war had never taken place.

The second issue and the central thesis of this chapter is that the Iran-Iraq war is linked to the outcome of Iraq's invasion of Kuwait or, in other words, to the successful U.S.-led containment and eviction of Iraqi forces from Kuwait. The first and second arguments of this chapter should be considered in tandem. Together they suggest that had the Iran-Iraq war not taken place, Iraq still might have invaded Kuwait, but that the outcome of the invasion would have been different.

Indeed, as shown here, the Iran-Iraq war contributed to the GCC's development and to an increase in Saudi influence. It provided added incentive for Riyadh to develop military facilities to handle the type of massive threat posed by Iraq's invasion of Kuwait. It helped reverse Egypt's isolation from Gulf security, enhance political and strategic co-ordination and trust between Arab-Gulf states and Washington, and push the United States to accelerate the development of Gulf-related military capabilities. In addition, it helped develop transatlantic security and political ties for Gulf contingencies. Together, these factors laid part of the foundation for Operations Desert Shield and Storm. The absence of the Iran-Iraq war and, thus, of all these inter-related and reinforcing consequences would have made the containment and reversal of Iraq's aggression in Kuwait much more difficult.

To be sure, this chapter does not show that Operations Desert Shield and Storm would have failed had the Iran-Iraq war not laid part of their political-security foundation. The successful containment and reversal of Iraq's invasion of Kuwait was probably tied more to the United States' general military superiority over Iraq, to its will to use its capability, and to Saddam's gross miscalculations than to antecedent factors. Rather, this chapter shows how antecedent causes, while perhaps not crucial in explaining the outcome of Desert Shield and Storm, were linked to it.

Some observers might argue that had the Iran-Iraq war never taken place, Iraq would have been much less capable militarily. Iraq would not have gained valuable battlefield experience, nor would it have had the incentive or opportunity to obtain as high a level of arms from the West. Therefore, it would not have posed as great a military threat as it did in 1990–91.

While there is, of course, some truth in this view, statistics show that the arms race between Iran and Iraq was fast-paced long before the outbreak of the Iran-Iraq war.[63] In addition, while Iraq would not have received massive loans from Kuwait and Saudi Arabia with which to buy arms had the Iran-Iraq war not taken place, it also would not have squandered its human resources and its own domestic means to buy arms. It is, therefore, reasonable to believe that while Iraq would not have had as many trained men under arms had the Iran-Iraq war not taken place, it still would have had developed a substantial military force with which to invade Kuwait.

The following two chapters of the book conclude the study of how conflict affected the evolution of regional politics, and in particular the U.S. role, in this broader scheme of things. While this chapter has focused on the connection between the Iran-Iraq war and Operations Desert Shield and Storm, chapter 6 examines the impact of these operations on U.S. regional security in the period from 1991 to mid-1994.

NOTES

1. See Lebow, *Between Peace and War*, 254–57; also see Emerson M. S. Niou and Peter C. Ordeshook, "Preventive War and the Balance of Power: A Game-Theoretic Approach," *Journal of Conflict Resolution* 31 (September 1987): 327–419.
2. See text of interview with King Fahd, in *London AL-HAWADITH*, FBIS: Near East and South Asia (NESA), 14 February 1992, 21.
3. For a more lengthy discussion of the origins of war, see MECS 14 (1990): 73–82.
4. For details, see Freedman and Karsh, *The Gulf Conflict 1990–1991*, 45–50.
5. For the text of the transcript of the Glaspie meeting, see "Excerpts from Iraqi Document on Meeting with U.S. Envoy," *New York Times*, 23 September 1990, A19.
6. For details of the Glaspie meeting and its potential implications, see Michael A. Palmer, *Guardians of the Gulf: A History of America's Expanding Role in the Persian Gulf, 1833–1992* (New York: The Free Press, 1992), 158–160.
7. For trends in Iranian and Iraqi military power from 1980 to 1988, see Cordesman, *The Gulf and the West*, 82.
8. See Kamran Mofid, "The Economic Reconstruction of Iraq," *Third World Quarterly* 12 (January 1990): 52–54.
9. See Efraim Karsh and Inari Rautsi, "Why Saddam Hussein Invaded Kuwait," *Survival* 33 (January/February 1991): 19.
10. See *Cairo MENA*, in FBIS: NESA, 13 August 1990, 5.
11. See *Manama WAKH*, in FBIS: MEA, 25 February 1982, C3.
12. For a description of these agreements, see *Manama WAKH*, in FBIS: MEA, 22 February 1982, C3. Also, see *Riyadh Domestic Service*, in FBIS: MEA, 24 February 1982, C5.
13. *Manama WAKH*, in FBIS: MEA, 7 February 1984, C1.
14. A good discussion of the tanker war's effect on GCC security appears in R. K. Ramazani, "Iran's Islamic Revolution and the Persian Gulf," *Current History* (January 1985): 41.

15. On the air attack, see Shahram Chubin and Charles Tripp, *Iran and Iraq at War* (London: I. B. Tauris & Co., Ltd., 1988), 167.

16. For this evidence, see Cordesman, *The Gulf and the West*, 370–71.

17. Iran's President Hashemi Rafsanjani quoted by John Kifner, "Iranian Officials Urge 'Uprooting' of Saudi Royalty," *New York Times*, 3 August 1987, A1.

18. For an interview with the prince, see *Kuwait Al-Siyasah*, in FBIS: NESA, 25 August 1987, J1–J5. A brief summary of the Saudi view of the Mecca riot appears in MECS 11 (1987): 589–91.

19. On the link between the Haj and U.S. reflagging, see Chubin and Tripp, *Iran and Iraq at War*, 175–76.

20. On the Saudi view, see *Paris Radio Monte Carlo*, in FBIS: NESA, 28 August 1987, J1. Also see comments by Saudi Prince Nayef, *Riyadh SPA*, in FBIS: NESA, 27 August 1987, J1–12.

21. For a summary of the post-Mecca crisis competition between Iran and Saudi Arabia for leadership of the Islamic world, see MECS 12 (1988): 177–80.

22. Quoted in Youssef M. Ibrahim, "Saudis Seeking an Arab Alliance Against Iran," *New York Times*, 16 October 1987, A9.

23. Ibid.

24. In *Riyadh AL-RIYAD*, in FBIS: NESA, 11 September 1990, 21.

25. Stephen M. Walt, *The Origins of Alliances* (Ithaca, NY: Cornell University Press, 1987), 29–31.

26. Scott Armstrong, "Eye of the Storm," *Mother Jones* (Special Report) 16 (November/December 1991): 31–32.

27. *Belgrade TANJUG*, in FBIS: NESA, 24 October 1990, 7.

28. Bob Woodward, "President Gave Saudis Word of Honor," *Washington Post*, 3 May 1991, A1, A16.

29. Author's interview with Dr. Paul D. Wolfowitz, under secretary of Defense for Policy, 1989–93, 26 August 1994.

30. Walter Pincus, "Secret Presidential Pledges over Years Erected U.S. Shield for Saudis," *Washington Post*, 9 February 1992, A20.

31. This paragraph is based on Palmer, *Guardians of the Gulf*, 27–29, 46–47.

32. The discussion of developments in the Saudi infrastructure is based in part on Armstrong, "Eye of the Storm," 30–35, and by the author's personal correspondence with Armstrong. Also see Scott Armstrong, "Saudis' AWACS Just a Beginning of New Strategy," *Washington Post*, 1 November 1981, A1, A12. In addition, for details on the importance of such facilities in the logistics build-up and sustainment of Operations Desert Shield and Desert Storm, see U.S. Department of Defense, *Conduct of the Persian Gulf War*, Appendix F.

33. For example, see former Secretary of State Alexander Haig, "Saudi Security, Middle East Peace, and U.S. Interests," *Current Policy* 323 (Washington, D.C.: Department of State, Bureau of Public Affairs, October 1981): 1–3.

34. See witness statement by George B. Crist, U.S. Congress, Senate, *Department of Defense Appropriations for Fiscal Year 1989*, Hearing Before a Subcommittee of the Committee on Appropriations (Washington, D.C.: GPO, 1988), Table 2, 178.

35. On these exercises, see U.S. Senate, Armed Services Committee, Witness Statement by General H. Norman Schwarzkopf, Commander in Chief of the U.S. Central Command, 8 February 1990 (hereafter cited as U.S. Senate, Schwarzkopf statement), 55.

36. See MECS 11 (1987): 33, 29–35 for a good summary of the reflagging mission.

37. See S. A. Yetiv, "How the Soviet Military Intervention in Afghanistan Improved the U.S. Strategic Position in the Persian Gulf," *Asian Affairs: An American Review* 18 (Summer 1990): 62–81.

38. See George C. Wilson, "Effort Is Launched to Beef Up U.S. Rapid Deployment Force," *Washington Post*, 28 September 1980, A17.

39. Statement by Nicholas Veliotes, former assistant secretary for Near Eastern and South Asian Affairs, U.S. Congress, House of Representatives, *U.S. Policy Toward the Persian Gulf*, Hearing Before the Subcommittee on Foreign Affairs and the Joint Economic Committee, 10 May 1982 (Washington, D.C.: GPO, 1982), 9.

40. In Ronald Reagan, *Public Papers of the Presidents of the United States* (Washington, D.C.: GPO, 1981) (hereafter referred to as Reagan Papers), 873. Also, for a clarification of this statement see 952.

41. On how the RDF was a response primarily to Afghanistan, see U.S. Congress, *Rapid Deployment Forces*, 11–15.

42. President Reagan referred to this lack of military readiness for Gulf contingencies as a "shame" in *Middle East Economic Digest*, 7 November 1980. He later aptly described the RDF as "neither rapid nor deployable and not much of a force." See Reagan Papers, 1982, I: 228, 254, 296.

43. For excellent details, see U.S. Senate, Schwarzkopf statement, 173–302. Also see U.S. Department of Defense, Caspar W. Weinberger, "Report of the Secretary of Defense to the Congress on the FY 1988/1989 Budget and FY 1988–92 Defense Programs," 12 June 1987 (hereafter cited as U.S. Department of Defense, Weinberger report), 36. In addition, see U.S. Department of Defense, *Conduct of the Persian Gulf War*, 368–69.

44. U.S. Department of Defense, Weinberger report, 36.

45. For more details, see *Strategic Sealift: Part of the National Defense Reserve Fleet Is No Longer Needed* (Washington, D.C.: U.S. General Accounting Office [GAO], October 1991), 14–15.

46. U.S. Senate, *Department of Defense Appropriations for Fiscal Year 1989*, 175; also see chart 8, 184.

47. U.S. Senate, Schwarzkopf statement, 58.

48. U.S. Senate, *Department of Defense Appropriations for Fiscal Year 1989*, 914.

49. Cordesman, *The Gulf and the Search*, 835.

50. For details on part of these costs, see U.S. Congress, *Rapid Deployment Forces*.

51. See "Soviet Buildup Near Iran Tested Carter," *New York Times*, 27 August 1986, A3.

52. On Egypt's possible role, see Philip H. Stoddard, "Egypt and the Iran-Iraq War," in *Gulf Security and the Iran-Iraq War*, ed. Thomas Naff (Washington, D.C.: National Defense University Press, 1985), 37–39.

53. David Ransom, Lawrence J. McDonald, and W. Nathaniel Howell, *Atlantic Cooperation for Persian Gulf Security* (Washington, D.C.: National Defense University Press, 1986), 81.

54. "Weinberger to Ask Help of NATO in Gulf Area," *New York Times*, 11 May 1981, A10.

55. See Lawrence S. Kaplan, "The United States, NATO, and the Third World: Security Issues in Historical Perspective," in *East-West Rivalry in the Third World*, ed. Robert W. Clawson (Wilmington, DE: Scholarly Resources, Inc., 1986), 17–18.

56. See U.S. Congress, Senate, *War in the Persian Gulf: The U.S. Takes Sides*, Staff Report to the Committee on Foreign Relations, November 1987 (Washington, D.C.: GPO,

1987), 29–30.

57. *Keesing's Contemporary Archives* (New York: Scribner, December 1987), 35597.

58. The British were already active in the Gulf since 1980 with the two-frigate Armilla Patrol, and France also had an Indian Ocean naval presence.

59. For a full line-up of the Western naval presence, see *Jane's Defense Weekly*, 26 September 1987, 671.

60. For a case-study analysis of allied naval intervention in the Gulf and for a consideration of a strategic option for future transatlantic policy toward this region, see Steve A. Yetiv, "The Transatlantic Dimension of Persian Gulf Security," *Naval War College Review* 44 (Autumn 1991): 45–58.

61. The WEU is composed of Belgium, France, West Germany, Italy, Luxembourg, the Netherlands, and the United Kingdom. Spain and Portugal joined the WEU in March 1990.

62. For an authoritative account of the WEU's role in European and Persian Gulf security, see WEU Secretary General Willem Van Eekelen, "Building a New European Security Order: WEU's Contribution," *NATO Review* 38 (August 1990): 18–23. Also, on the WEU's contribution during the Kuwait crisis, see Willem Van Eekelen, "WEU and the Gulf Crisis," *Survival* 32 (November/December 1990): 529–30.

63. See Michael Brzoska and Thomas Olson, *Arms Transfers to the Third World, 1971–85* (Oxford: Oxford University Press, 1987), 16–17.

6

THE MIDDLE EAST AFTER THE STORM

Iraq's invasion of Kuwait in August 1990 caught the world by surprise. It was not that Saddam Hussein had previously masked his brutal nature. Quite the contrary, his record even prior to his rise as president of Iraq in July 1979 reflected an individual willing and able to take violent measures to protect personal power and position. Rather, what was striking about Iraq's invasion was its ambition and extent.

Indeed, Saddam had options short of a full blown invasion by which to settle his score with Kuwait. The first was to use diplomacy to secure desired political and economic concessions from Kuwait, such as adherence to oil production quotas, renunciation of Iraqi war debts, and postwar credits for Iraqi economic reconstruction. While this strategy might not have achieved Iraq's goals in the short run, it may have succeeded over the long run.

Second, in combination with the first option or in lieu of it, Saddam could have threatened to use force against Kuwait by building military forces on the Iraqi-Kuwaiti border. He then could have parlayed his military position on the border into influence over Kuwait. In contrast to an outright invasion, this more limited strategy would have kept large-scale foreign forces from intervening in the conflict militarily, and would have bought Saddam time to hone his strategy of coercion against Kuwait.

Third, an even more ambitious option short of full invasion was to invade only those parts of Kuwait that were important to Iraq economically or strategically. Iraq might have taken control of the Rumaila oil field, over which Iraq and Kuwait laid joint claim, and Kuwait's strategically located Warba and Bubiyan islands, which Iraq had sought historically for increased access to Persian Gulf waters.

Had Saddam chosen option one, two, or even three, the global response probably would have been quite different. Unfortunately for Iraq, he chose option four—a full-scale, unabashed invasion of Kuwait. In the process, he dispossessed Kuwait of its property and identity, threatened the survival of neighboring Saudi Arabia, and raised the specter of Iraqi influence over a major portion of the world's oil supply. Although Western states and other actors could have possibly tolerated Iraq's temporary domination of northern Kuwait, Iraqi control of Saudi oil was another matter. It was this potentiality that generated much of the shock and fear that motivated U.S. action against Iraq and united the anti-Saddam coalition.[1]

The 1990–91 Persian Gulf war was a great event in strategic history but an unfortunate one in human history. One Arab state terrorizing and devouring another, hostages used as political pawns, and scuds falling on innocent civilians did not reflect a triumph of the human spirit. Under better conditions, nobler ways to solve disputes would have prevailed. But as it stood, Iraq's aggression was so blatant, Saddam so fatuously stubborn and recklessly over-ambitious, and the stakes so high that avoidable war became unfortunate reality.

ARGUMENT AND ORGANIZATION

Some observers argued that the outcome of the Gulf crisis for the U.S.-led coalition was nearly as unfortunate as the war. They pointed to such things as the festering Kurdish problem, Saddam's staying power, Baghdad's remaining military capability, Iraq's likely resurgence as a producer of weapons of mass destruction, the absence of regional democracy, the regional arms race, and the financial and human cost of the operation as evidence that Desert Storm was not such a great success. For instance, military analyst Jeffrey Record, a seasoned observer, argued that the Gulf war was

> a magnificent military victory barren of any significant diplomatic gains. It was fought to repel Saddam Hussein's challenge to the old order in the Persian Gulf, not to create a new one. Accordingly, future historians may regard the war as a complete failure.[2]

Adding to the criticism, another observer claimed that Saddam Hussein "not only remained in power, but that his position seemed to have been strengthened," and that in this sense Saddam won out over President Bush.[3] One widely cited book asserted that Desert Storm was a "Triumph Without Victory."[4]

This chapter concludes the story of the evolution of U.S. security in the Persian Gulf by examining the impact of the Gulf crisis at four levels of analysis: global, regional, intraregional, and state. In the process, it shows that the Gulf crisis, which hereafter refers to the invasion of Kuwait and the ensuing war, left the United States more secure in the region than it has ever been. More importantly, it shows why and how this was the case, and what it means in the broader evolution of Middle Eastern politics and U.S. regional security.

GLOBAL ACTORS AND REGIONAL POLITICS

The Iranian revolution, Afghanistan intervention, Iran-Iraq war, and the 1990 Gulf crisis affected the power and role of major global actors. Changes in their role affected the politics of the Middle East and, in turn, U.S. security in the Persian Gulf.

The Iran-Iraq war accelerated a trend toward the increased penetration of regional politics by actors outside the Middle East region. Prior to the Iran-Iraq war, the primary external actors were the United States and Britain, both of which played a secondary security role in the region. The Iranian revolution, however, collapsed regional security from within the Persian Gulf, and the Afghanistan intervention produced an external threat to the Gulf. Together, these events necessitated a direct U.S. role in regional security. Coming on the heels of these two events, the Iran-Iraq war further increased U.S. regional involvement and also increased the European role.

The Gulf crisis accelerated the globalization of regional politics by increasing the role of European states and Russia and almost institutionalizing the U.N. regional role. Desert Storm temporarily transformed the United States into a direct antagonist and moved it away from a third-party role. Although the United States as a third party was not initially involved in the dispute between Iraq and Kuwait, the United States eventually spearheaded military action against Iraq.

The United Nations and U.S. Regional Security

In the 1970s, the U.N. role in the region was minimal and remained so throughout the 1980s, notwithstanding the monitoring by U.N. peacekeepers of the cease-fire in the Iran-Iraq war. The Gulf crisis was a watershed. While Washington used the United Nations to forge the anti-Saddam coalition, the United Nations also became a more important actor in its own right. Increasingly, it could affect regional politics in a manner that its member states could not alone. This does not mean that the United Nations gained a life of its own independent of its member states, but it does mean that policy toward the Persian Gulf region was made under U.N. auspices more than it had been in the past.

In an idealistic world, increased U.N. intervention in any region would be viewed positively by sovereign actors. They would yield sovereignty to the United Nations, check their desire for increasing power, and allow collective security to protect their commonly held values. In reality, national and collective interests often conflict. As a supranational organization that represents a broad array of interests and ideologies, the United Nations has a different set of preferences than does, for instance, the United States as a sovereign state. When these preferences conflict, the freedom of maneuver for the sovereign actor can be circumscribed. While this was to some extent true for the United States in the Persian Gulf, the benefits of U.N. intervention far exceeded the costs.

In previous time periods, the internationalization of regional politics might have been a disadvantage to the United States. For several reasons, this was not the case from 1990 to 1993. First, the United States played a dominant regional role before the United Nations became involved in the Persian Gulf and thus was in a position to set the political-security agenda during the Gulf crisis. Second, the disintegration of the Soviet Union enhanced the United States' regional position and freedom of action in the United Nations, and enabled it to spearhead U.N. action without great concern for Russian opposition. Third, the United States as a sovereign actor and the United Nations as a supranational one shared similar goals with regard to Iraqi aggression. This decreased the potential for friction between the two actors and meant that U.N. action in the region would protect rather than challenge U.S. postwar interests. That is, it was unlikely that U.N. member states acting under U.N. auspices would try to take an anti-U.S. approach toward regional security or challenge the U.S.-led diplomatic and military agenda. Fourth, the United Nations offered the United States political cover that would have been harder to gain otherwise. Without the U.N. umbrella, U.S. action against Iraq would not have played as well in the Middle East and broader third world. The United States would have risked looking too much like an "imperialist" Western state, or a trigger happy superpower.

Europe and the Postwar Gulf

The increased role of European actors further globalized regional politics. Desert Storm, like the Iran-Iraq war, enhanced transatlantic military co-operation, thereby improving U.S. regional security. At the same time, Desert Storm further revealed significant political differences between the coalition partners, thus pointing to enduring constraints on transatlantic co-operation.

At the military level, Britain and France participated fully in the military campaign to liberate Kuwait after peaceful efforts to generate Iraqi withdrawal from Kuwait had failed. This enhanced transatlantic co-operation and paved the way for more effective co-ordination in the future. In the postwar period, France and Britain signed defense accords with Kuwait, which helped ensure their participation in a regional security framework that could deter regional aggressors or contain aggression in the event that deterrence failed.

At sea, European navies learned from their previous experience in the Gulf. Unlike during the Iran-Iraq war, the ministers of the WEU co-ordinated their respective areas of naval operation, exchanged intelligence, engaged in mutual protection of forces, and provided mutual logistical and operational support.[5] This helped in enforcing the economic embargo against Iraq and in conducting extensive mine-sweeping operations.

At the political level, however, the European Community failed to exhibit the type of strength in the face of an international crisis that many expected. The general perception in the United States was that Europe, with the exception of

Britain and perhaps France, benefited from the free-rider effect. Europe was provided a public good primarily by the United States—regional security and the free flow of oil at reasonable prices—without contributing its fair share in protecting that good. Germany, in particular, was singled out not only because it did not contribute troops to Desert Shield and Storm, but also because it seemed to treat the crisis with detachment. That German companies had supplied Iraq with substantial lethal technology facing Desert Shield troops only added fuel to the fire.

Furthermore, the Europeans, except for the British, were far ahead of the United States in the proclivity to appease Saddam. The United States and Britain refused to offer any carrots to Saddam in exchange for Iraqi withdrawal, which might have been construed as rewards for aggression. By contrast, the Russians and French, Iraq's number one and two arms suppliers respectively, were much more forthcoming. France went so far as to attempt a last-minute compromise with Saddam, even after the United States had staked its credibility on a formula granting him no rewards for aggression.

France's regional position was further undermined because the Iraqi invasion betrayed a flaw in French Middle East policy. France's policy had revolved around its relationship with Iraq much more than did the policy of any other Western actor. In the military and economic arenas, the French benefited from their interaction with Iraq and tended to support it politically. Saddam's brutal invasion hurt French influence in the region, despite France's postwar defense accord with Kuwait because it suggested that France had staked its regional fortunes on a reckless ally.

Desert Storm and U.S. Military Capability

While the improvement in transatlantic military co-operation benefited U.S. military capability indirectly, wars in the region, culminating with the 1990–91 conflict, also strengthened U.S. military capability directly. When the Shah of Iran was overthrown in 1979, Washington found itself unable to protect regional security. Although high-level plans for the development of the RDF were initiated by late 1979,[6] defense officials informed President Carter that the United States was virtually powerless to release the American hostages held in Iran.[7] The hostage crisis,[8] as well as concern about the broader Soviet threat, motivated serious U.S. defense efforts for Gulf contingencies. As noted earlier, while the Iranian revolution had undermined U.S. security from within the Gulf, the Afghanistan intervention threatened to capitalize on U.S. vulnerabilities from outside the Gulf. In part as a result of this dichotomy of threats, the RDF was funded, developed, and implemented,[9] the U.S.-operated naval and air base at Diego Garcia in the Indian Ocean was upgraded, the "scale and pace" of U.S. periodic naval force deployments increased,[10] and the United States gained access to key regional military facilities. Washington's ability to project force improved considerably between 1980 and 1991,[11] in response to the Iranian revolution, Afghanistan intervention, and the Iran-Iraq war.

But while significant steps were taken to improve U.S. rapid deployment capability in the 1980s, steps that proved critical in meeting the Iraqi challenge in 1990, many weaknesses remained. This was clearly reflected in the fact that it took the United States six months to develop the forces capable of launching Desert Storm. To be sure, Desert Shield was the largest movement of U.S. forces since World War II. But under more stringent time pressures, the operation would have been much more problematic, particularly if U.S. forces were tied up in another conflict. The Gulf crisis helped the United States identify and correct military weaknesses and gave it critical experience. Although postwar defense cuts produced some constraints on U.S. deployment capability, Washington's ability to project forces to the region increased from 1990 to 1993, and its ability to sustain them while in the region also improved. Improvements in U.S. military capability in the postwar period were so diverse and complicated that they cannot be described in this book. The goal here, rather, is to discuss these improvements at a level sufficient enough to provide a general sense of changes in U.S. capabilities.

In addition to changes in logistics capability and support, in training, and in interoperability of forces, Desert Storm helped the United States identify valuable technologies and improve or downplay less valuable ones. This further enhanced U.S. capabilities for long-range deployment and fighting in a desert environment.[12] Overall, the United States developed its military capabilities after Desert Storm, identified key weaknesses in its ability to protect and sustain a large military, and learned a number of valuable lessons that increased its ability to meet its three principal goals in the Persian Gulf region.[13]

The air force's ability to transport material required to supply Desert Shield troops, deployed or en route to the region, faced significant difficulties initially. But over time the Department of Defense and the air force devised some ways of alleviating these problems.[14] Improvements in the Civil Reserve Air Fleet program, which uses commercial aircraft to supplement the air forces' airlift capability, made future fleet activations more effective.[15]

Desert Shield and Storm also revealed problems in part of the U.S. mobility strategy referred to as "afloat prepositioning." This strategy was made necessary because of political problems associated with basing on Arab soil. It aimed to keep ships continuously loaded with combat equipment near potential conflict areas, thus increasing response time. Studies revealed that while equipment and supplies were delivered to Saudi Arabia eight days after the war began and almost two weeks before they could have been sealifted from the United States, some of the supplies most needed by the Marine Corps were not on the ships and that expansion of sealift capabilities was needed.[16] By 1994, prepositioning for one of two shore-based brigades was underway, with a third to be afloat,[17] and U.S. access to regional facilities as already noted improved.

When Iraq invaded Kuwait, U.S. military officials believed that the training of U.S. ground forces had been excellent. Experiences during the war revealed, however, that additional training in joint operations, deployment, and logistical and other support functions was needed.[18] In the postwar period, the scope of U.S. military exercises increased in a manner unimaginable prior to Desert Storm. In 1993 alone, the United States conducted seventy-seven naval, eight special forces, six army and six air force exercises.[19]

REGIONAL POLITICS AND SECURITY

Desert Storm not only generated changes in the role and power of major global actors, but also altered interaction between regional actors and between regional and global actors. In theory, postwar security plans aimed to deter Iraq and if necessary Iran through two or more of the following four strategies: the development of a joint GCC army; increasing the size of individual regional armies; collective security between GCC states, Syria, and Egypt; and bilateral security co-operation between Persian Gulf states and actors outside the Gulf.

In reality, the first three strategies, which were based on indigenous security approaches, faced serious obstacles. While these strategies aimed to help regional states protect their own security, the weaknesses of these approaches pointed to the continuing importance of the U.S. security role.

The GCC After Desert Storm: A Joint Army?

Prior to the Iranian revolution, Saudi security and political co-operation with other Arab Gulf states was minimal. The revolution generated interest among these states in forming some type of political-security union. The establishment of the GCC, however, was delayed by long-standing rivalries between the Arab Gulf states.[20]influence of Iran and Iraq, both of which wanted to dominate any such union, was a major stumbling block to its formation.[21]

The Iran-Iraq war not only gave Arab Gulf states added incentive to create the GCC in order to deal with the Iranian threat, but it also removed the Iran-Iraq obstacle by absorbing the energies of both states. Prior to the war, there was no significant military and political co-operation among Arab Gulf states. During the war, numerous bilateral security agreements were signed, and by 1984, the GCC council approved the formation of a GCC joint military force. The so-called Peninsula Shield, consisting of contingents from each of the six member states, was stationed in northern Saudi Arabia and numbered less than 10,000 men.

By underscoring regional dangers, the Iraqi invasion of Kuwait generated increased interest in GCC security, political, and economic co-operation. Saudi King Fahd, expressing broader sentiment, claimed that Desert Storm revealed the failure of "those who covet the territory of other states" and brought the GCC states closer together.[22]

The Gulf crisis, surprisingly, did not significantly increase GCC co-operation. The GCC states did agree to link radar networks in order to improve early warning capability and discussed developing the GCC as a military organization. The sultan of Oman advanced a proposal for the development of a 100,000-man joint GCC force that could raise the threshold level for U.S. regional intervention. This idea, one bandied about in the past, was widely viewed as overambitious.

The Omani plan faced several problems, including lack of manpower, interoperability of military forces, and budgetary constraints. These problems contributed to the perception among GCC leaders that the development of national armies was preferable to that of a major GCC force. The national army option was more simple, economically efficient, and realizable and also allowed states to retain autonomy and flexibility in cases where their national interests conflicted with those of the GCC as a whole.

Another stumbling block to closer military co-ordination was that the Persian Gulf war left some GCC states willing and able to resume historic rivalries. The war weakened Iraq enough to remove political and military constraints on Riyadh. Saudi Arabia proceeded to settle a long-standing territorial dispute with Qatar by forcibly occupying a small but significant part of its territory.

Meanwhile, Iran annexed the island of Abu Musa in August 1992, which generated fear across the Persian Gulf. Abu Musa had been jointly administered by Iran and the UAE under an agreement concluded in 1971, until Iran took control of it and two neighboring islands, the Greater and Lesser Tunbs. Disturbed by the Saudi position on its annexation of Abu Musa and interested in driving a wedge between Riyadh and other GCC states, Iran heightened fears in the Gulf that Riyadh sought to annex Qatar outright and to pursue its own hegemonic ambitions in the region and offered to sign a joint defense agreement with Qatar.[23]

Responding to failed diplomatic attempts to resolve the dispute, Qatar withdrew its military contingent from the joint GCC security force and refused to participate in regular GCC functions. This was the first such act by a GCC state since the GCC's formation in May 1981 and represented a threat to the fabric of the organization, an outcome that Iran had sought. Ironically, Iran's dramatic annexation of Abu Musa gave Saudi Arabia and Qatar some reason to settle the dispute in the name of pan-Arab interests.

Iraq's defeat also made serious GCC co-operation less important than it would have been had Iraq emerged from the crisis unscathed. To be sure, GCC states continued to fear Iraq even after Desert Storm. Kuwait's foreign minister, Shayk Sabah al-Ahmad al-Sabah stated that Iraq "continues to worry" the Arab Gulf states despite the time that has elapsed since the end of the war and that Iraq "still does not recognize the borders with Kuwait and refuses to free Kuwaitis it holds."[24] Kuwait, as well as other Gulf states, feared that if the United States decreased its regional presence, Saddam might attack again. Reflecting broader regional sentiment, Kuwait argued that the Gulf region would not experience peace and stability while Saddam remained in power and called on Saddam "to abandon his aggressive policy toward Kuwait."[25] The GCC stood behind Kuwait, and Saudi King Fahd urged the world community to make Baghdad comply with U.N. resolutions.

However, while GCC states remained wary of Iraq's intentions and moved to establish bilateral security arrangements with outside states against a future Iraqi threat, their confidence in the ability of the United States and other actors to contain Iraq also increased. The strong U.S. deterrent diminished the incentive to develop a major GCC force.

Developing Individual Armies

Although the strategy to develop a major joint GCC military force proved problematic, the second approach to long-term postwar regional security was more successful. GCC states sought to develop their own military forces through arms procurement, increases in army size, and military training exercises. Saudi Arabia was a case in point. By June 1991, Riyadh aimed, for perhaps the first time, to supplement its sophisticated air-defense system with a mobile, large-scale army. By some estimates, Riyadh increased its manpower in 1992 to around 60,000 to 70,000 men and planned in the next decade to double the size of its forces to about 200,000, so as to decrease reliance on the United States.[26]

But even major increases in the size of the Saudi army would leave the Saudis unable to mobilize their force structure, which is only one-tenth that of Iraq and Iran, and vulnerable to an all-out attack by Iraq or to serious challenges by Iran.[27] While the Saudis gained valuable experience during Desert Storm and developed a well-equipped air force, protecting their own security was still a job beyond their capability. Such a task was complicated by the huge territory that must be defended, Saudi internal security needs, budgetary constraints, problems in training forces for combat missions, and hostile, well-equipped adversaries.

Collective Security Takes a Back Seat

The third strategy in the approach to postwar regional security was strongly backed by the Bush administration[28] and involved an attempt at collective security under the so-called Damascus Declaration. This declaration was issued on March 6, 1991, and called for strategic collaboration between the GCC states, Egypt, and Syria.[29] In exchange for security support in the form of Egyptian and Syrian military contingents permanently stationed in the Gulf region, the GCC states would provide much needed capital for the Syrian and Egyptian economies.

Collective security, while initially successful, faced several obstacles. Whereas the Gulf states thought that Egypt and Syria were angling to get maximum money for minimal security, Egypt and Syria believed Gulf states wanted maximum security for minimal money. After initially supporting the security plan, the Saudis questioned the logic of assuming added financial burdens when facing budgetary constraints and of hosting foreign forces on their soil. The last time the Egyptians were involved on the Peninsula, the Saudis called on U.S. forces to deter them from challenging Saudi interests. The Saudis also feared that Arab states might become involved in royal family politics, thus undermining the regime.

The Kuwaitis were reluctant as well. A postwar poll taken in Kuwait found that 69 percent of the people polled wanted Kuwaiti security to be underwritten by the United States; only 17 percent choose security arrangements with Arab allies. By and large, Kuwaitis viewed the six-plus-two formula as a useless approach that would interject unstable Arab forces into the region.[30]

The security perceptions of regional actors also differed. Syria and Egypt sought to diminish the U.S. regional security role against the wishes of most GCC leaders. In addition, while Iran was steadfast against a U.S. regional presence, it also lobbied against a more involved role for Egypt, with which it had a long-standing rivalry. Given these rivalries, some Gulf leaders were concerned that Iran and Iraq would view the Damascus Declaration as an affront.[31] Iran's opposition to the plan, however, was of secondary importance to intra-Arab politics.

Egypt increasingly became annoyed with Saudi and Kuwaiti procrastination in implementing the accord[32] and, by early May, decided to follow in Syria's footsteps by withdrawing its 40,000 troops from Saudi Arabia and Kuwait. Even after the plan appeared dead, Iran's President Hashemi Rafsanjani stated in an interview in December 1993 his opposition to Egypt and Syria playing a regional security role and his desire that regional security rest with regional states.[33]

Arab states, reluctant to admit the failure of collective security,[34] sought to transform the Damascus Declaration into a framework for economic and political co-operation.[35] A concerned Iran responded to this initiative by inviting the GCC to set up a security committee to ease regional tensions without outside involvement.[36] While some GCC states were more sympathetic towards Iran than others, they did not trust Iran enough to allow it a significant security role in the GCC.

Kuwait Signs Bilateral Accords

The final strategy in the postwar period proved most successful. In the wake of the failure of collective security, regional actors sought the backing of outside actors—primarily the United States. Kuwait, the least secure regional actor, was in a similar position to Iraq as France was to Germany after World War I. In both cases, the weaker actor, fearing a resurgence of its nemesis, aimed to sign defense accords with various powerful actors. As noted earlier in this chapter, Kuwait managed to sign defense accords with Britain, France, and Russia. These accords aimed at preserving regional peace and deterring further aggression through defense co-operation, training and exercises, and arms sales.

By enlisting Russia, Kuwait increased its leverage with Iraq because post-Cold War Russia had greater influence with Iraq than any other great power. Prior to the end of the Cold War, a defense accord of this sort would have seriously threatened U.S. security. Kuwait, the Gulf state most confident in its ability to play the superpowers off each other in the early 1980s, provided the stepping stone to an enhanced Soviet regional position. The end of the Cold War, however, altered the implications of Russian regional involvement and changed the United States' perception of the Russian threat. In the best case scenario, post-Cold War Russia could help the United States maintain the regional status quo. But, at a minimum, it was not in a position in the near future to do much damage to U.S. regional interests, particularly given the United States' improved standing after Desert Storm.

The problems associated with the first three approaches to postwar regional security made it clear that the United States would remain the ultimate guarantor of regional security. Even Kuwait's defense accords with Britain, France, and Russia, while significant, were secondary to the U.S. security role.

The United States and the GCC

Improvements in U.S.-GCC relations complemented the enhancement of U.S. military capability. The strength and nature of U.S. relations differed with each GCC state as a function of numerous factors such as domestic politics in regional states, geopolitics, and intra-Arab politics. But, in general, U.S. relations with the GCC improved immensely. Desert Storm played an important role in this evolution. Although Kuwait had been the least pro-U.S. GCC state, its position began to change significantly when the United States reflagged Kuwaiti tankers during the latter part of the Iran-Iraq war. After Desert Storm, the U.S.-Kuwait Defense Cooperation Agreement was signed in September 1991 and provided for U.S. access to Kuwaiti military facilities, prepositioning of defense material for U.S. forces, and joint exercises and training. While the agreement did not mandate automatic U.S. protection of Kuwait, it raised strategic relations to a level unimaginable prior to Desert Storm.

The United States also updated its access agreement with Oman and concluded accords with Qatar and Bahrain. Bahrain, which served since 1949 as host of the United States' small Middle East Force, renewed its access and prepositioning agreement with Washington in October 1991. Qatar in turn signed a twenty-year defense co-operation agreement on June 23, 1992, which also allowed U.S. access and prepositioning[37] and increased the number of Qatari officers in U.S. schools fortyfold after Desert Storm.[38]

U.S.-Saudi efforts to enhance security co-operation were more complicated. U.S.-Saudi relations were defined by a complex mix of variables that could not easily be reduced but which revolved around a U.S. need for Saudi oil and Saudi reliance on U.S. security. Riyadh's dependence on the United States was primarily a function of the level of threat it faced. Alternately, the United States depended on Saudi Arabia for its support against anti-U.S. regional threats and for its role in providing oil at reasonable prices. Changes in the level of need on either side affected relations between the two nations.

While U.S.-Saudi relations were correct throughout the early and mid-1970s, they worsened in 1978–79 for a number of reasons. First, the Camp David accords created a major rift, which then U.S. secretary of state Cyrus Vance described as "very clear and sharp."[39] Second, the United States was viewed as unable to stop Soviet gains in South Yemen, Ethiopia, and Afghanistan in 1978, prior to the actual Soviet invasion in 1979, to prevent the downfall of the Shah of Iran[40] and to deal effectively with the Iranian hostage crisis. While some members of the Saudi royal family continued to stress that U.S.-Saudi relations remained strong,[41] it was clear that the events of 1978 and 1979 had taken their toll. Already strained U.S.-Saudi relations were aggravated by a Saudi loss of confidence in the United States and by U.S. doubts about Saudi stability.[42]

The Afghanistan and Iran-Iraq wars reversed this trend. As discussed in chapter 4, the intervention undermined Moscow's attempts to woo Riyadh and made Saudi Arabia more important strategically to Washington. The Iran-Iraq war impeded Iran's efforts to undermine Saudi influence by absorbing Iran's energies and by giving Riyadh the opportunity to spearhead the development of the GCC. The war also made the United States strategically more important to Riyadh, despite Riyadh's desire to keep it at arms length. These increasing mutual interests benefited U.S.-Saudi relations throughout the 1980s.

Other war-related developments also enhanced U.S.-Saudi co-operation. Riyadh agreed to overbuild its security facilities for U.S. use during a major regional crisis and to use its U.S.-built radar surveillance equipment for the purpose of providing air protection for U.S. reflagged Kuwaiti tankers.[43] While this might have been expected given U.S. protection of Saudi interests, the Saudis were not averse to manipulating the U.S. connection to suit their fluctuating security needs.[44] Thus, factors that made Riyadh more amenable to co-operation with Washington were important. While problems in U.S.-Saudi relations did not disappear, the co-operation catalyzed by the war contrasted starkly with the unstable relations that existed prior to the Gulf war. By 1988, U.S.-Saudi relations had reached heights unimaginable in 1979.

If the Iranian threat at times pushed Riyadh into Washington's arms, Iraq's invasion of Kuwait put the two states in full embrace. The Saudis were initially hesitant about requesting U.S. support against Iraq, but the crisis generated unprecedented U.S.-Saudi co-operation and gave both states invaluable political and military experience. In the postwar period, however, the United States encountered long-standing problems with Riyadh. The Saudis and the UAE proved much more reluctant to engage in formal defense interaction with Washington than were other GCC states. This reluctance, however, should not have come as a surprise. In the words of one seasoned diplomat, U.S. optimism about a defense pact with Riyadh was "silly because such formal and inevitably public arrangements, smacking of outside influence, had been unacceptable to Riyadh throughout the history of U.S.-Saudi relations."[45] This was true despite the fact that the Saudis, like other Gulf Arabs, had never suffered colonial rule common to the broader Arab experience.

In characteristic fashion, Riyadh distanced itself from Washington when the regional threat diminished. This is primarily because the security benefits of the U.S. connection decreased when the Iraqi threat diminished, while its political costs at home and in the Arab world increased. With the external threat diminished, Saudi domestic politics became more important. The establishment ulama and some senior al-Saud princes, such as Abdallah who aligned with Syria and Iran and whose role in royal family circles was as a challenger to accepted thinking,[46] bolstered the opposition against a strong postwar U.S. connection.

From its perspective, the United States valued a defense pact with Saudi Arabia because it would have allowed Washington greater access, predictability, and deterrence capability against a potential aggressor. The Pentagon, however, was forced to defer plans announced in April 1991 to place a forward headquarters element of U.S. rapid deployment forces in Saudi Arabia. Efforts in May 1991 by U.S. secretary of defense Richard Cheney to store substantial U.S. ground equipment in Saudi Arabia were rebuffed. Even Saudi Prince Khaled, who was considered among the most pro-U.S. of Saudi military officials and who led Saudi forces during Desert Shield and Storm, was skeptical of an increased U.S. presence.[47]

Although Riyadh rejected the notion of a U.S. stockpile, the two actors did use an obscure 1977 military training pact in order to expand co-operation in the postcrisis period. U.S. military planners sat down with their Saudi and Kuwaiti counterparts in 1991 and 1992 to review the entire military structures in these countries and to make needed improvements. They increased joint exercises and training, and Riyadh provided more port access for the U.S. Navy and more ground support for the U.S. Air Force.[48]

While the U.S. commitment to Saudi security was long-standing, Desert Storm raised the U.S. commitment to the level of a security guarantee, absent written formalities. Indeed, when asked in testimony before Congress what the difference was between this form of a commitment and an actual treaty, high-level state department official John Kelly stated that a treaty has to be "ratified by the Senate of the United States."[49] Desert Storm was clearly a watershed rather than just one more significant event in the evolution of U.S.-Saudi relations. Although the Iran-Iraq war increased Saudi confidence in the United States, which had been in doubt in the late 1970s and early 1980s, Desert Storm showed that the United States had the will and capability to launch a major, sustained military operation. Desert Storm, thus, produced a "qualitative" change in U.S.-Saudi relations.[50]

Perhaps the greatest movement in U.S.-Saudi relations, however, occurred in the economic arena. Desert Shield and Storm elevated U.S.-GCC economic relations to new heights. The Clinton administration attempted to extend the spirit of free trade to its Arab economic relations, and for their part, GCC states became much more likely to make economic concessions to the United States. The Saudis doubled their purchases of U.S. goods from 1987 to 1992, with major increases in the post-Gulf crisis period.[51] Total U.S. exports to Saudi Arabia, which were $6.6 billion in 1991, were 26 percent ahead of 1991 figures in the first quarter of 1992.[52] Even President Bill Clinton successfully intervened to get the Saudis to buy $6 billion worth of U.S. passenger planes rather than the European air bus.[53]

THE MILITARY BALANCE OF POWER RESTORED

U.S. regional security was enhanced not only by improvements in U.S. relations (with GCC states), but also by major changes in the regional distribution of power. As Table 6.1 shows, Iraq and Iran were relatively balanced prior to the Iranian revolution. The revolution, however, shifted the balance in Iraq's favor in two ways. It virtually severed Iran's link to the United States and Saudi Arabia, and weakened Iran's military. Contrary to popular belief, Ayatollah Khomeini shunned military power. Whereas the Shah obsessively bought billions in U.S. weapons, Khomeini reversed this practice. He shut down U.S. military facilities on Iranian soil, executed or imprisoned scores of his top military personnel, and spurned Soviet arms offers. As Iran's spiritual leader, Khomeini placed most trust not in the regular Iranian military, but in the Pasdaran, Iran's Revolutionary Guard, an outfit motivated more by faith than by military power. Although Khomeini used force internally, even the export of Islam was to be conducted nonmilitarily.[54]

Iraq's invasion of Iran was predicated in part on the belief that it was better to deal Iran a knock-out blow while it was vulnerable rather than face it later when it regained strength.[55] But Iraq grossly miscalculated, and as the war proceeded, Iran threatened to shift the regional balance of power to its favor. In 1986, a major Iranian military victory at the Faw Peninsula created the specter of Iraqi defeat, which sent shock waves throughout the Gulf. GCC states not only feared Iran but also Iraq, which increased its demands for GCC economic and military support.

Iraq managed to hold off Iran with indirect support from the United States and moderate Arab-states. But this balancing behavior strengthened Iraq and contributed to an imbalance of power between Iran and Iraq by the war's end in 1988. Although Iraq's economy was more devastated by the Iran-Iraq war than was Iran's, Iraq's military grew in strength substantially. Along with other factors, this predisposed Iraq to invade Kuwait, which, in turn, generated a chain of events that culminated in the serious diminution of Iraq's military capability. This left Iran with a freer hand in the region.

Table 6.1. The Regional Military Balance, 1978–1993

	Men (1,000s)*				
Country	Total	Army	Tanks	Artillery	Combat Aircraft**
1978					
Iran	413	25–285	1,720–1,775	782–1,225	459–470
Iraq	212	180–200	1,800–2,450	956–1,160	450–470
1980					
Iran	240	150	1,735	1,000	445
Iraq	243	200	2,750	1,240	332
1988					
Iran	604	550	500–600	875	60–165
Iraq	1,100	1,000	5,500	2,800	500–800
1993					
Iraq	400	350	2,200	1,650	300
Iran	600	440	700+	2,300	265
Saudi Arabia	100	68	696	700	296

*Includes Revolutionary Guards forces and Popular Army forces.
**Excluding the 112 aircraft flown to Iran during the Gulf War.

Sources: U.S. Department of Defense, *Conduct of the Persian Gulf War: Final Report to Congress* (Washington, D.C.: Government Printing Office, April 1992), 154, 157; *The Military Balance, 1993–1994* (London: International Institute for Strategic Studies, 1993); Anthony H. Cordesman, *After the Storm: The Changing Military Balance in the Middle East* (Boulder, CO: Westview Press, 1993), 382.

Overall, the Iranian revolution and the Iran-Iraq war created imbalances in military capability, while the Persian Gulf war helped restore the military balance. The Iranian revolution, the Iran-Iraq war, and the Persian Gulf war produced lower levels of Iranian and Iraqi military capability than otherwise would have been the case, thus leaving the United States and Saudi Arabia in a relatively stronger position. The Persian Gulf war, however, left Iran politically dominant and produced potential for a shift in the balance of military capability in Iran's favor.

Saudi Stability and Regional Conflict

Increases in Saudi regional influence and capability benefited U.S. security as did changes in the balance of power. After the Iranian revolution, Saudi stability and relations with the United States were shaky, revolutionary Iran was emergent, and the Soviets were gaining momentum. This changed in the 1980s. The Saudis spearheaded the development of the GCC, expanded their military capability, improved political and military relations with the United States, and assumed a more assertive foreign policy. Desert Storm further enhanced Riyadh's position by strengthening its military capability, improving its relations with Iran, and weakening Iraq.

From Bipolarity to Tripolarity: The Saudi Pole Emerges

The Iran-Iraq war and Desert Storm transformed the regional distribution of power by weakening Iran and Iraq and by strengthening the Saudis. Prior to these events, Iran and Iraq were the major powers in a bipolar regional structure. By 1991, bipolarity had turned into something closer to tripolarity, with the Saudis becoming an important, albeit weaker, third pole. The United States remained superimposed above this structure at the global level in an even more definitive manner than it had been in the late 1980s.

This change in the distribution of power had political and military implications. In theory, many scholars would predict that a tripolar military distribution of power would be less stable than a bipolar one in part because rivalry for power would increase between regional actors. In the Persian Gulf, however, the weakening of Iran and Iraq and the strengthening of Saudi Arabia engendered stability, despite the move toward tripolarity. This is because Iran and Iraq, the more radical states, were weakened yet remained relatively balanced between each other, while the status quo Saudis were strengthened. The issue of whether bipolarity or multipolarity was more stable, then, had to do with more than the distribution of power. It also depended on the direction of the power shift. Power shifts toward moderate actors and away from immoderate ones, which result in tripolarity, can be expected to produce more rather than less stability. This is precisely what occurred in the Persian Gulf region from 1980 to 1993. Tripolarity enhanced rivalry between Iran and Saudi Arabia and between Saudi Arabia and Iraq by making the Saudis more able to challenge these actors. It also elevated the strength of moderate states, while weakening that of revisionist ones. The United States' enhanced position at the global level reinforced the positive effect of tripolarity by further checking the two revisionist powers in the triangle, Iran and Iraq, and bolstering the weaker third pole, Saudi Arabia. By diminishing Iran's main rival, Iraq, the Persian Gulf war revived Iran as a major regional actor.

The Saudi-Iranian Roller Coaster

While Iran emerged from the Gulf crisis a comparatively stronger actor, its postwar foreign policy remained contradictory and confounding. In part, this reflected the internal struggle in Iran between radicals and moderates. Iran sought a rapprochement with Saudi Arabia and other GCC states and aimed to develop economic relations with the West. This made sense. The Iran-Iraq war had left Iran economically devastated and war weary, and political isolation had crippled its foreign policy.

Despite its apparently assertive postwar foreign policy, Iran's leader Hashemi Rafsanjani repeatedly stressed the importance of economics over ideology. While less moderate elements in Iran argued for a more confrontational foreign policy, the regime had virtually no support for renewed conflict with its neighbors.[56] Iranian moderates did well in elections for Iran's Fourth Islamic Majlis in April and May 1992. The elections were a resounding victory for Rafsanjani, whose supporters won an absolute majority in the Majlis.[57]

But while Iran showed a moderate side, it also flexed its regional muscles and continued to seek a dominant security role, flaunting the United States and GCC states in the process. Despite severe economic problems, Iran embarked on a postwar five-year, $10 billion military rebuilding program. It acquired modern conventional weapons mainly from Russia, China, and North Korea and continued to develop its biological and nuclear weapons programs and its already effective chemical weapons program.

While wary of Iran, the Saudis aimed to develop workable relations from 1990 to 1992. Saudi-Iranian relations had ebbed and flowed from 1980 to 1993, but were strengthened. During the Iran-Iraq war, Riyadh chose the lesser of two evils in supporting Iraq against revolutionary Iran. Although Riyadh gave Iraq financial and military support in its war against Iran, the Saudis also sought at times to appease Iran for security purposes. But the threat from Iran increased significantly after its major military victory at the Faw Peninsula in early 1986. The rising Iranian threat coupled with Riyadh's increasing confidence in U.S. regional power and in its own capability, were important factors in pushing the Saudis to assume a more confrontational policy toward Iran. This policy included the severing of diplomatic ties with Iran in April 1988 in response to the Mecca crisis, closer political-military ties to the United States, and increased assertiveness in the face of Iranian military threats.[58]

The 1988 cease fire in the Iran-Iraq war created opportunities for a Saudi-Iranian rapprochement. Prior to Iraq's invasion of Kuwait, however, relations continued to be bedeviled primarily by lingering tensions over the Iran-Iraq war and by Iran's continuing political challenge to Saudi authority as the protector of Islam's holy sites. Although the Persian Gulf war undermined Saudi-Iraqi relations, it proved to be an important turning point in Saudi-Iranian relations. Both states had much to lose if Saddam's gamble in Kuwait paid off and much to gain by increasing their co-operation. The invasion impressed upon the Saudis the importance of Iran's balancing role against Iraq. It also gave Iran the opportunity to shore up its relations with Arab Gulf states and to make the case that the real threat to the Gulf had always come from Iraq.

Saudi-Iranian diplomatic relations were restored in March 1991, and tensions over Mecca were largely set aside. Prince Saud al-Faisal, Saudi foreign minister, became the first senior Saudi official to visit Teheran in twelve years, and for the first time, Iran was invited to sit in on the meetings of the GCC. Despite the shock of Iraq's invasion, the Saudis ruled out military co-operation with Iran but agreed to consult it on regional security and to increase political and economic co-operation. The overall improvement in relations was significant, although Iran remained disturbed by the Saudi-U.S. connection, and the Saudi monarchy continued to be openly criticized in some quarters in Iran. By June 1992, Teheran's first ambassador to Riyadh described Iran and Saudi Arabia as "two wings without which the Islamic world cannot fly."[59] From Iran's perspective, the invasion of Kuwait never would have occurred had Saudi-Iranian relations been stronger in August 1990.[60]

Despite improvement in relations, prospects for a serious and lasting rapprochement between Iran and GCC states such as Saudi Arabia remained doubtful. In addition to opposing a U.S. regional role and criticizing the Gulf monarchies for having too much wealth and not enough scruples, Iran continued to support populist Islam, which the more conservative Saudis considered a threat. Bridging this ideological divide proved difficult with "radicals" affecting Iran's foreign policy agenda.

Saudi-Iranian strategic rivalry was also accelerated by the Gulf crisis, which knocked Iraq out of regional competition temporarily. As noted in the foregoing analysis, Iran moved to annex Abu Musa in 1992, which disrupted Saudi-Iranian relations. Iran's action at Abu Musa was linked to the Persian Gulf war in two basic ways. First, the war undermined Iraq's influence and left Iran a freer hand in the region. Second, it generated defense agreements between the United States and Kuwait, Bahrain, and Qatar, which Iran condemned as threatening to its position, and attempted to use as justification for its occupation of Abu Musa.[61]

Through 1993 and well into 1994, Iran continued to assert its sovereignty over the three islands of the Greater and Lesser Tunbs and Abu Musa, to which it held a historic claim. Gulf states repeatedly asked Iran to withdraw from the islands, or to agree to international arbitration to resolve its territorial dispute with the UAE. Although GCC states were unable to influence Iran over Abu Musa, the speed and unity of their response may have given Teheran pause in considering additional moves against the islands.[62]

The row over Abu Musa reflected the broader rivalry between Iran and Saudi Arabia, each attempting to fill the power vacuum left after the defeat of Iraq. This rivalry extended beyond the Persian Gulf to Central Asia. Indeed, Iran launched a diplomatic offensive to convert Central Asian republics to its particular brand of Islam. In response, the Saudis, reflecting an increasingly assertive foreign policy, sent Saudi foreign minister Prince Saud al-Faisal to tour the region in order to push the Saudi position.[63] This relatively new arena of rivalry for these states added yet another dimension to the complex international politics of the Middle Eastern region.

Saudi-Iraqi Relations

Iraq's defeat by the Desert Storm coalition further strengthened Saudi Arabia by weakening a feared rival. Until the mid- to late-1970s, Iraqi foreign policy was generally revisionist and pro-Soviet, which proved problematic for the conservative Saudis. While Iraq began to moderate its policies and to turn to the West for economic assistance and arms in the mid-late 1970s, it also continued to oppose the U.S. regional presence and the U.S.-Saudi link, in part because Baghdad sought regional hegemony.[64]

The Iranian revolution pushed Saudi Arabia closer to Iraq not only because Iraq appeared more powerful than Iran but also because Iran was perceived as the major threat. Prior to the Iran-Iraq war, Iraq had been feared by the Saudis and other Arab states. Oman, for instance, felt it necessary to mollify Iraq after allowing the United States access rights in 1980.[65] And most Gulf states accepted Iraq's February 1980 Pan-Arab Declaration that underscored Iraq's major regional ambitions, rejected any foreign regional influence, and presented an implicit challenge to the U.S.-Saudi relationship and to Saudi influence.[66] Iraq's influence had risen to such an extent that Riyadh's concerns about U.S. resolve, and its fears of Iran, overrode traditional Saudi mistrust of Iraq and pushed Riyadh to side with Iraq for security purposes.[67]

While Saudi concerns about Iraq continued throughout the 1980s, the Iran-Iraq war transformed Iraq from a powerful regional actor into one strapped by the exigencies of conflict. Saudi Arabia, which had been challenged by Iraq politically prior to the war, became one of its primary financiers. In the prewar period, Baghdad stridently objected to a U.S. regional presence. By contrast, during the war it supported a stronger U.S. role in order to push Iran to end the war. The U.S.-led reflagging of Kuwaiti tankers in 1987–88 greatly benefited Iraq by limiting Iran's strategic maneuver, protecting Iraq's Gulf Arab "allies" from Iranian military reprisals, and ultimately leading to several U.S.-Iranian military engagements that damaged Iran's military power.[68]

The Iran-Iraq war left Iraq in a position to extend its regional influence relatively unfettered by its rivalry with war-ravaged Iran. Despite the fact that Iraq depended on Riyadh for postwar economic reconstruction, the Saudis feared Iraq and signed a nonaggression pact with it. Saddam's assertive postwar foreign policy presaged Iraq's invasion of Kuwait, which left Saudi-Iraqi relations at an unprecedented low. Although most members of the Saudi royal family never trusted Saddam even as they supported him, they did not believe that he could annex Kuwait and physically threaten Saudi security. His removal from power remained a *sine qua non* for any meaningful improvement in Saudi-Iraqi relations.

WAR AND DOMESTIC POLITICS

Wars not only have significant effects on relations between states, but also on the domestic politics of states. The Gulf war was no exception. It affected the domestic politics of states across the region and beyond it. Two cases, however, were particularly relevant to U.S. regional security—Saudi Arabia and Iraq. At the state level, wars enhanced Saudi stability and constrained Iraq in ways that benefited U.S. regional interests.

Saudi Domestic Stability

Saudi Arabia's status as the linchpin of U.S. regional security made its domestic stability important. The more stable the kingdom was, the better off was regional security. While wars had a mixed impact on Saudi stability, in general they increased it.

Prior to the Iranian revolution, there were no indicators of serious domestic instability in Saudi Arabia; the primary domestic concerns were with managing the fast-paced modernization process and reconciling rivalry within the royal family.[69] This changed in the post-revolutionary period. In the most serious challenge to the royal family's authority in several decades, a group of armed men seized the Grand Mosque in Mecca in November 1979.[70] This was followed by major Shiite demonstrations in the eastern Saudi oil province, the first of their kind, and anti-regime demonstrations in 1980 at Mecca and Medina. Although the 1979 Mecca attack was probably linked much more to dislocations created by the modernization process than to the Iranian revolution,[71] the 1980 demonstrations were more closely linked to the revolution.[72]

The Iran-Iraq war, which erupted in September 1980, had two major effects on Saudi stability. First, it dramatized the potential for domestic instability created by the Iranian revolution. Although Khomeini called for the overthrow of Arab Gulf monarchies, which he viewed as illegitimate, Iran did not pursue this end militarily. Iraq's brutal attack on Iran and the ensuing war combined Iran's political threat with a military one.

Second, while the Iran-Iraq war fueled the revolution in the short term, it weakened Iran over time, thus making it less able and inclined to undermine Saudi domestic stability. In 1984, Khomeini engineered a reversal in Iranian foreign policy in which Iran would stop actively confronting the West and exporting the revolution regionally. This turnaround was directly related to the war. Iran was suffering military setbacks, was unable to obtain spare parts and equipment thanks to U.S. pressures, and wanted to generate international support for its war position. In response to Iran's foreign policy shift, Riyadh sent Saudi foreign minister Saud al-Faisal on a formal visit to Iran. This visit marked the beginning of improvement in relations.[73]

The shaky rapprochement, however, was disrupted by the war-related Mecca crisis in 1987, which represented the most serious threat to Saudi stability in the 1980s. Partly in retaliation for Saudi support of U.S. reflagging of Kuwaiti tankers, Iran attempted to challenge the Saudi regime and its authority over Islam's holy sites by instigating a riot at Mecca that left 400 Iranian pilgrims dead. As discussed in chapter 5, the Mecca incident seriously damaged Saudi-Iranian relations. But it brought the Saudis increased support from the Arab world and the United States and totally backfired on Iran politically. Overall, the Iran-Iraq war undermined Iran's power, clearly weakened its will and ability to export the revolution,[74] and decreased its long-term threat to Saudi domestic stability.

While Iran attempted to solve war-related economic problems in part by slowly reintegrating itself into the regional and world economy, Iraq decided that an invasion of Kuwait would do the trick more quickly.[75] The ensuing Gulf crisis produced no serious manifestations of Saudi domestic instability, but it did reignite the internal debate over the nature of Saudi rule and caused economic dislocation in the kingdom.

The Internal Debate: To Reform or Not?

In December 1990, King Fahd received a "Secular Petition" from forty-three religious and secular leaders, which was followed three months later by "The Religious Petition" from scores of top religious leaders.[76] The ultra-conservative religious forces expressed their strong concern over royal family corruption, nepotism, and favoritism, and royal monopoly control over decision making.[77] At the same time, liberal democratic forces pushed for democratic reforms.

In a surprising move, the royal family responded with royal decrees, calling for a Consultative Council of commoners nominated by the king, adherence to the rule of law, and an enlarged body of princes to select a new monarch. King Fahd linked these measures directly to the Persian Gulf war and described them as a "kind of partnership between the grassroots and the leadership."[78]

The debate over reforms was neither acrimonious nor divisive, and King Fahd was widely acknowledged as the legitimate arbiter. In some Saudi quarters, the reforms were viewed as devoid of content in that they did not "presage any political reform or bring any change to the method of government."[79] Certainly, they did not represent a Saudi embrace of Western democracy or even of democracy in general. Indeed, King Fahd stated that the "democratic systems prevailing in the world are systems which in their structure do not suit this region and our people" and that "the system of free election is not part of Islamic ideology."[80] The Clinton administration, however, continued to explore the possibility of introducing democracy and submitted an official document to the Arab Gulf states in February 1994 encouraging pluralism and democracy. The Gulf states, however, expressed serious reservations.[81]

While the Saudi reforms were not remarkable, they also were not entirely insignificant. The Saudis had been promising to establish a Consultative Council since 1962[82] but had failed to do so until after the Persian Gulf war. Although the measures fell far short of meaningful democratic reform, they represented modest concessions to Saudi democratic forces. These forces had been pushing for more democratic institutions prior to the Iranian revolution, but their efforts gained momentum only after Iraq's eviction from Kuwait.[83] Conservative forces in the kingdom also gained from the decrees. While the royal measures did not accommodate their desire for strict imposition of Islamic laws, it did accommodate their demands for greater decision-making participation and for such things as regulations to eliminate corruption.[84]

King Fahd also moved in mid-1993 to appease Saudi Shiites who number 700,000 out of a population of 12 million and are concentrated in the eastern oil province. Although the process was delicate, Fahd promised to improve relations and, in turn, the Shiite minority—in particular an exiled Muslim opposition group—agreed to suspend some forms of antigovernment activity.[85]

Whether the general reform process assumes meaningful dimensions depends chiefly on the regime, which is unlikely to promote any serious diminution of its control over the kingdom. Indeed, previous attempts at reform in 1962 and 1980 were abandoned when internal and external pressures for them were reduced.[86] The reforms, however, contributed to Saudi domestic stability by at least charting a path for more meaningful reform and lowering the level of domestic discontent.

Overall, while regional wars threatened the kingdom in the short term, they contributed to Saudi stability in two ways. The Iran-Iraq war undermined the Iranian challenge to Saudi rule sparked by the Iranian revolution, and the Persian Gulf war pushed the Saudis to appease discontented domestic elements.

War and Economics

While the Iran-Iraq war imposed costs on the Saudis, Desert Shield and Storm produced serious economic dislocation. Although Saudi oil income in 1991 was over $40 billion dollars due to windfall profits from increased prices and production related to the Gulf crisis, Saudi war expenses were estimated at 60 to 70 billion dollars.[87] Riyadh's financial woes were exacerbated by a downturn in the global economy and a general decrease in the price of oil on the global market. Saudi Arabia's economic problems necessitated the withdrawal of substantial monies from U.S. banks, which hurt Saudi credit ratings in the United States. It also pushed the Saudis to stretch out payments for billions of dollars worth of weapons it agreed to buy from U.S. defense contractors.[88]

Riyadh's financial position was linked to domestic stability. Because the Saudis used money to maintain internal and external security, financial troubles threatened to increase short-term instability. By offering the kingdom's 4,000 princes easy access to the banking system and government subsidies, financial resources helped Riyadh keep rivalries in check in the royal family and also helped stave off popular dissatisfaction. It also allowed the Saud family to buy off potential enemies and to persuade allies not to stray from the Saudi line.[89] Although strained budgets decreased Riyadh's ability to exercise domestic and foreign policy, the regime retained the ability to restore economic vitality through huge oil reserves, some of which were newly found, substantial foreign investments, and little foreign debt that could decrease financial flexibility.

Postwar Constraints on Iraq

Critics of Desert Storm pointed to Saddam's survival and Iraq's postwar defiance of U.N. resolutions as evidence that Desert Storm was a questionable victory. To be sure, Iraq displayed short-term success in recovering from Desert Storm. Despite the war and stringent postwar U.N. sanctions, Saddam was not overthrown and actually oversaw an ambitious program of postwar economic and military reconstruction. His resilience complicated U.S. regional policy. As one former high-level U.S. official asserted, as long as Saddam survives, "he paralyzes our policy."[90] Iraq's short-run achievements notwithstanding, Desert Storm imposed severe constraints on Iraq.

U.N. Sanctions Against Iraq

In the postcrisis period, the United States stressed that it respected Iraq's territorial integrity and sovereignty, did not wish to see it fragmented as a state, and had no quarrel with the Iraqi people. But in the U.S. view, Iraq remained a political and military threat to the region. U.S. policy under President Clinton, which was backed by all GCC states and members of the European Union,[91] aimed to force Iraq to comply with all U.N. resolutions and to stand "firmly behind the security and the integrity of the states in the area against any future aggression."[92]

U.N. Resolutions 687 and 707 called for critical U.N. sanctions against Iraq and seriously impeded Iraq's ability to restore its military capabilities. Referred to as the "mother of all resolutions" for its record length, Resolution 687 was passed by the Security Council on April 3, 1991. It forced Iraq to accept a U.N. demarcated border with Kuwait, the inviolability of Kuwaiti territory, and U.N. peacekeepers on the Iraq-Kuwait border. It also mandated full disclosure of all of Iraq's ballistic missile stocks and production facilities (over 150 kilometers range), all nuclear materials, chemical and biological weapons and facilities, and co-operation in their destruction. Paragraphs 10 through 12, furthermore, required Iraq to "unconditionally undertake not to use, develop construct, or acquire" weapons of mass destruction. Iraqi compliance with Resolution 687 was a prerequisite for lifting or reducing sanctions against it.[93]

The ban on the sale of oil deprived Iraq of an estimated 12 to 15 billion dollars with which it could rebuild its conventional capabilities and develop nonconventional weapons. U.N. sanctions prohibiting arms transfers and related materials further hindered Iraq's ability to restore its conventional capability to prewar levels. And, the ban on the sale or supply of commodities and products added to Saddam's problems by generating internal discontent and forcing him to divert monies from reconstruction toward providing goods for important domestic constituencies.

Iraq's Response to U.N. Sanctions

Iraq assumed a two-pronged approach toward U.N. sanctions. On the one hand, it accepted Resolution 687, acted or pretended to meet some of its obligations, and then called for the lifting of the U.N. embargo.[94] On the other hand, Saddam left little doubt about his enduring ambitions. While the Iraq-Kuwait border dispute was settled in legal terms in the postwar period, Iraq was dissatisfied. The U.N. commission that was designated to redraw the border redrew it in a manner that caused two serious friction points. Kuwait was given a larger portion of the Rumaila oil field over which Kuwait and Iraq lay joint claim and retained control over Warba and Bubiyan islands. Sovereignty over these islands allowed Kuwait to control Iraq's only current access point to Persian Gulf waters. Kuwait considered the area its rightful possession, one usurped by Iraq in 1932 and 1973.[95]

Iraq continued to assert that it would eventually conquer Kuwait. Despite warnings from the United Nations Iraq-Kuwait Observer Mission (UNIKOM), the Iraqi army repeatedly violated Kuwaiti territory and threatened the Saudi border as well. For instance, on July 1 and 3, 1993, Iraqi forces shot machine guns along the Saudi border, which alarmed the royal family.[96]

Furthermore, Iraq displayed "no apparent intention" of giving up its efforts to develop weapons of mass destruction. Rather, it engaged in sporadic concealment and "pretended cooperation."[97] Saddam also refused to allow the United Nations to control Iraq's overseas sales and to use proceeds for humanitarian purposes and for funding U.N. operations in Iraq.

Restraining Saddam

Iraq's defiance was generally unsuccessful. At the political level, the United States and other actors, particularly the Saudis, worked to isolate Baghdad. Iraq sought to break this isolation by re-establishing relations with its arch rival Iran, which despite its purchases of Iraqi oil, rebuffed Iraq.[98] Iraq had limited success with Oman, the only GCC state to maintain relations with Iraq after the Gulf war, and Qatar. Qatari Television aired video reports from inside Iraq on the negative effect of economic sanctions on Iraqis, an action that caused Kuwait to recall its ambassador in Qatar for consultations. Riyadh criticized these two states for their attempted rapprochement with Iraq, arguing that Iraq was "working to divide the GCC."[99]

At the economic level, U.N. sanctions deprived Iraq of oil revenues and a role in affecting decision making in global oil markets. Economic deprivation also exacerbated Saddam's internal problems. He not only had to quell the troublesome Kurds and Shiites but also to keep his own officers content, a task that became increasingly more difficult. Iraq's living standards were cut to half the prewar level, inflation reached 250 percent over prewar levels, and the Iraqi dinar was devalued over 900 times its value from 1990 to 1993.[100] Deep dissatisfaction with the regime resulted among the Iraqi people, army, and even within Saddam's Tikriti ruling family. In the view of key experts, Desert Storm made Iraq more vulnerable to a coup or internal family problems than ever before.[101]

At the strategic level, Desert Storm and postwar U.N. sanctions weakened Iraq in the conventional arena, undermined its nuclear program, and damaged to some extent its biological and chemical programs. Prior to Desert Storm, Iraq had a formidable conventional force, which enabled it to affect events in the Persian Gulf region and the broader Middle East. By the war's end, the world's sixth largest air force had been decimated, and Iraq's army was halved in size. Iraq lost an estimated 2,633 tanks of 5,800; 2,196 artillery pieces of 3,850; and 324 fixed-wing combat aircraft of an estimated 650 to 700. Its navy, which was not particularly formidable but nonetheless dangerous, was destroyed. Furthermore, postwar U.N. sanctions decreased Iraqi capabilities by reducing the operational readiness of forces that survived Desert Storm. Although seriously weakened, Iraq did retain about 50 to 60 percent of its prewar conventional military capability and reconstituted a total of 28 of its prewar 57 divisions. As a result, it remained the strongest military in the Persian Gulf region.[102]

In the nuclear area, postwar U.N. inspections revealed that Iraq had been closer to developing nuclear weapons than had been expected. Inspectors found a multi-billion dollar nuclear program that could have produced its first nuclear weapon not in ten years as some U.S. intelligence agencies had thought, but in three to four years had Iraq not invaded Kuwait.[103] While Iraq initially defied the U.N. resolution requiring full disclosure of nuclear materials, over time the U.N. Special Commission and the International Atomic Energy Agency (IAEA) made substantial progress toward eliminating its programs of mass destruction.[104] Experts believe that all major parts of Iraq's nuclear program were destroyed or seriously damaged either by Desert Storm or by U.N. inspection teams. This included Iraq's nuclear reactor, major nuclear labs, calutron project, and centrifuges. Its uranium mine was also located and its processes for turning uranium ore into oxide controlled.

Despite suffering severe and perhaps irreparable damage, Iraq's nuclear program remained potentially viable. Baghdad retained the human intelligence capability to support a major nuclear program, including substantial dual-use technology and working designs for a centrifuge system. In the 1980s and before, it had developed experience in how to defy internal inspections and to protect its program from external attack. Furthermore, some analysts speculated that Iraq retained an underground reactor or centrifuge cascade, despite the failure of U.N. inspectors to identify such facilities.[105] While highly improbable, Iraq could also buy nuclear fuel and technology, or even a nuclear weapon from former Soviet republics. At a minimum, Saddam's continuing interest in obtaining nuclear weapons necessitated long-term monitoring as described in U.N. Resolution 715 to prevent Iraq's program from taking off again.

Prior to the Gulf war, Iraq had the most advanced chemical warfare program in the Arab world. After Desert Storm, Iraq retained the ability to produce chemical and biological weapons, despite the severe damage imposed by allied air forces on its principal chemical agent facility located at Samarra and its main biological warfare research complex at Salman Pak. Were U.N. sanctions to be lifted, Iraq could restore its former chemical weapons production in less than one year (it may be able to do so even with sanctions in place), and produce biological weapons within weeks. Indeed, according to CIA Director James Woolsey, neither the war nor postwar inspections were enough to degrade seriously its chemical and biological capability.[106]

Saddam's problems extended to maintaining sovereignty over Iraqi territory. In northern Iraq, the Kurdish insurrection succeeded for the first time in taking several major urban centers, including the oil facilities at Kirkuk, and, at the height of their rebellion, a majority of Kurdistan territory. Although Saddam crushed the rebellion, it sapped Iraq's energy and created nearly one million refugees in early April 1991, concentrated primarily on the Iranian and Turkish borders. This human tragedy generated support for an international effort, code-named Operation Provide Comfort, and led the coalition allies to create safe havens against Iraqi attacks. The influx of allied troops further compromised Saddam's freedom of action in his own country.

In the south, Saddam met the postwar Shiite uprising with a unprecedented crackdown. Even during the Iran-Iraq war, the Baathi party and Saddam's state police maintained control of southern Iraq. But Desert Storm changed this by weakening Iraq's military capability and logistics as well as Saddam's credibility, while raising the spirits of his detractors. U.S. concern with Iraq's gross human rights violations in this area led the United States, Britain, and France to declare a no-fly zone over southern Iraq in August 1992, which applied to fixed-winged aircraft and helicopters. While the United States was not ready to create a security zone in southern Iraq similar to that in northern Iraq, it did cooperate with the United Nations to identify human rights abuses.

WAR AND PEACE: INTRAREGIONAL DYNAMICS

War in the Persian Gulf helped generate the peace process in the Arab-Israeli arena, which in turn, benefited U.S. security in the Persian Gulf. The Gulf crisis was linked to the regional peace process in several ways.

First, the United States clearly saw a link between diminished Iraqi power and the peace process. Even before Desert Storm, President Bush viewed Arab-Israeli peace as part of the overall concept of a New World Order. Desert Storm put the United States in a position to spearhead the peace process. The war demonstrated that Washington could orchestrate an international response against a worse case scenario threat in the Persian Gulf region and improved U.S. regional standing. This had serious implications for politics in the Arab-Israeli arena. It reinforced the U.S. ability to convince Arab states that it could influence Israel to make serious concessions for peace and raised the potential pay-off for Arab states engaging in the peace process.

At the same time, U.S. power gave Israel more confidence that its concessions for peace would not compromise its security. U.S. influence could help ensure Arab compliance to a peace agreement or provide Israel with support in the event that peace collapsed after it had made territorial concessions. By strengthening Israel comparatively, the defeat of Iraq also made it more safe for Israel to make concessions for peace. Moreover, Iraq's scud missile attacks on Israel brought home the message to some Israelis that territorial depth was less significant in the ballistic missile age than it had been before, thus making territorial concessions more palatable.

Second, Desert Storm helped strip Arab nationalist and radical states of a military alternative to the political process. Iraq and Syria had been the only actors that could prosecute a serious military option against Israel. By weakening Iraq militarily and discrediting it politically, Desert Storm removed Iraq in the short term as a serious antagonist and political force in the Arab world. Meanwhile, Syria's involvement in Desert Shield made it more likely to assume a role in the peace process. This was not only because Syria joined the U.S.-led alliance, but also because co-operation with the West as opposed to steadfastness with the Arab radical front made more sense after the success of Desert Storm. The loss of Moscow as a principal patron and arms supplier no doubt added to Syria's interest in choosing negotiation over continued conflict, as did its history of utter failure in attempting to destroy Israel military.

Third, Arab Gulf states were more inclined to support the peace process after Desert Storm. In part this was because they were indebted to the United States for checking Saddam's growing regional influence, remained dependent on U.S. security support, and did not want to be seen as undermining the peace process. Desert Storm also improved the public Arab attitude toward Israel and clearly made GCC states more willing to participate constructively in the Middle East peace process. Reflecting broader Arab sentiment, the Saudi daily, *Al-Riyadh*, asserted that "Israel and the Arabs must put away their historic enmity and resort to the logic of interests."[107]

All GCC states attended the multilateral peace talks in Moscow and committed themselves to participation in the working groups created there.[108] The Saudis in particular played an active role in these talks, urging moderation on all sides. For the first time, excluding Nasser's challenge on the Arabian peninsula in the

1960s, Arab Gulf states and Israel had similar interests in seeing an Arab state checked. This added to the movement toward peace.[109]

The peace process had a positive effect on U.S. standing in the Persian Gulf. In the past, Gulf states circumscribed their level of co-operation with the United States in part because of its strong association with Israel. Close interaction with the United States made them vulnerable to domestic and regional criticism that they were lackeys of the United States and were betraying the Arab and Palestinian cause. The launching of the peace process, the United States' vital security role against Iraq, and Israel's serious movement toward peace decreased their vulnerability to such criticism. Regardless of whether the peace process succeeds, its mere initiation has benefited U.S. security in the region.

CONCLUSION

The Gulf crisis produced profound changes in the regional and international politics of the Persian Gulf at multiple levels of interaction. Together, these changes significantly increased U.S. ability to protect its three principal regional interests: ensure the flow of oil at reasonable prices, maintain Saudi stability, and deter and contain anti-U.S. states.

At the global level, the Gulf crisis further internationalized regional politics. The U.N., United States, and European states developed their ability to enhance regional security through joint and independent efforts. Although the Iran-Iraq war had already motivated such efforts, the Persian Gulf war formalized and expanded them.

While developments at the global level facilitated U.S. efforts to protect its three major interests in the Persian Gulf, regional events had a similar effect. Attempts at creating effective indigenous security structures fell short in the postwar period, but intelligent attention was focused on how regional actors could protect their own security. In lieu of developing a joint GCC military force or pursuing the Damascus Declaration formula for collective security, GCC states aimed to develop their own individual armies, while increasing co-operation and co-ordination with each other and outside states.

Shifts in the regional balance of power further added to regional stability. The Iran-Iraq and Persian Gulf wars weakened Iran and Iraq, respectively, and strengthened the Saudis. This shifted the distribution of regional power away from bipolarity based on competition between Iran and Iraq and toward tripolarity. More importantly, it enhanced the power of moderate states over revisionist ones.

At the domestic level, Iraq was severely constrained. Although it did reconstitute part of its army, Iraq faced crippling U.N. sanctions, suffered from serious economic problems, and was unable to break regional and global isolation. The war and U.N. sanctions greatly impeded Iraq's ability to threaten regional security. While Desert Storm constrained Iraq at the domestic level, it left the Saudis not only less vulnerable to external threats but also more stable internally. To be sure, the Gulf crisis hurt Riyadh's short-term economic position and generated social and political ferment. But it also pushed the Saudis to take measures to appease discontented domestic elements, thus decreasing the potential for internal instability.

At the intraregional level, war was the midwife of the Middle East peace process. The peace process in the Arab-Israeli arena contributed in turn to U.S. regional security in the Persian Gulf arena. From the Arab perspective, Israel became less of a liability in the U.S. effort to forge stronger relations with Gulf states, and from Israel's standpoint, U.S. relations with GCC states became less worrisome.

NOTES

1. For critical documents leading to the authorization by the U.S. Congress of force against Iraq, see U.S. Congress, House of Representatives, Committee on Foreign Affairs, *The Persian Gulf Crisis: Relevant Documents, Correspondence, Reports*, Report prepared by the Subcommittee on Arms Control, June 1991 (Washington, D.C.: GPO, 1991).

2. Record, *Hollow Victory*.

3. Roger Hilsman, *George Bush vs. Saddam Hussein: Military Success! Political Failure?* (Novato, CA: Lyford Books, 1992).

4. U.S. News and World Report, *Triumph Without Victory: The Unreported History of the Persian Gulf War* (New York: Times Books, 1992).

5. For an authoritative account of the WEU's role in European and Persian Gulf security, see Van Eekelen, "Building a New European Security Order," 18–23. Also, on the contribution of the WEU during the Gulf crisis, see Van Eekelen, "WEU and the Gulf Crisis," 529–30.

6. See Johnson, *The Military as an Instrument of U.S. Policy*, citing statements by Robert Komer, former under secretary of defense.

7. Ibid., 9.

8. U.S. House, *Chronologies*, 1979, 208.

9. See U.S. Congress, *Rapid Deployment Forces*, XIV, 4, 8, 11. Also, see interview with Secretary of Defense Harold Brown in *Wall Street Journal*, 1 July 1980, 22.

10. Address by Secretary Brown, DSB 80 (May 1980): 66.

11. For details, see U.S. Senate, Schwarzkopf statement, 173–302.

12. On technological gains, see Thomas A. Keaney and Eliot O. Cohen, *Gulf War Air Power Survey: Summary Report* (Washington, D.C.: GPO, 1993), chap. 9.

13. On lessons learned, see "Desert Shield/Desert Storm—Logistics Lessons Learned," *Air Force Journal of Logistics* 15 (Fall 1991); U.S. Congress, House of Representatives, Committee on Armed Services, *Defense for a New Era: Lessons of the Persian Gulf War* (Washington, D.C.: GPO, 1992).

14. See "Desert Shield/Storm: Air Mobility Command's Achievements and Lessons for the Future" (GAO/National Security and International Affairs Division (NSIAD)-93-40, 25 January 1993).

15. "Military Airlift: Changes Underway to Ensure Continued Success of Civil Reserve Air Fleet" (GAO/NSIAD-93-12, 31 December 1992).

16. "Military Afloat Prepositioning: Wartime Use and Issues for the Future"

(GAO/NSIAD-93-39, 4 November 1992).

17. Fred Smith, defense department official, "Remarks at the Meridian International Center" (hereafter cited as Smith address), Washington, D.C., 18 May 1994, 6.

18. "Operation Desert Storm: War Offers Important Insights into Army and Marine Corps Training Needs" (GAO/NSIAD, 92-240, 25 August 1992).

19. Smith address, 7.

20. Personal correspondence with Ambassador Richard Murphy, assistant secretary of state for Near Eastern Affairs under the Reagan administration, 26 May 1994.

21. See Nadav Safran, *Saudi Arabia: The Ceaseless Quest for Security* (Cambridge, MA: Harvard University Press, 1985), 373.

22. For King Fahd's view of postwar security, see *Saudi Arabia, The Monthly Newsletter of the Royal Embassy of Saudi Arabia* 9, no. 2 (February-March 1992): 1–2.

23. *Cairo MENA*, in FBIS: NESA, 5 October 1992, 12.

24. *Paris AFP*, in FBIS: NESA, 21 December 1993, 25.

25. *Kuwait KUNA*, in FBIS: NESA, 20 December 1993, 33.

26. Youssef M. Ibrahim, "Gulf Nations Said to Be Committed to U.S. Alliance," *New York Times*, 25 October 1991, A9.

27. For details, see Anthony H. Cordesman, *After the Storm: The Changing Military Balance in the Middle East* (Boulder, CO: Westview Press, 1993), 572–74.

28. U.S. Congress, House of Representatives, Committee on Foreign Affairs, *Developments in the Middle East*, Hearing Before the Subcommittee on Europe and the Middle East, 17 March 1992 (Washington, D.C.: GPO, 1992).

29. The text of the Damascus Declaration appears in *Journal of Palestine Studies* 20 (Summer 1991): 161–63.

30. See Joseph Kechichian, "Political Reforms in Kuwait and the GCC States," *Middle East Insight* 18 (September/October 1991): 40–41.

31. See *Cairo AL-SHA'B* in FBIS: NESA, 7 January 1993, 2.

32. Caryle Murphy, "Egypt's Pullout Signals Discord with Gulf," *Washington Post*, 11 May 1991, A18.

33. For the text of the interview, see *Beirut Tele-Liban*, in FBIS: NESA, 3 December 1993, 47–48.

34. See, for instance, the interview with high-level Kuwaiti officials in *AL-Shariqah AL-SHURUQ*, in FBIS: NESA, 18 January 1994, 21.

35. *Damascus SANA*, in FBIS: NESA, 11 January 1994, 6.

36. *London AL-SHARQ AL-AWSAT*, in FBIS: NESA, 17 February 1994, 44.

37. U.S. Congress, House of Representatives, Committee on Foreign Affairs, *Developments in the Middle East*, 24 June and 30 June 1992 (Washington, D.C.: GPO, 1992), 9.

38. Smith address, 6.

39. Quoted in "Vance Sees Decline in U.S.-Saudi Links," *New York Times*, 9 May 1979, A10.

40. See *Kuwait AR-RA'Y AL-AMM*, FBIS: MEA, 12 January 1979, C1; MECS 3 (1978–79): 22, 751. Even the Shah blamed Washington for his demise. Sick, *All Fall Down*, 179.

41. *Riyadh SNA*, in FBIS: MENA, 30 May 1979, C2.

42. On Riyadh's lack of confidence in the United States, see Cordesman, *The Gulf and the Search*, 260–61. Also see *Middle East Economic Digest*, 9 March 1979, 13.

43. For details, see David B. Ottaway, "Saudis Agree to Widen Gulf AWACS

Patrols," *Washington Post*, 23 June 1987, 14.

44. Safran, *Saudi Arabia*, 412.

45. Author's interview with Ambassador Richard Murphy, assistant secretary of state for Near Eastern Affairs under the Reagan administration, 26 May 1994.

46. Personal correspondence with Ambassador Richard Murphy.

47. Judith Miller, "Saudi General Sees No Need for Big American Presence," *New York Times*, 29 April 1991, A9.

48. Smith address, 5.

49. U.S. Congress, House of Representatives, Committee on Foreign Affairs, *United States Policy Toward the Middle East and the Persian Gulf*, Hearings Before the Subcommittee on Europe and the Middle East, 17 June and 26 June 1991 (Washington, D.C.: GPO, 1991), 35 (hereafter referred to as U.S. House, *U.S. Policy Toward the Middle East*, 1991.)

50. Interview with Dr. Paul D. Wolfowitz, 26 August 1994.

51. Gerald F. Seib and Peter Waldman, "Best of Friends: U.S.-Saudi Ties Grow, Benefiting Americans but Troubling Some," *Wall Street Journal*, 26 October 1992, 1.

52. U.S. House, *Developments in the Middle East*, 10.

53. Robert Pelletreau, assistant secretary for Near East and South Asian Affairs, Address to the American Business Community (hereafter cited as Pelletreau address), Abu Dhabi, 8 May 1994, 12.

54. See Richard W. Cottam, "Revolutionary Iran and the War with Iraq," *Current History* 80 (January 1981): 5–9.

55. See text of interview with King Fahd, in *London AL-HAWADITH*, FBIS: NESA, 14 February 1992, 21.

56. See Youssef M. Ibrahim, "Rebounding Iranians Are Striving for Regional Leadership in Gulf," *New York Times*, 7 November 1992, 6.

57. Farzin Sarabi, "The Post-Khomeini Era in Iran: The Election of the Fourth Islamic Majlis," *Middle East Journal* 48, no. 1 (Winter 1994): 104.

58. Steve A. Yetiv, "The Outcomes of Operations Desert Shield and Desert Storm: Some Antecedent Causes," *Political Science Quarterly* 107 (Summer 1992): 201–05.

59. Cited in *Tehran IRNA*, FBIS: NESA, 2 June 1992, 49.

60. *Tehran IRNA*, in FBIS: NESA, 2 June 1992, 49.

61. See *Paris AFP*, in FBIS: NESA, 4 September 1992, 23.

62. Personal correspondence with Ambassador Richard Murphy.

63. Youssef M. Ibrahim, "To Counter Iran, Saudis Seek Ties with Ex-Soviet Islamic Republics," *New York Times*, 22 February 1992.

64. On Iraq's ambition, see Chubin and Tripp, *Iran and Iraq at War*, 154.

65. Herman F. Eilts, "Security Considerations in the Persian Gulf," *International Security* 5 (Fall 1980): 102.

66. For the text of the Pan-Arab Declaration, see MECS 4 (1979–80): 224–25. Also, see *Al-Thawrah*, in JPRS: NENA, 15 April 1980, 127–28.

67. See MECS 3 (1978–79): 61.

68. On these military clashes, see Cordesman, *The Gulf and the West*, 393–401.

69. MECS 2 (1977–78): 679.

70. For details on Saudi instability during this period, see MECS 3 (1978–79): 736–55, 358–59.

71. See Safran, *Saudi Arabia*, 225–26.

72. See U.S. House, *Saudi Arabia and the United States*, 24.

73. On Iran's foreign policy during this period, see Gary Sick, "Iran's Quest for Superpower Status," *Foreign Affairs* 65 (Spring 1987): 697–715.

74. On the waning of the revolution, see Judith Miller, "Islamic Radicals Lose Their Tight Grip on Iran," *New York Times*, 8 April 1991, A1.

75. Statement by Iraq's foreign minister, Tariq Aziz, in *Cairo MENA*, in FBIS: NESA, August 1990, 5.

76. The text of these letters appear in "Empty Reforms: Saudi Arabia's New Basic Laws," *Middle East Watch* (May 1992): 59–62.

77. For a brief discussion of their views, see Caryle Murphy, "Saudi Wealth Stirs Discontent," *Washington Post*, 27 March 1992, A23, A29.

78. See text of interview with King Fahd, in *London AL-HAWADITH*, FBIS: NESA, 14 February 1992, 22.

79. See interview with King Fahd, in *London AL-Quds AL'-ARABI*, in FBIS: NESA, 26 March 1992, 9–10.

80. Cited in MEES 35, no. 27 (6 April 1992): C3.

81. *Paris AFP*, in FBIS: NESA, 29 April 1994, 25.

82. See MECS 2 (1976–1977): 570.

83. On a letter to King Fahd outlining the democratic reforms sought, see *Amman AKHIR KHABAR*, in FBIS: NESA, 29 April 1991, 9.

84. For the text of the royal decrees, see "Empty Reforms."

85. Caryle Murphy, "Saudi King Reconciles with Shiite Opposition," *Washington Post*, 16 October 1993, A15.

86. Ibid, 5–6.

87. David Ottaway, "Saudis Said to Owe $64 Billion, Scrape to Meet Obligations," *Washington Post*, 3 April 1991, A25.

88. Christopher Whalen, "The Saudi Well Runs Dry," *Washington Post*, 29 August 1993, C2.

89. On the Saudi postwar economic condition, see "Saudi Stability Hit by Heavy Spending Over Last Decade," *New York Times*, 22 August 1993, A1.

90. Author's interview with Ambassador Richard Murphy, 26 May 1994.

91. *Kuwait KUNA* in FBIS: NESA, 9 May 1994, 2–3.

92. Statement by Edward P. Djerejian, assistant secretary for Near Eastern and South Asian Affairs. U.S. Congress, House of Representatives, Committee on Foreign Affairs, *Developments in the Middle East, March 1993*, Hearing Before the Subcommittee on Europe and the Middle East, 9 March 1993 (Washington, D.C.: GPO, 1993), 4.

93. The texts of major U.N. resolutions adopted in 1991 appear in U.S. House of Representatives, *U.N. Security Resolutions on Iraq: Compliance and Implementation, Report to the Committee on Foreign Affairs by the CRS*, March 1992 (Washington, D.C.: GPO, 1992).

94. For the text of such an argument, see "Iraq Calls for Lifting of UN Embargo," MEES 35, no. 42 (20 July 1992): D1.

95. On Kuwait's position, see *Cairo MENA*, in FBIS: NESA, 24 April 1992, 13. Also, see *Cairo MENA*, in FBIS: NESA, 7 May 1992, 15–16.

96. *Riyadh SPA* in FBIS: NESA, 12 July 1993, 16.

97. Address by Ronald Neumann, Director, Office of Northern Gulf Affairs, Department of State, "United States Policy Toward Iraq" (hereafter cited as Neumann address) (Washington, D.C.: Meridian International Center, 27 January 1994), 1.

98. *London AL-AWSAT*, in FBIS: NESA, 3 March 1994, 38.

99. *Paris AFP*, in FBIS: NESA, 4 April 1994, 26.

100. U.S. Congress, House of Representatives, Committee on Foreign Affairs, *Developments in the Middle East, July 1993*, Hearing Before the Subcommittee on Europe and the Middle East, 27 July 1993 (Washington, D.C.: GPO, 1993), 26; Smith address, 2.

101. Neumann address, 6; Smith address, 2; also, see U.S. Congress, House of Representatives, Committee on Foreign Affairs, *U.S. Policy Toward Iraq 3 Years after the Gulf War*, Hearing Before the Subcommittee on Europe and the Middle East, 23 February 1994 (Washington, D.C.: GPO, 1994), 15.

102. On Iraq's conventional capability, see Department of Defense, *Conduct of the Persian Gulf War*, 148–159; Michael Eisenstadt, "Like a Phoenix from the Ashes?: The Future of Iraqi Military Power," Policy Paper No. 36 (Washington, D.C.: Washington Institute for Near East Policy, 1993), chap. 3; also Smith address, 3.

103. See David Albright and Mark Hibbs, "Iraq's Bomb: Blueprints and Artifacts," *The Bulletin of the Atomic Scientists* (January/February 1992): 30–40.

104. See statement by Robert L. Galluci, assistant secretary for Politico-Military Affairs, Department of State, to the Subcommittee on Europe and the Middle East. U.S. Congress, House of Representatives, *Iraq's Nuclear Weapons Capability and IAEA Inspections in Iraq*, 29 June 1993 (Washington, D.C.: GPO, 1993).

105. See Eisenstadt, "Like a Phoenix from the Ashes," 24.

106. Woolsey, cited in Eisenstadt, "Like a Phoenix from the Ashes," 33. This paragraph is based on ibid, 30–34.

107. Quoted in Youssef M. Ibrahim, "Most Arab Capitals Welcome Talks," *New York Times*, 20 October 1991, 10.

108. Pelletreau address.

109. In September 1994, GCC states announced that in light of the peace process they would abandon the secondary and tertiary economic boycotts of Israel, while maintaining the primary boycott.

7

MISSED OPPORTUNITIES

In the fields of observation chance favors only those minds which are prepared.

—Louis Pasteur[1]

The successes and failures of states, like that of individuals, are sometimes determined by their ability to seize the right opportunity at the right time. Doing so can change their trajectory in history and enhance their welfare, while failing to do so can send them down a much less appealing path. In the competitive realm of international politics, states that can take advantage of opportunities can advance themselves over others in sometimes enduring and critical ways. This would not be the case were world politics characterized by substantial and predominant co-operation between states. In such a world, seizing opportunities would be less important, and more emphasis would be placed on collective rather than individual state welfare. In modern world politics, however, states are acutely aware of their relative power position and are extremely concerned with preserving and advancing their own security, particularly when failing to do so leaves them potentially vulnerable to the exploits of others.

To be sure, states do co-operate on a range of issues when they feel that this will advance their position in the short or long run. In some cases, they will even risk their security in order to generate co-operation over the long term. But at the core, they are mindful of their own welfare because no government or police force above them can ensure their security. This is the distinctive feature of international politics. In such a world, gains made by one's adversary often translate into one's losses; analysts sometimes refer to such interaction as zero-sum.

At times, the interaction between the United States and the Soviet Union, Iran, and Iraq tended to be zero-sum. The gains of the Soviet Union, Iran, and Iraq in the Middle East context often translated into U.S. losses during the period from 1979 to 1993. Fortunately for the United States, its adversaries were ineffectual at seizing opportunities and scoring political and strategic gains.

Chapters 1 through 6 suggested that conflict constrained Iran, Iraq, and the Soviet Union, but the theme of missed opportunities was not developed. Yet, the rise of U.S. power and standing in the Persian Gulf region had much to do with opportunities missed by its adversaries. Were it not for regional conflicts, U.S. adversaries would have had much better chances to protect and advance their interests and that of their allies and to undermine the objectives of the United States as a third party to conflict.

WAR AND OPPORTUNITY COSTS

Wars in the Middle East created numerous costs. Some of these costs were direct, such as military and civilian casualties and damage to industrial infrastructure. Others were indirect. The opportunity costs of war, for instance, were significant in terms of foregone social programs, educational and cultural enhancement, and economic development. Indeed, one study concluded that in the absence of the Iran-Iraq war, Iraq could have become another Kuwait with massive foreign exchange reserves by 1990.[2] But wars in the Middle East were significant not only for their actual consequences and for typical foregone domestic gains, but also for the foreign policy opportunities that they made actors miss.

In the course of history, foreign policy opportunities are sometimes fleeting. Seizing them often requires decisive and planned action and freedom from constraint. The greater the constraints on an actor, the less likely it will be to seize opportunities that can enhance its welfare. While all states face economic, political, and military constraints, these constraints fluctuate widely based on innumerable factors. Actors involved in conflict, particularly extended conflict, are usually under more constraints than uninvolved actors. They must focus their strategic attention on their adversary and on means by which to deter, control, or defeat their adversary; their military and economic resources, depending on the type and intensity of conflict, will be earmarked toward victory; their people, having been in conflict, will be less eager to engage in foreign adventures, particularly if the nation's efforts in conflict bear little fruit. Under such conditions, the actors in conflict are not only more likely to overlook potential foreign policy opportunities but also more likely to let them pass. Indeed, the constraints of conflict alter the priorities of states in a manner that makes boldness in seizing foreign policy opportunities less important, unless these opportunities relate to victory in conflict.

To be sure, the impact that conflict has on the principal antagonists is case-specific. The less significant and intense the conflict, the fewer the constraints on the antagonists, provided one side does not lose altogether. The impact also depends on which actor one examines. The victor, if one results, will be more free to seize opportunities once the conflict is over than it may have been prior to the conflict, provided that the victory was clear and not too taxing. In general, however, both actors are much more likely to face constraints while in conflict than they otherwise would face. They must use their political, economic, and sometimes military capabilities to defeat their competitor and cannot so easily focus their attention and efforts on identifying and capitalizing on opportunities. Because this is largely true, particularly in intense conflicts where victory is elusive, we can fairly say that an important and often overlooked cost of conflict for antagonists is that they are less likely to seize opportunities than are less involved actors.

This was the case for Iran, Iraq, and the Soviet Union in the 1980s. They had much greater difficulty advancing their agendas while caught in conflict than they otherwise would have had. Meanwhile, the United States in its third-party capacity was more free from constraint and, therefore, better able to capitalize on opportunities to protect and advance its welfare and that of its allies. As a third-party actor not initially involved in conflict, it was more able to husband its resources, bide its time, develop its regional strategy, and avoid the draining costs of extended and intense conflict. Third-party status conferred upon it important political and strategic benefits.

IRAQ'S WASTED CHANCES

The Iran-Iraq war constrained both Iran and Iraq at times when they otherwise might have increased their power. Prior to the war, Iraq's regional influence was strong and rising. Its arch enemy, Iran, was in revolutionary chaos and had scarcely settled its domestic political course, much less its foreign policy. Moreover, Iraq had launched a successful propaganda campaign for leadership in the Arab world based in part on pan-Arabism and anti-Americanism. Arab Gulf actors were intimidated enough by Iraq to avoid challenging Saddam's political and military position on key issues such as co-operation with the United States. At the global level, Iraq's Soviet patron appeared to be gaining momentum against the United States, whose credibility was wavering after the Iranian revolution, the Iranian hostage crisis, and the invasion of Afghanistan. Because the Soviets were Iraq's superpower patron, Moscow's rise in standing further elevated Baghdad in Arab politics.

Iraq's move toward greater influence in and perhaps domination of the Arab world, with all its attendant benefits, was impeded by the Iran-Iraq war. The war transformed Iraq from a state with much regional influence into one that, while still influential, depended on Arab largesse, and toward the latter part of the war, on indirect U.S. support. Iraq's dependence on others decreased its ability to push its anti-U.S. and anti-Saudi prewar foreign policy agenda. It would have made little sense for Saddam to advance his revisionist agenda against the interests of states that supported Iraq or could support Iraq against Iran. Saddam had to wait for a cease fire in the Iran-Iraq war before he could resume pursuing the opportunistic foreign policy agenda that he had set in 1979.

Had Iraq not attacked Iran in September 1980, Iraq could have used the threat posed by the Iranian revolution to elicit support from Arab states and to further fuel its regional ambitions. Such a threat would have accelerated rather than stymied Iraq's trend toward increased power in the Arab world because it would have highlighted Iraq's importance as a bulwark against Iran. In such a case, it is possible that Iraq would have undermined U.S. security before Washington had a chance to improve its regional position. Riyadh, for instance, would have been extremely reluctant to support U.S. political and security efforts over Iraq's veto, particularly since Iraq would have remained crucial to containing Iran. Pro-Iraqi members of the Saudi family would have had an easier time making the case that Riyadh should support Saddam's position in the Arab world, his anti-U.S. views, and his hardline stance against Iran. Iraq's invasion of Iran and the ensuing war not only weakened Iraq economically and decreased its regional leverage, but also weakened Iran and thus made Iraq less important as a bulwark against it.

If Iraq's invasion of Iran seriously constrained Iraq, its invasion of Kuwait put Baghdad in a straight jacket. Prior to the Gulf crisis in 1990–91, U.S. security had increased as a result of developments initiated or accelerated by the Iran-Iraq war. Iraq, however, remained both able and predisposed to disrupt the regional status quo and to challenge U.S. regional interests. Indeed, although the Iran-Iraq war prevented Iraq from seizing foreign policy opportunities and devastated its economy, the war strengthened Iraq militarily and weakened Iran. This put Iraq in a more formidable military position. Meanwhile, rather than moderating its foreign policy position in order to gain Western economic support for postwar economic reconstruction, Iraq chose to revert back to the immoderate position it had assumed in 1979 and 1980 when it issued the anti-U.S. Pan Arab Charter. With Iraq willing and able to challenge U.S. security, U.S. standing would have remained vulnerable through the 1990s and beyond. Post-cold war decreases in U.S. military spending and preparedness would have made the United States even more vulnerable to a resurgent Iraq. Iraq's invasion of Kuwait was one of the few events that could have helped the United States identify and deal with the Iraqi threat before it became unmanageable. Without the invasion and Desert Storm, Iraq would have retained immense military capability and continued to increase its power, while the United States scaled back its capabilities.

Desert Storm came at a propitious time for the United States and moderate states in the Middle East for another reason as well. Baghdad was well on its way to developing a nuclear weapon prior to its invasion. Iraq's clandestine program was sophisticated and consisted of a well-financed approach to multiple paths for producing highly enriched weapons grade uranium. Desert Storm drastically altered the course of Iraq's nuclear program. All "known" activities toward the production of such uranium were stopped either by the war or by postwar U.N. inspection teams.

Prior to Iraq's invasion of Kuwait, the IAEA consistently rated Iraq's compliance with its inspections as "exemplary." As a signatory of the Nuclear Non-Proliferation Treaty, Iraq was required to allow such inspections. The problem, however, was that the IAEA was only inspecting locations where Iraq was not building the bomb and was unaware of the other sites that Iraq failed to declare for inspection. In the absence of Desert Storm, it is highly unlikely that U.N. inspectors would have identified Iraq's nuclear sites.[3]

For its part, U.S. intelligence was aware prior to Desert Storm that Iraq was developing different methods for producing nuclear weapons. But its knowledge of Iraq's program was limited. Without Desert Storm, experts believe that it is probable that Iraq's uranium enrichment program would have continued and produced enough highly enriched fuel for one or more weapons by 1992. Iraq also would have continued to develop its array of centrifuges used to purify uranium to weapons grade. Iraq may have produced a centrifuge cascade in a few years that would have offered it another path toward the development of nuclear weapons. Indeed, despite Desert Storm and postwar U.N. inspections, the IAEA stated that if Iraq's nuclear technical expertise were held together in the post-Desert Storm period, "the design and organization process, and possibly small scale research activity, may continue with a low probability of being discovered," in the absence of "extraordinary luck or the defection of knowledgeable Iraqi personnel."[4] If the IAEA needed such luck in the postwar period when it benefited from intrusive inspections, one need only imagine how compromised its position would have been without Desert Storm.

Had Iraq developed nuclear capability in the absence of Desert Storm, Middle Eastern politics would have been transformed. Baghdad could have used a nuclear weapon to blackmail regional actors, deter foreign interventions such as Operations Desert Shield and Storm, or, under unlikely circumstances, attack another Arab state, Iran, or even Israel. The mere possession of such weapons would have probably made most regional and extraregional actors more likely to accommodate Saddam than to confront him.

In this sense, Iraq's invasion of Kuwait was a major strategic blunder and a godsend for its adversaries. Given what we know about Iraq's program, IAEA inspections, and the impact of the Persian Gulf war and postwar inspections, no development other than war could have conceivably removed the Iraqi nuclear threat. While Israel did succeed in bombing Iraq's Osirak nuclear reactor in 1981, Iraq's nuclear program diversified and went underground by 1990. Moreover, Iraq learned how to protect its program from air strikes and sabotage. Even if the United States and the IAEA realized how far along Saddam had come by 1990, they still would have had serious difficulty destroying Iraq's nuclear potential, particularly without clear provocation from Saddam.

IRAN: OVEREXTENDED AND UNDERWHELMING

While wars constrained Iraqi foreign policy and made Baghdad miss opportunities to enhance its regional position at U.S. expense, the Iran-Iraq war also had a negative impact on Iran. Although Iraq attacked Iran in September 1980 and not vice versa, it was Khomeini who refused to sue for peace after 1982 when Iraq had tired of the war. This had serious implications for Iran's welfare.

After the Iranian revolution, Iran sought to export its revolution throughout the Gulf and broader Middle East and was willing to make political and economic sacrifices in the process. It aimed to transform the regimes of the Gulf Arab monarchies to its brand of conservative Islam and to undermine U.S. regional influence. By 1984, however, the war had taken a major toll on Iran's domestic and international position, pushed Iran to moderate its foreign policy, and reduced its ability to advance its political agenda.

The war also aroused fear of and focused attention on Iran's revolution, which made it more difficult for Khomeini to "vouchsafe" Islamic fundamentalism without provoking considerable alarm. In the absence of war, Iran could have attempted to export its revolution in a nonmilitary and less provocative fashion behind the tacit threat of its feared military hand. The war, however, forced Iran to play this hand, to deplete its military arsenal, and, in the process, to isolate itself further from the Arab Gulf states and the international community.

To be sure, GCC states were not inclined to commit national suicide to please Iran's antimonarchical ideological agenda. But there was room for political maneuver for Teheran in some Arab capitals. Some Arab leaders such as Prince Abdullah of Saudi Arabia preferred a stronger connection to Iran and a weaker connection to the United States rather than vice versa. Furthermore, the GCC states did not trust Iraq, despite siding with it against revolutionary Iran. As a major regional military and economic power, Iran therefore had opportunities to make inroads on the Arab side of the Gulf. Such inroads might have given it a base from which to further increase its influence in regional politics.

Iran's immoderate foreign policy during the 1980s not only closed off its opportunities in that time period, but continued to do so in the 1990s. In the aftermath of Desert Storm, GCC states looked to numerous actors for military support. Iran would have been a likely candidate to play some security role in the region, given its aversion to Iraq and its interest in checking it.

To some extent, GCC states took steps to increase Iran's role in regional security. But serious questions arose as to whether Iran and GCC states could develop a basis for co-operation over the long term. In part, this was because Desert Storm had weakened Iraq and left Iran looming more powerful, but it was also because Iran played a revisionist role in the region in the 1980s, and its internal struggle between radicals and moderates remained unsettled. Memories of Ayatollah Khomeini and Iran's revolutionary zeal were not soon to be forgotten, particularly given that such zeal was alive in Iran well after the Ayatollah's death.

MOSCOW: SHOOTING ITSELF IN THE FOOT

While conflict undermined the ability of Iraq and Iran to advance their foreign policy agendas at a time when the United States was vulnerable, the Afghanistan intervention, which spanned most of the 1980s, damaged Moscow's ability to exploit regional opportunities. The period 1976 to 1979 was one of increasing Soviet influence in the larger Gulf region. On the periphery, the Soviets gained a military foothold in Ethiopia; closer to the region's center, they benefited from a consolidation of ties to South Yemen in 1978–79 and from the Iranian revolution. While Iran hardly embraced the Soviets, it moved quickly to dissolve the basis of U.S.-Iranian strategic relations, which had served the United States in the 1970s. By challenging the regional status quo, the Iran-Iraq war created additional instabilities that could have been beneficial to the Soviet Union. The United States was clearly on a path to regional decline. If Moscow aimed to enhance its position in the region substantially, the period 1979 to 1980 was the most propitious.

The Soviet Union, however, failed to capitalize on U.S. regional vulnerability. This failure was related to regional dynamics, to long-standing regional aversion to communism, and to Soviet inability to compete with the West at the economic level. The negative effects of the Soviet occupation of Afghanistan were also contributory.

The Afghanistan invasion of December 1979 sent shock waves worldwide. While the Soviet Union might have considered the potential for dominating South Asia and the Persian Gulf in its decision to invade Afghanistan, three reasons suggest that its intentions were much more limited. First, the Persian Gulf oil fields of Iran and the Gulf states are on the western edge of Iran, while Afghanistan is on its far eastern edge, with much mountainous country in between. If the Soviet Union wanted to gain direct or indirect influence over the region's oil, it probably would have gone directly through Iranian Azerbaijan. Second, Moscow was obsessed with secure borders. In Afghanistan, it faced the rise of an anti-Soviet regime on its border. In assessing its intentions, therefore, we can note that from its standpoint, the Soviet Union had a compelling motive for invading Afghanistan but not necessarily the Gulf region.

Third, if Moscow had bigger ambitions, we would expect it not to have been genuinely surprised by the opposition it provoked. However, as Thomas Watson, former ambassador to the Soviet Union, put it, Moscow thought Washington considered Afghanistan to be relatively unimportant and would not be "disturbed greatly."[5] This explains why its leaders were "surprised at the strength of denunciation" by the West and "reacted with tough defiance."[6] While Moscow prepared itself for handling the military tasks of the actual invasion, it was not prepared for the opposition it provoked.[7] Other actors viewed Soviet actions as potentially more ambitious than the Soviet Union probably intended them to be.

The Iran-Iraq war increased the U.S. military and political presence in the region, particularly during the U.S. reflagging of Kuwaiti tankers. This presented the Soviets with an opportunity to paint the United States as "imperialistic," an effort to which Moscow had devoted much energy in the past. That some of the Gulf states were predisposed to view the United States as "imperialistic" added potential to such a Soviet ploy. Soviet propaganda efforts, however, failed in part because Moscow was oppressing Afghan Muslims. Political attacks on the United States sounded hypocritical and fell on deaf ears.

The Afghanistan intervention also decreased Soviet leverage with Saudi Arabia and Iran at a time when both actors sought external support for their position during the Iran-Iraq war and, thus, might have accommodated some of Moscow's interests in the region. As discussed in chapter 4, while all Muslim states strongly condemned the Soviet involvement in Afghanistan, only Saudi Arabia and Iran took credible action to undermine Soviet efforts there. This was not surprising because the Saudi and Iranian stake in supporting things Muslim, such as the Afghan rebels, was greater than that of the other Gulf states; the legitimacy of the Saudi and Iranian regimes rested, in large part, on adherence to basic Islamic principles. Moscow's presence in Afghanistan clearly prevented it from making political inroads with Riyadh and Teheran. Seizing such an opportunity would have given Moscow much increased leverage in the Persian Gulf and Middle Eastern region. Indeed, Saudi Arabia and Iran were critical actors in the Middle East and in the Islamic world writ large. Even modestly improved relations with either state would have benefited the Soviet Union significantly in the region.

Regional states also viewed the intervention as part of a broader Soviet attempt to encircle the Gulf and became more suspicious of the Soviet Union. Thus, they were less inclined to support any Soviet initiatives and more inclined to take steps to weaken Soviet power. This further decreased Moscow's ability to take advantage of U.S. vulnerability in the Persian Gulf and to enhance its own regional influence, as did the fact that the Soviets became bogged down in Afghanistan. Even if they had entertained ideas of influencing Persian Gulf politics in invading Afghanistan, their debacle prevented them from doing so.

The Afghanistan case illustrates the famous security dilemma theory of international politics. This theory states that one actor's attempt to increase its security may decrease the security of other actors, thus pushing them to take countermeasures that result in no gain or a loss for the initial actor. The Soviet Union's efforts to improve its security by invading Afghanistan decreased the security of countries in and outside the region. This produced effects that probably left the Soviets in a worse regional strategic position than they would have been had they not invaded Afghanistan. The Soviet Union may have just wanted, or had the ability, to secure Afghanistan under a pro-Soviet government, but the West understandably assumed and planned for the worst. The result was strategic and political countermeasures that constrained Moscow and benefited U.S. strategic interests.

MODERATE POWERS: CLOSING WINDOWS

Regional wars not only weakened and constrained Iran, Iraq, and the Soviet Union, thus making them miss important opportunities, but also bolstered Saudi Arabia and the United States. The rise of these moderate powers placed yet another check on Iran, Iraq, and the Soviet Union and further decreased the probability that they could take advantage of windows of opportunity.

As established in chapter 5, conflict bought the United States much needed time. U.S. security and power were at a low following the Iranian revolution. Had Iraq, for instance, invaded Kuwait in 1980 instead of Iran, the United States would have had difficulty responding effectively. It would have lacked military capability for regional contingencies, extensive access arrangements and logistics facilities, strong and developed relations with the Saudis and European allies in the region, and effective Egyptian support. By 1990, however, regional conflicts had pushed the United States to prepare itself for the Iraqi challenge. Indeed, conflict in the 1980s put Washington in a position to shut down Iraq's opportunity in Kuwait in 1990.

Prior to the Iran-Iraq war, Saudi influence and power was also negligible. Riyadh lacked military capability, its stability appeared shaky, U.S.-Saudi relations were troubled, and its foreign policy was characteristically unassertive. Regional conflict pushed the Saudis to develop their military capability, to assume a more assertive foreign policy role, and to develop stronger and more durable relations with the United States. While the Iranian revolution presented primarily a domestic-level threat to Arab-Gulf states, the Iran-Iraq war added a military one. While the Iran-Iraq war represented a regional threat to Gulf security, the Afghanistan intervention added an external one. Together, these two wars significantly heightened U.S. and regional threat perceptions. This had an important effect on U.S.-Saudi relations.

While the United States was more concerned with the Soviet threat than with Iran's in 1980, the Saudis were more concerned about Iran than Moscow. These threat perceptions helped generate U.S.-Saudi co-operation. Because each side now perceived a serious threat to its interests and understood that the other side did as well, both sides were given good reason to expect that the other would be willing to co-operate seriously. It was easier to trust common interest than professed intentions.

Initial increases in co-operation generated expectations that more co-operation could be developed and sustained. Thus, whereas in 1979, tensions in U.S.-Saudi relations and Iraq's rising influence must have made the Saudis wonder whether it made sense to assume the political costs of closer association with the United States, by 1981 expectations of co-operation improved and so did the perceived benefits of the U.S. connection.

Heightened threat perceptions also motivated significant improvements in U.S. and Saudi military capabilities for Gulf contingencies. This increased the benefits of co-operating with the United States even more; a policy of confronting rather than appeasing threatening regional actors became more plausible. The Saudi shift to a more confrontational policy, in turn, made its back-up U.S. security connection even more important. When Iraq invaded Kuwait, these effects contributed to Riyadh's vital decision to confront rather than appease Saddam.[8]

The enhanced position of the United States and Saudi Arabia made it much less likely during the 1980s and into the 1990s that Iran, Iraq, and the Soviet Union could meet their regional objectives. In this sense, the rise of the United States as a third party created more than a one-time check on Iran and Iraq. It created a check of longer duration with significant implications in the historical process.

CONCLUSION

By using force, Iraq, Iran, and the Soviet Union closed off certain paths in the historical process that if chartered might have benefited their welfare significantly. It is not simply that they lost wars or failed to achieve their war objectives, or that they suffered incredible domestic-level opportunity costs. Their loss was greater than that. They missed significant foreign policy opportunities to undermine U.S. regional security and to strengthen their own position. Any explanation of regional politics must take these missed opportunities into account because they figured prominently in the failures of Iran, Iraq, and the Soviet Union and in the rise of U.S. power and standing.

NOTES

1. Louis Pasteur, inaugural lecture as professor and dean of the faculty of sciences, University of Lille, Douai, France, 7 December 1854, from Suzy Platt, ed., *Respectfully Quoted* (Washington, D.C.: Congressional Quarterly, Inc., 1992).

2. See Mofid, "The Economic Reconstruction of Iraq," 52–53.

3. Statement by Gary Milhollin, U.S. House, *Iraq's Nuclear Weapons Capability and IAEA Inspections in Iraq*, 56.

4. Written statements submitted by the IAEA, in ibid, 154.

5. Cited in Thomas T. Hammond, *Red Flag over Afghanistan: The Communist Coup, the Soviet Invasion, and the Consequences* (Boulder, CO: Westview Press, 1984), 139.

6. Bradsher, *Afghanistan*, 189.

7. For details, see ibid., 189–204.

8. For a more detailed discussion, see Yetiv, "The Outcomes."

8

CONCLUSION

When states have differences that cannot be resolved easily, they sometimes resort to political, economic, and/or military measures to realize their objectives. The resulting conflict often assumes its own dimensions, envelopes its antagonists, and affects the surrounding political-security environment. The third party, an actor not initially involved in conflict but one that is seriously affected by it, constitutes a critical part of this environment. Chapter 1 developed a basic approach for analyzing how conflicts affect the third party in the short and long run. It is worthwhile revisiting this approach and providing summary answers to the major questions associated with it.

The third-party approach has five basic parts. The first is to identify a third party on which to focus, such as the United States in the Middle Eastern context. The third party need not be a great power to be of interest, but should be clearly identified. Its position relative to the conflict should also be specified and explained.

Second, rather than focusing on the two primary antagonists to conflict, the third-party framework broadens the scope of analysis to examine how non-state actors, political and military processes, and other third parties are affected by conflict. Third, through this broader analysis, the approach focuses on how and why conflict affects the position, welfare, and trajectory of the third party in the historical process. Does conflict between two actors leave the third party weaker or stronger once the conflict is over? Fourth, the third-party approach identifies the implications of changes in the power and security of the third party. What do these changes mean over the long term? How do they affect the subsequent role of the third party and the politics or issue context in which the third party plays a role? Fifth, the third-party framework explores the policy- and theory-oriented implications of changes in the power and security of the third party.

The final aspect of the approach is its methodology. This methodology is applied implicitly in the book and discussed explicitly in chapter 1 and in the appendix. In brief, the goal of the methodology is to identify and evaluate the relationship between conflict, its consequences, and changes in the security and power of the third party. While in this book the strength of U.S. regional security was made operational and compared through time, this approach could also apply in other cases. For instance, one might want to see how Japan's interests are affected by a trade conflict between the United States and the European Union. In such a case, identifying and operationalizing Japan's interests and comparing how well it realizes its interests before and after conflict would be sensible.

IDENTIFYING THE THIRD PARTY

The first part of the third-party approach involves identifying a third party. In the broader Middle East region, the United States represented the third party to conflicts between the Soviet Union and Afghanistan, Iran and Iraq, and Iraq and Kuwait. In each case, the United States was not initially involved in the conflicts but was greatly affected by them.

As previously suggested, while this book focused on the United States in the conflictual Middle East, the third party of interest will differ with each issue or context. Observers of Russian politics might examine the impact of war between Serbs and Croats on Russian security; scholars of the presidency might explore how conflict between Democrats and Republicans in Congress affected the president's power; those interested in international organizations such as the United Nations might evaluate the impact of war between Iraq and the U.S.-led coalition on the United Nation's international role and influence. But in any case, the analyst will broaden the scope of analysis and ask how conflict between two actors affects the power, welfare, and security of the third-party actor in the short and long term. This brings us to the interesting story of the evolution of U.S. standing in the Persian Gulf region, a story about unexpected twists in history and paradoxical turns of war.

CONFLICT AND THE RISE OF U.S. STANDING

Great powers seldom leave their national security to their adversaries, but in some regards U.S. security in the Persian Gulf region was defined as much by the foreign policy behavior of its adversaries as by Washington. Indeed, it was Moscow that intervened in Afghanistan in December 1979; Iraq that invaded Iran in September 1980 and Kuwait in August 1990; and Iran that renounced the United States as the "Great Satan" and refused to accept a cease fire in the Persian Gulf war until July 1988. Neither the United States nor any of these other actors foresaw the strange and paradoxical twists that conflict would take.

Although the United States took decisive political, military, and economic measures in response to conflict, it was reacting primarily to the pressures and actions imposed upon it by its adversaries. Indeed, the rise of U.S. regional power was caused in part by the miscalculations of its competitors, miscalculations that ignited prolonged conflicts that generated significant and unexpected consequences.

Through broadening the scope of analysis in line with the second part of the third-party framework, it becomes clear that conflict reversed U.S. regional decline and elevated U.S. security. This section of the conclusion focuses on the third part of the third-party framework and explains how and why conflict affected the position, welfare, and trajectory of the third party in the historical process.

The occurrence within a similar time frame and geographical area of the 1978–79 Iranian revolution, the Afghanistan intervention, and the Iran-Iraq war (1980–88) raised the specter of U.S. regional decline. Analysts feared an increase in Soviet influence or an outright military invasion of the region by Moscow; the spread of Islamic fundamentalism; the ascendance of Iran or Iraq to regional hegemony; an alignment of anti-U.S. radical forces around Syria, Libya, and Iraq; and the weakening or collapse of the generally pro-U.S. Saudi regime. There was little reason to believe that regional conflicts would strengthen U.S. regional security and much reason to predict that they would leave the United States marginalized. This scenario, however, never came to pass. Quite the contrary, as this book has shown, U.S. regional decline was reversed. Snapshots of the nature of U.S. security and power from 1978 to 1993 reveal how and why this is so.

Prior to the Iranian revolution, relations between key Persian Gulf actors were correct, despite long-standing rivalries and border disputes. Relative stability decreased the potential for Iraq, South Yemen, and the Soviet Union to advance their interests at Washington's expense. In addition, the balance of power between Iran and Iraq was fairly even; this helped deter either side from attacking the other or smaller Gulf states, efforts that might have succeeded at the time were one side much stronger than the other.

Furthermore, despite the rigors of the modernization process and the usual instability associated with state building and political and economic jockeying in the Arab world, Saudi Arabia was more or less stable, and U.S.-Saudi relations were at least co-operative, if not strong. Although Washington lacked sufficient military capability to deal with serious regional contingencies such as the invasion of Kuwait, the twin pillars of Iran and, to a lesser extent, Saudi Arabia played a role in protecting regional security. Hence, U.S. military weakness was not as important as it would become after the Iranian revolution when the twin pillar strategy fully collapsed. In general, U.S. regional security was relatively stable prior to the Iranian revolution.

The revolution, however, seriously weakened the U.S. position. It undermined relations between Iran and most Arab Gulf states, disrupted the regional balance of power such that Iraq gained the upper hand over Iran, and threatened Saudi stability. It also sounded the death knell for the twin pillar policy by transforming U.S.-Iranian relations from co-operation to confrontation. This placed the burden for Gulf security directly on U.S. shoulders for the first time in regional history. Unfortunately, the United States was in a poor position to assume this responsibility. It could not count on the Saudis for political and military support because Saudi regional influence had decreased and because of anti-U.S. regional currents. Riyadh was reluctant to associate closely with Washington because of the negative reaction in the Arab world to the Camp David accords, rising anti-U.S. fervor generated by the Iranian revolution, and fear of the growing influence of hardline anti-U.S. Arab states such as Iraq, Libya, and Syria. In addition, the perception of Soviet political and military gains in Angola, Ethiopia, South Yemen, and Afghanistan, coupled with the U.S. loss of Iran as an ally, damaged U.S. credibility.

To worsen matters, the United States lacked the military capability to cope with major threats to regional security. The U.S. rapid deployment force, which would play a critical role during the 1990–91 Persian Gulf crisis, had not been developed. The regional military facilities that hosted the forces of Operations Desert Shield and Storm in 1990–91 had not been built to any significant extent. Finally, regional actors were not disposed to provide logistics or political support for U.S. military efforts.

Against this backdrop, the December 1979 Soviet invasion of Afghanistan appeared particularly ominous. At the time, there was ample opportunity for states in and outside the region to improve their position at U.S. cost. Ironically, the intervention in Afghanistan would help reverse this negative trend rather than worsen it.

Over time, the intervention spurred the United States to improve its deterrent in the Gulf, to revive foundering defense alliances, and to focus intelligent attention on defending its regional interests. To some extent, it damaged Soviet relations with important Muslim states and catalyzed some level of intra- and inter-regional defense co-operation between generally pro-U.S. actors. Afghanistan also exhausted Soviet resources and will, which otherwise may have been exploited to challenge U.S. regional security. These effects, which would enhance U.S. security over time, were put in motion slowly. In the meantime, Iraq would invade Iran in September 1980 and seriously contribute to regional chaos.

While the Iran-Iraq war generated potential for future conflict in part by producing an imbalance of power between Iran and Iraq, it also enhanced U.S. security and prepared the United States for Operations Desert Shield and Storm. Unlike the Afghanistan intervention, which focused U.S. attention on deterring external threats to the region, the Iran-Iraq war drew U.S. attention to internal threats as well.

The Iran-Iraq war motivated the United States to accelerate the development of power projection capability and pushed Arab Gulf states, which were also important third parties to conflict, to form the GCC in May 1981. In addition, the war contributed to Saudi interest in funding and building the military facilities that would be used against Saddam in 1990–91, enhanced U.S.-Saudi relations undermined by the Iranian revolution, and reintegrated an isolated Egypt into the Persian Gulf security system. In addition, the war enhanced U.S. security and political relations with its European allies and improved transatlantic co-ordination in dealing with regional threats, an area which had been shaky. Thus, when Iran finally agreed to a cease fire in 1988, U.S. security had increased dramatically. Washington could count on a reasonably solid political-security foundation.

Iraq's invasion of Kuwait posed yet another significant threat to U.S. regional power and security. The U.S.-led response of Operations Desert Shield and Storm aggravated relations between Saudi Arabia and Yemen, which supported Iraq in the crisis. It also put Iraq at loggerheads with Arab Gulf states and, by weakening Iraq, left Iran the most dominant regional actor. This was problematic because Iran had more room for strategic and political maneuvering, despite the fact that the Iran-Iraq war had left it economically devastated and militarily weak. Teheran proceeded to impose its sovereignty on the Arab Gulf islands of Abu Musa and the Upper and Lesser Tunbs, which caused regional and international alarm.

While the Gulf crisis created new forms of regional instability and worsened old ones, it also generated and contributed to developments that enhanced U.S. regional security. At the global level, the Gulf crisis further globalized regional politics. Global-level actors including the United Nations, European states, and the United States enhanced their ability to protect Gulf security through joint and independent efforts. While the Gulf crisis revealed significant weaknesses in U.S. sealift and airlift capabilities, it also gave Washington invaluable experience in the conduct of long range contingencies and resulted in greater U.S. access to regional facilities. Although the Iran-Iraq war had already motivated global-level efforts related to Gulf security, the Persian Gulf war formalized and expanded them.

While developments at the global level facilitated U.S. efforts to protect its three major interests in the Persian Gulf, regional events had a similar effect. Efforts at producing indigenous security strategies fell short in the postwar period. Intelligent attention, however, was focused on how regional actors could protect their own security. In lieu of developing a major joint GCC military force or pursuing the Damascus Declaration formula for collective security, GCC states developed their own individual armies, while increasing co-operation and co-ordination with each other and outside states. Iraq's invasion demonstrated to the Saudis in unforgettable terms where their security ultimately rested. This gave them a greater appreciation of the importance of U.S. capability in the region.

Improvements in U.S.-Saudi relations coincided with important changes in the regional balance of power. Although the Persian Gulf war left Iran with more freedom to pursue its regional interests, it also left Iraq with less military capability. This represented an improvement in the balance of power because Iraq's ability to dominate the region was checked at least in the short term. Although Iraq still had more capability than Iran, the move was toward a balance of power at lower levels of military capability. This decreased Iran's and Iraq's threat to other regional actors. Meanwhile, Saudi power increased in the 1980s and shifted the distribution of regional power away from bipolarity based on competition between Iran and Iraq and toward tripolarity. More importantly, changes in the distribution of power favored moderate states over revisionist ones. From the U.S. standpoint and that of actors that sought to preserve regional stability, this was about the best outcome that could have been expected. Immoderate potential hegemons were weakened, and the status quo Saudis were bolstered. At the domestic level, Iraq was severely constrained. While it did reconstitute part of its army, it faced crippling U.N. sanctions, suffered from serious economic problems, was prevented from selling oil with which to fuel its recovery, and was unable to break regional and global isolation. The war and U.N. sanctions undermined Iraq's ability to develop and deploy weapons of mass destruction and greatly impeded Iraq's ability to threaten regional security.

While Desert Storm constrained Iraq at the domestic level, it benefited Saudi Arabia. Desert Storm left the Saudis not only less vulnerable to external threats but also more stable internally. To be sure, the Gulf crisis hurt Riyadh's short-term economic position and generated social and political ferment. But it also pushed the Saudis to take measures to appease discontented domestic elements, thus decreasing the potential for internal instability. At the intraregional level, war generated a move toward Middle East peace. This, in turn, contributed to U.S. security in the Persian Gulf by increasing co-operation between Arab Gulf states and Washington and decreasing tensions between Israel and these states.

As the foregoing discussion suggests, there was a stark difference in U.S. power and security in 1979 and in 1993. In 1979, Saudi stability was in doubt, the regional balance of power had shifted to Iraq's favor, and the ability of moderate states such as the United States and Saudi Arabia to handle threats to the status quo was limited. By 1993, Saudi stability had increased, the balance of power was restored, and the ability of moderate states to handle threats to the status quo was unprecedentedly high.

Iran did emerge from the Persian Gulf war in a dominant position over Iraq but, like Iraq, was severely weakened politically, economically, and militarily. Whereas in 1979 either Iran or Iraq had the potential to challenge seriously U.S. regional security, by 1991 their ability to do so had decreased substantially. The Soviet Union, which was a threat to U.S. security in 1979, slowly became bogged down in Afghanistan in the 1980s before becoming defunct altogether. Egypt, which was ostracized in the Arab world in 1979 for making peace with Israel and, therefore, could not play an effective role in Gulf security, assumed significance during the Gulf crisis as a critical pro-U.S. Arab actor. In 1979, moreover, transatlantic political and security links were dubious, but by the time of Operations Desert Shield and Storm they had improved substantially. Finally, while Saudi stability was in doubt in 1979, by 1993 it had increased notably, and the GCC, which was nonexistent in 1979, had developed by 1993 into a potentially effective transnational organization.

THE THIRD PARTY, HISTORY, AND THE CAUSES OF OUTCOMES

The improvement in the United States' position as a third party had important implications in the historical process, which need to be explored in line with the fourth part of the third-party framework. Regional war created the potential for future conflict, but it also produced important stabilizing effects such as improvements in U.S. military capability and in the regional military infrastructure. These effects strengthened U.S. security and made subsequent war, concluding with Iraq's invasion of Kuwait, more containable than it otherwise would have been. Thus, the impact of conflict on the Middle East in general and on the United States as the third party in particular, not only had short term implications but also long-term consequences.

The Afghanistan war produced effects that not only strengthened U.S. security in the Gulf,[1] but also undermined Moscow's foreign policy in the region.[2] This facilitated U.S. containment of Iran during the Iran-Iraq war. The Iran-Iraq war, in turn, produced effects that, as shown in chapter 5, were clearly linked to the U.S.-led containment and eviction of Iraqi forces from Kuwait in 1991.[3] For its part, Iraq's invasion of Kuwait caused regional upheaval, but also temporarily eliminated Iraq as a major regional threat. Thus, the regional status quo was reinforced, making it extremely difficult for Iraq or any state to dominate the Gulf by military or political means.

As described in chapter 7, the U.S. rise to power in the Persian Gulf region was related not only to events that took place in regional and global politics, but also to developments that never transpired. Indeed, conflicts caused Iran, Iraq, and the Soviet Union to miss significant foreign policy opportunities. Were this not so, they would have been in a much better position to undermine U.S. regional security and to enhance their regional position. Missed opportunities played a significant role in changing the outcome of regional politics in the 1980s and thereafter.

While the story of the rise of U.S. power and security in the Persian Gulf region is interesting, it is also important to ask what it means more generally. Scholars have focused much attention on what causes conflict, but they have done much less to explore the causes of the outcomes, or results, of conflict. This is peculiar because it stands to reason that knowing why some event occurred is no more important than knowing why the event resulted in a specific outcome. At a basic level, we can explain the outcomes of developments in world politics by appealing to proximate or antecedent causes. Proximate causes of outcomes can be viewed as a major part of the conflict. Thus, a proximate cause of the U.S.-led victory over Iraq was the development of a strong coalition against Saddam. By contrast, antecedent causes of conflict outcomes are events and developments that take place long before the conflict begins and that help explain its outcome.

Through its long-term perspective, the third-party approach focuses attention on and illumines antecedent causes of outcomes. In this book, the third-party framework helped show how the first Gulf war (1980–88) produced short- and long-term effects that contributed to the successful containment and eviction of Iraqi forces from Kuwait in 1990–91. This linkage became clear only after examining the impact of the Iran-Iraq war on the United States as a third party and then analyzing what this meant for regional politics over the long term. That is, the Iran-Iraq war bolstered U.S. regional standing in the 1980s and prepared Washington for Desert Shield and Storm in 1990–91.

The linkage drawn in this book between the first and second Gulf wars emphasizes the importance of antecedent causes. Failure to account properly for the role of antecedents is problematic because it can lead to an exaggeration of the role of more immediate causes. Thus, without understanding the linkage between the Iran-Iraq war and the outcome of the second Persian Gulf war, too much emphasis can be placed on the role of individual actors or on the strategies of states in explaining the outcome. This tended to be true of the Gulf crisis. Much focus was placed on the behavior of presidents George Bush and Saddam Hussein and less on the antecedent context that helped govern their behavior. Because antecedents are important in understanding outcomes and are relatively neglected, it follows that they deserve more attention. Antecedents, for instance, helped explain why Iraq's invasion of Kuwait was contained and reversed successfully.

IMPLICATIONS FOR POLICY AND THEORY

Identifying and understanding how antecedent causes are related to conflict outcomes is important for gaining a proper appreciation of history. But, it also enhances policymaking and evaluation, and theory building. This is because such efforts depend fundamentally on ascertaining what produces observed outcomes or, in particular, where the causes of policy successes and failures lie. Policy successes and failures might not be a product primarily of the nature of policy, but of other factors put in motion long before the policy was implemented. Inability to recognize the cause of a policy success or failure can lead to two main problems of policy analysis and evaluation.

The first problem arises in believing that a policy failed because it was poorly developed and executed, when in reality it failed because of antecedent causes, causes that long preceded the policy and that would have produced a negative outcome, regardless of the policy. Under such conditions, we will assume that the policy failed because it was a bad policy. As a result, we will probably attempt to change the policy, waste resources, and produce a different policy that is less likely to succeed than the original one. Indeed, as Robert Jervis points out, a common lesson that analysts draw is to avoid policies that have failed in the immediate past and to adopt tactics that are opposite of those tried.[4]

A second problem also arises in ignoring the important role of antecedent causes of outcomes. The causes of a successful policy outcome might be misspecified. That is, a good outcome might naturally be viewed as caused by an intelligent policy, when in reality the policy success is linked to antecedent causes that have little to do with the policy. In such a case, we will be inclined to use the same policy again but face a less favorable outcome. This book suggests, for instance, that it is unwise to assume that the success of U.S. intervention in the Persian Gulf could be easily repeated elsewhere. As discussed in detail in chapter 5, it was clearly related to prior events such as the Iran-Iraq war. The effects of this war, such as the development of regional military facilities and the improvement of U.S.-Saudi relations, were antecedent causes of the successful containment and eviction of Iraqi forces from Kuwait in Operations Desert Shield and Storm. Thus, Washington benefited from developments that were particular to the regional and international politics of the Persian Gulf region and from the political-security foundation laid prior to the actual Gulf crisis. In the absence of such a foundation for the large-scale use of force, an approach such as Desert Shield and Storm will be much less likely to succeed. This is a lesson worth remembering even if threats as serious and unambiguous as that posed by Iraq in 1990–91 are rare.

The Usefulness of Force

While the third-party perspective is useful in explaining policy failure and success, it may also produce a more accurate view of the usefulness of foreign policy instruments, such as military force. As discussed in chapter 1, analysts have discovered repeatedly that force works and that economic statecraft fails in world politics. In other words, they have found that states that use force are likely to be victorious and that those that apply economic sanctions against others are unlikely to succeed. These analysts only examined short-run outcomes, however, or in other words, did not explore the long-term consequences of the use of force and economic statecraft. By contrast, the third-party approach emphasizes long-term analysis in the broader context of conflict and, thus, might lead to different conclusions.

In this book, for instance, the third-party approach revealed a profound cost of the use of force on the part of Moscow, Baghdad, and Teheran, which analysts overlooked: The United States, the primary third-party competitor in each of these conflicts, was strengthened through a number of inter-related developments over time. In identifying the link between Iraq's use of force in 1980 against Iran, which triggered the Iran-Iraq war and Iraq's defeat in 1990–91, this book demonstrates a point not often shown: how the costs of force can manifest themselves in the long term. Indeed Saddam sowed some of the seeds of Iraq's demise in 1990–91 long before he ever invaded Kuwait. It just took some time for the effects he helped put in motion to play out in the historical process.

This analysis suggests the benefits of exploring the long-term implications of the use of force (or of other foreign policy instruments). This type of analysis would provide two possible gains. First, it would offer a more accurate picture of the consequences of the use of these instruments. Such knowledge is currently lacking. In an inventory of research on the subject, Patrick J. McGowan and Howard B. Shapiro found that "the effect of the foreign policy tool used has been a neglected area of research." They expressed both surprise and concern about this finding and asked an interesting question: "Since the purpose of foreign policy is to bring about some consequence . . . why study foreign policy if you are going to ignore the outcomes which decision-makers hope to bring about with that policy?"[5]

The second benefit of exploring the long-term consequences of statecraft is that it will increase our understanding of the value of one foreign policy instrument relative to another, in an increasingly more interdependent world. Is military force more useful than economic statecraft? Under what conditions might it be? Should actors use the stick or the carrot, force or economic sanctions, diplomatic pressure or the withdrawal of foreign aid? Answers to these questions are to some extent related to what we know about the consequences of the use of each of these instruments. Presumably, the more we know about these consequences, the more prudent will be our policy choices.

Naturally, problems arise in attempting to establish long-term causal connections. After all, how we can we be sure that event X caused effect Y some time later? The answer, of course, is that we cannot be. However, because short-term successes are sometimes transformed over time into modest successes or even failures, it is important to consider long-term effects.

To be sure, we might also find that the long-term effects of the use of force can benefit its user or that the failure to use force can produce significant negative long-term effects for the foreign policy actor. The argument here, however, is not that we have overestimated the value of the use of force, but that the finding that force generally works is worthy of further consideration.

The Third Party and the Future

While conflicts enhanced U.S. regional security, they also burdened the United States with responsibilities that it otherwise would not have had. This was apparent when Washington sent out an armada of naval ships to protect "reflagged" Kuwaiti tankers and, in the process, clashed with Iranian military forces. It was even more evident following the second Persian Gulf war. Although its effort in Operations Desert Shield and Storm was subsidized largely by regional actors, Washington suffered the brunt of enforcing the U.N.-brokered cease fire agreement between Iraq and the U.S.-led military coalition and of protecting Iraqi Kurds and Shiites.

The United States' entrenchment in the region in the 1980s and early 1990s was necessary but in some ways a drawback. A more appealing scenario could be imagined. Regional actors would have solved their disputes in the 1980s without war and recognized that their welfare and security would be best preserved through co-operation. Iran and Iraq would have turned their attention to economic development rather than to the self-defeating pursuit of regional hegemony and would have devised an arms control regime to deal with chemical, biological, and nuclear arms proliferation in the region. The monies saved could have been used to improve the lives of their people, to develop stable institutions, and to promote human rights.

In order to maintain elements of regional stability, the GCC and Egypt would have co-operated politically and military so as to protect regional security, with the United States playing an unobtrusive back-up role. At the same time, the wealthy GCC states would have offered economic and political incentives to Iran and Iraq. This combination of carrots and mild sticks would have ensured peace until long-term, more stable institutions and security frameworks were developed.

While attractive in theory and desirable from a U.S. standpoint, this story line or its close variants were largely fantasy. The anarchic nature of the region, the politics of oil, the many lingering territorial disputes and interstate rivalries, the delusions of regional grandeur in both Baghdad and Teheran, and the upheaval generated by the Iranian revolution made the probability of conflict high and the chances of long-term regional co-operation low. They also made a more involved U.S. role in the region necessary. Without it, the potential for Iran or Iraq to dominate the region would have increased substantially, with attendant negative consequences for the broader Middle East and the international theater.

Although it may seem counterintuitive, conflict produced the set of circumstances and developments that improved U.S. regional security. It is almost unimaginable that any other set of events could have weakened Iran and Iraq, defanged a near-nuclear Iraq, set Iran's nuclear program back several years, deprived U.S. adversaries of key opportunities to challenge the U.S. regional position, and produced throughout the 1980s the many facets of the political-security foundation that would serve the U.S.-led coalition against Iraq in Operations Desert Shield and Storm and into the 1990s. Little about the Persian Gulf region, or of theory in general, suggests that these sets of developments could have occurred in the absence of the serious shocks produced by conflict.

Alternatives to U.S. Regional Power

The rise of U.S. power and standing in the Persian Gulf region bodes well for regional stability into the 1990s. But, at the same time, it smacks of the type of domination that would be preferable to avoid were there other reliable means by which to strongly supplement the U.S. security role. That, however, is the rub. Other alternatives have proven problematic.

One alternative to an U.S.-dominated security structure has been a larger role for the GCC. The GCC developed considerably from its inception in 1981 and showed a postwar desire to become a more legitimate security organization. The GCC, however, remains incapable of deterring or even significantly impeding a major attack on one of its members, chiefly because it lacks the manpower and combat training, but also because it is not effectively unified. Repeated attempts by GCC states in the postcrisis period to develop a more effective military arm fell short.

Another alternative was referred to as the six-plus-two formula. This formula was put in motion under the Damascus Declaration, which was signed by the GCC states and Egypt and Syria on March 6, 1991.[6] It was based on political and security co-operation between the six members of the GCC, Egypt, and Syria. The idea is that Egypt and Syria would provide the manpower and experience that the GCC lacks, in exchange for financial assistance from GCC states. Egyptian and Syrian troops would be stationed in Kuwait, Saudi Arabia, and other Gulf states in order to back a smaller GCC military force against Iraq, Iran, or other threats to Gulf security.

While the six-plus-two formula was not without reason, it failed to materialize. Gulf states, uncomfortable with entrusting their security to Egypt and Syria, did not find the security arrangement economically feasible. They preferred to rely on the U.S. security umbrella and independent military efforts. Thus, while GCC states continued to interact with Egypt and Syria in the political and economic arenas, they downplayed the military side of the Damascus Declaration.

A third alternative was for GCC states to develop their own individual armies for purposes of self-protection. In theory, this would decrease the threshold for U.S. regional intervention. But while efforts toward this goal have been made, even under the best scenario, GCC states would need a major U.S. back-up role against an Iranian or Iraqi threat.

A fourth alternative faced even more significant obstacles than the first three alternatives and could not conceivably be implemented until major changes took place in Iran. This alternative is to include Iran indirectly in a regional security framework based on co-operation between the GCC and Teheran. The logic here is that Iran would be less inclined to challenge U.S. regional security because it would feel itself part of the security structure. Through the politics of inclusion, Iranian foreign policy would become more moderate and responsible. In addition, with the United States playing a less important security role, Iran would feel less threatened and challenged by U.S. power and thus would become less aggressive toward Western interests. However, it remains unclear whether Iran would use its newly acquired security position to co-opt other Gulf states, seek regional hegemony, and slowly decrease the ability of the United States to protect regional security in the event that Iran (or Iraq) seriously challenge U.S. interests in the future.

Although the Iran alternative seems highly doubtful in the 1990s, it is not altogether a dead letter into the next century. Forces of moderation in Teheran have risen intermittently, and Iran has attempted to shore up its relations with the Gulf Arabs, notwithstanding its clumsy behavior regarding the Arab islands of Abu Musa and the Upper and Lesser Tunbs. It is possible, albeit unlikely, that in five to ten years the risks of including Iran in a Gulf security arrangement will decrease enough to make the potential benefits of such a move exceed the potential costs. It is necessary, however, to see whether changes in Iran's domestic, regional, and global environment give it real and stable incentives to play a positive long-term security role. In the absence of such incentives and changes, Iran cannot be counted on as a partner in regional security.

The Advantages of Third-Party Status: Practice and Theory

At first glance, the more prominent U.S. regional role and the dubious nature of security alternatives suggest that the United States should pursue a vigorous foreign policy to maintain its position and fend off future challengers. While such an approach makes sense, Washington must be concerned about undermining its third-party role. The United States was strengthened by regional conflict partly because it was positioned to play the third-party role. Third-party status conferred upon it strategic and political benefits that are instructive in the U.S. experience and of potentially broader relevance.

First, U.S. third-party status made predicting the U.S. response more difficult for its competitors. While the aggressor can more or less expect the target either to accommodate or oppose it, a third party's behavior is often less predictable because its interests in relation to the conflict are more ambiguous. The antagonists, thus, might either mistakenly predict the severity of the third-party response or fail to foresee it. This offers a third-party latitude during conflict which it otherwise would not have.

Second, in addition to benefiting from greater latitude, the United States did not face well-prepared actors. When Moscow, Baghdad, and Teheran initiated or pursued conflict, they might have considered how the United States as a third party would respond to their use of force, but it is safe to say that they were more concerned with how to beat their adversary. Their objectives, logistics preparation, alliance-making, strategic deception, and propaganda were conceived and developed chiefly with the primary target in mind. As the third party, then, the United States gained an advantage inasmuch as its competitors were not particularly well prepared politically and/or militarily to deal with its response to their statecraft.

Third, as a third party, the United States could sit back and observe its competitors. What were their intentions and objectives? Did they act out of fear or ambition? With whom did they ally? How capable were they? Answers to such questions helped the United States decide if and how to intervene in the conflict. Otherwise its decision would have been more ad hoc and prone to mishap.

While primary antagonists also learn about their competitors by observing their behavior during conflict, they gain less from this type of feedback than do third parties. This is because the intense involvement of the primary antagonists in conflict makes objective analysis for them more difficult. It also constrains their ability to alter their policies based on the knowledge they gain during conflict. The Soviets, for instance, probably realized by 1981 that they had underestimated the Afghan resistance, but they were stuck in Afghanistan. Unlike a third party, their credibility was on the line and their troops were deployed.

Fourth, in the present case, long-term conflict weakened U.S. competitors, Iran, Iraq, and the Soviet Union. It diverted and absorbed their resources and made them less likely to seize political and military opportunities. In general, the main antagonists to conflict are much more likely to deplete their treasure than are third parties and to miss foreign policy opportunities to enhance their economic, political, and strategic position. To be sure, this need not always be the case. Under some conditions, conflict may strengthen the third party's competitor. The shorter the conflict, for instance, the less likely it will be that the third party's competitors will be weakened. They will avoid a protracted struggle while retaining the possibility of meeting short-term goals. Balancing behavior in world politics, however, mitigates against the chance that conflict will strengthen the third party's competitor in any significant way. That is, history shows that states usually attempt to stop any other actor from becoming too powerful.

Fifth, conflict often generates instability and threats that make alliances important for the principal antagonists and a range of third-party actors. Inasmuch as any particular third party is in a position to support other threatened actors, it stands to gain influence with which to improve its standing. This is because a third party, particularly one as powerful as the United States, can provide other actors with security support. The more threatened these actors feel, the more valuable is such support.

Finally, as the third party, the United States could take steps to defend its interests and strengthen itself with less risk of making others insecure. Ordinarily, the anarchic, self-help nature of world politics makes this difficult. Because no government exists above states to enforce international law and norms, states are highly sensitive to threats to their security and to the need to protect their own interests. Thus, in line with the famous security dilemma theory, attempts by one actor to improve its security often decrease the security of others, pushing them to take countermeasures, thus possibly leaving the first actor with no net gain.[7]

By virtue of its initial position outside the conflict, however, the third party may escape this dilemma. The extent to which it can do so depends on many factors, such as the nature of the conflict and its antagonists and the values at stake for the third party. But, in general, the third party gains freedom of maneuver in this respect. In this book, for instance, the U.S. political and strategic response to the Afghanistan intervention was not offset by another round of challenges from the Soviet Union and its allies, despite the fact that the United States, like the Soviet Union, was trying to improve its security in an environment of instability and virtual anarchy. While actors in the Middle East and South Asia, such as Iran and India, did not view the U.S. response with great favor, their opposition was either muted, symbolic, or surprisingly mild. Although this was largely due to their own concerns about the Afghanistan intervention, the United States' third-party role was also a factor. Because the United States was not the initial aggressor, its response was generally viewed as defensive rather than offensive and thus as more justified than the Soviet invasion. That the balance of power at the global level appeared to be shifting strongly against the United States also gave it more freedom in responding without triggering a counter-response. Therefore, U.S. efforts to redress this imbalance with various countermeasures was more understandable than it otherwise would have been.

Maintaining Third-Party Status

While regional conflicts strengthened the United States, they also threatened to move it away from third-party status. Every U.S. president since the Second World War has understood the importance of the Persian Gulf to the United States. But up until the administration of President Reagan, they have let others protect U.S. regional interests. This ended with the Iranian revolution, which undermined the twin pillar policy of the 1970s and pushed the United States to consider how it might protect its own regional goals.

The Afghanistan intervention, while tying down Moscow in a prolonged struggle, motivated the Carter Doctrine, which was a military commitment to protect the region against outside forces. The Reagan Doctrine issued during the Iran-Iraq war further expanded U.S. regional commitment. It committed the United States to protect Gulf security, particularly the stability of Saudi Arabia, from internal as well as from external threats.

In the aftermath of the Persian Gulf crisis, the Bush administration articulated a vision of Gulf security that represented an even higher level of U.S. commitment and an unprecedented U.S. role.[8] The United States sought to fashion a New World Order and a stable Middle East. Following in the trend of increased U.S. involvement in the region, the Clinton administration unveiled a policy called "dual containment." In the past, Washington aimed to prevent either Iraq or Iran from gaining regional hegemony by balancing one state against another. A primary example was in the mid-to-late 1980s when Washington lent Baghdad political, technological, and indirect military support in its eagerness to contain revolutionary Iran. Dual containment sought to replace balance-of-power policy, which was widely viewed as having contributed to the creation of a powerful Iraq under Saddam. Under dual containment, the United States would use its resources and those of its allies to contain both Iraq and Iran. In the words of President Clinton's national security adviser, Anthony Lake, the United States aimed to "neutralize, contain, and, through selective pressure, perhaps eventually transform these backlash states into constructive members of the international community."[9]

In some respects, dual containment made sense. Iran and Iraq remained hostile to U.S. interests in the mid-1990s, aimed to develop weapons of mass destruction, opposed the Middle East peace process, promoted international terrorism, and did not appear likely to moderate their foreign policies in the near term. Containing both of them, therefore, had appeal, particularly given that balance-of-power policy in the postwar Gulf presented obvious problems. As Phebe Marr, a noted expert on Iraq pointed out, it certainly did not make sense to tilt toward Saddam in order to balance against Iran or to tilt toward revolutionary Iran in order to balance against Iraq.[10] While dual containment made sense in certain issue areas such as the proliferation of weapons of mass destruction, it was more problematic as a general policy.

In its ambition, dual containment pitted the United States against both Iran and Iraq, thus making it more of a primary antagonist than a third party to potential conflict. This threatened to divert the attention of Iran and Iraq away from each other and toward the United States and the attention of the United States away from how it could affect indirectly the course of the ongoing Iran-Iraq rivalry to how it could directly suppress both states. By diverting the attention of Iran and Iraq from each other and by creating the perception of a United States bent on regional control, dual containment threatened to bring Iran and Iraq closer.

To be sure, Iran and Iraq were unlikely bed fellows. Another war between them was as likely as sustained co-operation. But they disliked the United States at least as much as they hated each other. And if convinced that they would fall alone if they did not stand together, they could have been pushed into co-operation, if only to deal Washington a blow so that they could resume their own regional rivalry unfettered by the United States.

U.S. ambition also threatened to give "radicals" in the region ammunition in their domestic struggle with moderates, to dissuade more "pragmatic" leaders such as Iran's president Rafsanjani from making conciliatory moves toward the West, and to push Islamic and secular radicalism into an anti-U.S. alliance.

While no actor alone could have easily challenged the United States, a coalition might have been successful.

The United States should be careful about projecting the image of a regional hegemon in the postwar Persian Gulf. In part, this is because the events of the last decade have thrust it into a position of greater regional prominence. And great powers are perceived by others differently than are smaller powers. Others tend to be more sensitive to the ambitious actions of great powers because they wield more influence than do smaller powers. The United States emerged from Desert Storm with much elevated power and thus can expect others to be more sensitive to the prospect of U.S. regional domination than they would have been had it emerged a weaker actor from regional conflicts.

One major implication of the U.S. rise as a third party is that it should be careful about appearing bent on hegemony because the benefits of doing so are not high. Under conditions where the United States faces significant threats, has questionable allies, and doubts its own capabilities, projecting a strong image is useful. It helps pacify doubtful allies and deter would-be aggressors. While these conditions may develop in the region in the next decade, they do not characterize the postwar Persian Gulf. In particular, conventional threats to U.S. interests are not significant enough to warrant a high-profile role.

Military opportunism on the part of Iran or Iraq is unlikely to succeed. Quite the contrary, as this book shows, such opportunism is likely to put in motion developments that further reinforce the regional status quo and strengthen the United States. This decreases the risks to the United States of choosing a general policy that leans more toward a low-key regional profile than toward a more visible, aggressive role. Such a policy seeks to avoid the appearance of ambition, while still meeting critical goals such as checking the spread of weapons of mass destruction to Iraq and Iran, enforcing U.N. sanctions against Iraq, and, preventing Iran or Iraq from dominating the region in the future.

While the developments of the past ten years make such domination unlikely in the 1990s, selective balance-of-power policy remains a suitable antidote to regional adventurism. Its failure in the 1970s and 1980s had less to do with the policy itself than with its implementation. The United States, for instance, supported Iraq against Iran in 1986–87 when it appeared that the latter might dominate the Gulf. This policy was reasonable. But U.S. support did not stop there. Washington continued to bolster Saddam in the postwar period, despite the fact that the balance of power had shifted to Iraq's favor and despite strong indications that Saddam sought regional domination. This was not a problem with the logic of balance-of-power policy. It was a problem with how this policy was practiced. The United States did not balance against the stronger and more threatening actor in the region. It helped it. Washington could just as easily have decided to balance against Iraq in the postwar period.

Maintaining third-party status in a region as critical to U.S. interests as the Persian Gulf is no easy task. In developing foreign policy, it is difficult to strike the mean between being strong enough to deter regional aggressors yet not so strong that they are threatened into provocative actions they otherwise would not take. Doing so requires a mix of strategies that combine strength and conciliation. Determining to what extent strength should be the mainstay of such a strategy depends on existing conditions and on the issue area in question.

Given the history of the region and the U.S. role in this wider scheme of things, it seems wise that the United States consider the following ways by which to help preserve its third-party status. First, it should refrain from making official, sweeping, and aggressive statements of policy that are directed at particular actors. Such statements are useful only for purposes of one-time deterrence. Thus, if Iraq again threatens to invade Kuwait, a strongly worded message would help deter it. But such statements are not often useful in the Middle East as basic policy in the absence of clear threats. Their deterrence effect wears off, they generate antagonism without really accomplishing a clear strategic goal, and they become the political baggage of interstate relations that makes future accommodation difficult. Historically speaking, regional states have responded poorly to the pressures imposed on them by external powers.

Labeling Iran an "international outlaw" as the Clinton administration did in early 1993 might have made sense if this would have increased short- and long-term international pressure on its regime to moderate its foreign policy. But such pressure was unlikely to accomplish this goal and likely to put the United States on record as the lead state against Iran. In other words, it threatened to move Washington away from a third-party role. While such a move would be warranted if it offered significant benefits to offset costs, the prospects for such benefits would need to be established clearly.

Second, the United States should avoid positioning itself militarily as if it aimed to be a primary antagonist in the region as opposed to a powerful third party. Indeed, the military positioning and strategy of states communicates to other actors how aggressive that state intends to be. Actors that are aware of how their strategy affects others are more likely to be able to strengthen their own security without threatening the security of others. In the Persian Gulf, the United States must position itself well enough to defend its interests in the event that deterrence fails, but not so much so that it can defend against phantom threats, while threatening and provoking regional actors into aggressive actions that they otherwise would not take. In such a case, Washington will waste resources, meet an objective that need not be met, provoke countermeasures, and deprive itself of the advantages of third-party status as discussed in the foregoing analysis.

Third, Washington can trust the logic of balance of power. History reveals repeatedly that states balance against powerful and/or threatening actors. The Persian Gulf is no exception. Iran and Iraq have a natural tendency to balance each other. The United States should let this process work as a means of meeting its regional objectives. This does not mean that the United States can relax. It must play an important role in the balancing process when Iran or Iraq prove unable to check each other effectively. But given postwar conditions, it need not take a high-profile, lead role in containing both actors. It also need not help one actor balance against the other. Rather, it can organize its allies for purposes of ensuring that neither Iran nor Iraq can reach a point where they might be able to overturn the regional status quo.

The logic of statecraft is to meet maximum national objectives with minimal expenditure. Dual containment, while sensible in some ways, threatens this logic. Because it is difficult and costly to contain Iran and Iraq at once over the long term, it is worthwhile seeing whether they can balance each other off at their own expense, with the United States and regional actors rounding off any imbalances that might emerge. Clearly, such a balance will not prevent either state from developing weapons of mass destruction and engaging in terrorism. This means that the United States needs different strategies for different issues areas, based on a proper mix of carrot and stick. In the areas of weapons of mass destruction and terrorism, it makes sense to contain both Iran and Iraq, while relying on a guided balance-of-power policy at the conventional level.

APPLYING THE THIRD-PARTY PERSPECTIVE

The rise of U.S. standing and security in the Persian Gulf is the story of the failures and fortunes of a major third party; not a basic one. The United States' superpower status clearly affected how it behaved in the Persian Gulf as a third party and how conflict affected it. As a major third party to regional conflicts, the United States was more likely to play a role in affecting the course of conflict than it would have been had it been a weaker third party. Yet, in 1979 after the Iranian revolution, even the United States as a major power was quite vulnerable to the vagaries and instabilities of conflict.

The paradox of conflicts is that instead of further weakening the United States at a time when it was vulnerable, conflicts reversed U.S. decline, prepared it to meet the Iraqi challenge in 1990–91, and left it more secure than it otherwise would have been. The U.S. rise as a third party benefited regional security and implied several insights for history, policy, and possibly theory that have been elaborated upon in this chapter.

But, while this book has focused on how conflict affected the United States in the Middle Eastern context, the third-party approach it developed can apply in other contexts as well. Indeed, almost every conflict seriously affects at least one third party, and some conflicts affect scores of third parties. The Gulf crises, for instance, affected the economies of states from Western Europe to Japan to the Horn of Africa.

We have seen how major conflicts affected the security, interests, and power of the United States in the Middle East. In other contexts, the impact of conflict on the third party will differ from the present case. Given the great diversity in world politics, this is hardly a profound point. No two situations are alike. Yet, an accumulation of cases on conflict and third parties may create a basis for developing theory, by illuminating the conditions under which the third party is weakened or strengthened by conflict. In the process, we may learn more about the utility of statecraft, the politics of rapidly changing conflictual regions of the world, conflict processes and outcomes, and conflict avoidance and resolution. Indeed, the study of the third party will tell us something about the third party itself be it a state, an international organization, or some other actor in world politics. It can also inform us about the context in which the third party plays a role, the long-term role of the third party in that context, other contexts which the third party affects, and the nature and impact of conflict in general.

NOTES

1. For detailed evidence, see Yetiv, "How the Soviet Intervention in Afghanistan Improved the U.S. Strategic Position in the Persian Gulf."

2. See S. A. Yetiv, "Persian Gulf Security: A Bivariable Analysis," *Defense Analysis* 6, no. 3 (September 1990): 289–98.

3. For details, see Yetiv, "The Outcomes."

4. On the lessons decision makers learn from history, see Robert Jervis, *Perception and Misperception in International Politics* (Princeton, NJ: Princeton University Press, 1976), chap. 6.

5. Cited in David A. Baldwin, *Economic Statecraft* (Princeton, NJ: Princeton University Press, 1985), 11–12.

6. For the text of the Damascus Declaration, see *Damascus Domestic Service*, in FBIS: NESA, 7 March 1991, 1.

7. See Robert Jervis, "Cooperation under the Security Dilemma," *World Politics* (January 1978): 169.

8. See comments by Richard Cheney, *The Soref Symposium: American Strategy After the Gulf War* (Washington, D.C.: Washington Institute for Near East Policy, 1991), 45.

9. Anthony Lake, "Confronting Backlash States," *Foreign Affairs* 73, no. 2 (March/April 1994): 46.

10. "Symposium on Dual Containment: U.S. Policy Toward Iran and Iraq," *Middle East Policy* 3, no. 1 (1994): 15.

APPENDIX: METHODOLOGY

The present methodology consists of two basic canons of empirical research: the comparative method and operationalization. The comparative method is used to identify the effects of conflict, and operationalization is applied to measure indirectly the strength of U.S. regional security. By offering a basis for examining the strength of U.S. security, and by comparing the strength of U.S. security before and after the outbreak of each conflict, reasonable judgments can be made about how conflict affected U.S. security in the short and long term.

COMPARING U.S. REGIONAL SECURITY THROUGH TIME

As E. H. Carr once put it, "Past, present and future are linked together in the endless chain of history."[1] This has profound implications for anyone who seeks to understand the sequence of cause and effect in history. Because history is continuous, we must break it down in order to understand it. Otherwise, cause and effect would blur into indistinction.

The Iranian revolution, the Afghanistan intervention, the Iran-Iraq war and the Iraqi invasion of Kuwait each had major effects on U.S. regional security. To understand the impact of each event, it is necessary to distinguish to the extent possible its effects from the effects of other events, and from the broader historical process.[2] Otherwise, we might attribute to one conflict the effects of another or exaggerate a causal relationship that did exist.[3] That is, we might think that the Iran-Iraq war caused a change in U.S. regional security, which in reality resulted from the Afghanistan intervention, or that the Iran-Iraq war did more to change U.S. regional security than was truly the case. We might also fail to understand how the Afghanistan intervention affected the course of the

Iran-Iraq war in a way that then affected U.S. regional security, or how both these conflicts interacted to create new effects on Middle Eastern politics and on U.S. regional security. While separating out the effects of conflict is difficult, it is necessary in the effort to understand the role of each conflict in the evolution of U.S. regional security.

The comparative method of difference associated with John Stuart Mill is used in this book to identify the effects of conflict.[4] While in statistics one variable can be held constant while others fluctuate, such manipulation is not possible when analyzing the impact of conflict in the historical process. One cannot change history to eliminate and then recreate the occurrence of any conflict, thus controlling for it. Consequently, it is necessary to improvise methodologically.

In this book, the strength of U.S. regional security before and after the outbreak of war is compared. The simple idea here is that war, being a dramatic event, represents the major change between the periods before and after war. Thus, changes in U.S. regional security in the period after war erupts might be attributed to war. Through case study analysis, it is possible to judge to what extent this is true.

Scholars apply the comparative method either cross-nationally[5] or diachronically. The cross-national approach involves a comparison of entirely separate but similar cases, while the diachronic approach involves analysis of one case through time. This book uses a diachronic approach. It compares the same variable, U.S. regional security, before and after the Iranian revolution, the Afghanistan intervention, the Iran-Iraq war, and the Iraqi invasion of Kuwait. The diachronic application of the comparative method offers a better solution to the problem of controlling variables than do cross-national studies because it involves more constants and fewer variables.[6] That is, fewer variables change over just time than they do over both time and area.

In this book, U.S. regional security is examined in the period prior to the January 1979 departure from Iran of the Shah of Iran; from January 1979 when the Shah departed from Iran to December 24–27, 1979, when the Soviets invaded Afghanistan; from December 28, 1979, to September 22, 1980, when the Iran-Iraq war erupted; from September 23, 1980 to the Soviet withdrawal from Afghanistan; in the period between the cease fire in the Iran-Iraq war (August 1988) and the Iraqi invasion of Kuwait (August 1990); and, finally, in the three-year period following the Iraqi invasion of Kuwait.

In order to determine the effects of each conflict, principal emphasis is placed on the time period immediately preceding and following the outbreak of each conflict. The important effects of conflict are then traced through time in terms of their impact on U.S. regional security. The Iran-Iraq war, for instance, began nine months after the Soviets invaded Afghanistan. Thus, ongoing effects that began between December 1979 and the September 1980 outbreak of the Iran-Iraq war may be attributed to the Afghanistan intervention but not to the Iran-Iraq war.

The different nature of the present conflicts also helps separate out their effects. Strategically, the Afghanistan invasion was viewed as a global-level threat to the Persian Gulf, while the Iran-Iraq war was a regional-level threat. The Afghanistan intervention was a potential, although unlikely, air and land threat, while the Iran-Iraq war was a more serious air, land, and also naval threat. The former was perceived as directly challenging the United States at the superpower level, while the latter was an indirect challenge to the United States at the regional level. The Afghanistan invasion was an ideological affront to most of the Islamic world, whereas the Iran-Iraq war was a military threat to some Islamic states. The former was perceived as most threatening in 1980, whereas the latter was perceived as most threatening after 1982, and particularly after Iran's successful Faw offensive in February 1986.

The difference in nature of these two wars tells us something about their likely effects. This is because it stands to reason that a cause will have certain properties that are related to the effect it engenders. Thus, if the Afghanistan intervention is an external threat to the Persian Gulf, its effects are likely to be characterized by some feature that is related to the deterrence of an outside threat. Bearing this general notion in mind decreases the potential for confusing the effects of one event with those of another.

OPERATIONALIZING U.S. SECURITY
IN THE PERSIAN GULF

The approach described above is useful in identifying the effects of conflict, but it does not tell us if these effects strengthened or weakened U.S. regional security. Thus, it is important to operationalize U.S. regional security so that it can be measured indirectly and compared systematically at different time periods. This is how one understands how conflict affects the third party in the short and long term.

U.S. regional security from 1978 to 1993 depended on the unimpeded flow of oil to the United States and its allies, the protection of the stability of pro-U.S. Gulf states, and the control of anti-U.S. influences. But if these were the general goals of the United States, then what variables can measure the extent to which they were secure? In other words, what variables measure the strength of U.S. regional security? While the strength of U.S. regional security is not directly observable, six variables can measure it indirectly: the level of Saudi domestic stability, the strength of U.S. military capability relevant to the protection of U.S. regional security, the strength of U.S. relations with key regional states, the strength of Soviet relations with key states in the Middle East, the strength of relations between Arab Gulf states, and the regional balance of power between Iran and Iraq.

While these variables are useful in general for indirect measurement, they must be supplemented by historical analysis, interpretive logic, and common sense. This is true for two reasons. First, as a complex concept, U.S. regional security is not amenable to precise measurement. Indeed, most of the present operationalization employs qualitative variables on the assumption that they offer insight into important aspects of U.S. security that cannot be examined quantitatively.

Second, although the six variables to be presented do indicate the strength of U.S. regional security, they must be examined in context. For instance, U.S. access to regional military bases reflects positively on U.S. security because it is a prerequisite for dealing with major regional military threats. A large U.S. regional military presence, however, can create unacceptable political costs. Thus, the fact that the United States gained significant access to regional military bases does not tell us enough about U.S. regional security. In simple terms, then, operationalization systematizes the present empirical analysis but does not replace it. Operationalization is a guide to reality, a vehicle through which to compare and to make sound judgments, but it cannot be an intellectual strait jacket. World politics is too complex and varied to allow such an application.

The Level of Saudi Domestic Stability

Conflict can increase, decrease, or fail to affect the domestic stability of states. Since Saudi Arabia has been the linchpin of U.S. regional security, its domestic stability is vital to U.S. security. The stability of other states in the Persian Gulf is far less important because they either challenged U.S. regional security or were not in a position to affect it greatly. Indicators of instability in Saudi Arabia include coups, mass demonstrations, and identifiable incidences of internally and externally motivated subversion. If conflict can be linked to increases in these indicators, then this suggests U.S. security was weakened (*ceteris paribus*). For instance, the demonstrations against the Saudi regime in November 1979 in the eastern oil province are linked to the Iranian revolution. They indicated a decrease in Saudi stability and, in turn, a threat to U.S. regional security. Subtle changes in Saudi stability that cannot be accounted for by the present indicators are examined in the broader case-study analysis.

The Strength of U.S. Military Capability Relevant to the Protection of U.S. Regional Security

Conflicts can enhance, damage, or fail to affect the military capability of states. I define U.S. military capability as its ability to protect by military means its interests in the Persian Gulf region with limited allied assistance. This definition distinguishes the strength of U.S. military capability as a variable from the strength of U.S. relations with key regional states (Variable 3).

Based on this definition, U.S. force projection capability is the critical indicator of U.S. military capability. Long distances, the absence of a permanent U.S. military facility in the region, and a questionable regional military infrastructure made rapid deployment vital for the protection of U.S. regional security. I define force projection capability as the product of how fast and how much military equipment and troops Washington can deploy to the Persian Gulf from the U.S. mainland or from non-Persian Gulf staging areas.

The Strength of U.S. Relations with Key Regional States

U.S. military capability has been defined here as independent of allied assistance. But the nature of U.S. relations with regional states is critical to U.S. security. U.S. regional interests are more secure when its relations with key regional states such as Saudi Arabia, Iran, Egypt, and Iraq are stronger.

This variable is made operational based on the extent of U.S. access to regional strategic facilities, U.S. military maneuvers with regional states, and U.S. diplomatic contact with regional states. Official and unofficial statements in the Middle East press reflecting the nature of U.S. relations with key states are also examined. In the absence of any concrete state action such as joint military maneuvers or the signing of military accords, it is important to assess such statements. This is often the only way to identify subtle but important changes in the nature of bilateral relations. Interviews with policymakers offer additional insight into the nature of U.S. relations with regional actors.

The Strength of Soviet Relations with Key States in the Middle East

The Soviet Union played a key role in affecting U.S. security in the Persian Gulf from 1978 to 1989. Thus, it is impossible to understand the evolution of U.S. regional security without understanding the regional role of the Soviet Union. Soviet relations with key states fluctuated as a function of conflict. The stronger they were, the weaker was U.S. security (*ceteris paribus*). This assumption is plausible inasmuch as the Soviet Union's interest for most of the time period under examination here was to limit the U.S. regional military presence, undermine U.S. relations with regional states, and build a political and strategic foothold in the area.[7] Soviet relations with key regional states such as Iraq, Iran, Saudi Arabia and the Yemens are operationalized as are U.S. relations with key states in variable (3) previously discussed.

The Strength of Relations Between Arab Gulf States

Conflict seriously affected relations among the eight Gulf states. U.S. security was served better by stronger as opposed to weaker relations among six of these states: Saudi Arabia, Qatar, Oman, Kuwait, the United Arab Emirates, and Bahrain. Two reasons support this point.

First, these states tended to support the U.S.-favored regional status quo. Thus, it was in the United States' interest that they co-operate in political and security areas. Second, for purposes of protecting their security against threatening regional actors, these states often pursued simultaneously a policy of appeasing Iran, Iraq, and the Soviet Union on the one hand, and relying on the United States on the other. Factors that made these states more likely to lean toward the United States, rather than to appease threatening regional actors tended to benefit U.S. security. I argue that increased unity among and co-operation between these six states was such a factor.[8]

The strength of these Arab-state relations is indicated by the extent of military treaties or agreements, joint strategic maneuvers, and intelligence co-operation. Official and unofficial statements in the Middle East press reflecting the nature of U.S. relations with key states are also examined. Interviews with key policymakers also offers information on intra-Arab relations which is not obtainable elsewhere.

The Regional Balance of Power

Based on balance-of-power logic, the more closely balanced are Iran and Iraq, the region's two strongest states, the less likely either would attempt to or could dominate the Persian Gulf either politically or militarily. It is also better for the balance to exist at lower levels of capability on each side than at higher levels because then the relative military capability of more moderate states such as Saudi Arabia will be higher. Indicators of the balance of power include the number of aircraft, main battle tanks, and major naval combatants on each side.

THE CHOICE OF VARIABLES AND EVENTS

Because any operationalization is somewhat subjective, it is useful to explain the choice of variables. The variables previously discussed were chosen based on the belief that they best reflect what we mean by "U.S. regional security." Thus, when considered together, they offer a rough indication of the strength of U.S. security. While other variables are also important in measuring U.S. security, the view here is that their inclusion would not add enough to the analysis to be sensible.

Since this book involves a comparative analysis, it is also necessary to apply the same variables across time so as to avoid comparing apples and oranges. In this sense, the six variables are chosen not only because, when considered together, they indicate the strength of U.S. security, but also because they best reflect the strength of U.S. security from 1978 to 1993. Thus, even though

Variable 4, Soviet relations with regional states, is irrelevant in the current international climate, it is included because of its importance for most of the time period under consideration in this book.

NOTES

1. Edward Hallet Carr, *What Is History?* (New York: Vintage Books, 1961), 179.

2. On the general methodological problems associated with such a task, see Donald T. Campbell, *Methodology and Epistemology for Social Sciences* (Chicago, IL: University of Chicago Press, 1988), 226–27.

3. On the paradoxes of isolating causal series, see Mario Bunge, *Causality and Modern Science* (New York: Dover Publications, 1979).

4. This method was previously discussed by William of Ockham in the thirteenth century. On Ockham, see A. C. Crombie, *Augustine to Galileo*, vol. 2 (Cambridge: Harvard University Press, 1961), 31–32. Mill never believed that the method of difference could be applied to social science research, but the view here is that it is better to apply this method imprecisely than not at all.

5. For a good example of this approach, see Skoçpol, *States and Social Revolutions*.

6. Arend Lijphart, "Comparative Politics and the Comparative Method," *American Political Science Review* 65 (September 1971): 689.

7. See Yetiv, "Persian Gulf Security," 289–98.

8. For a discussion of factors affecting power alliance strategies, see Glenn H. Snyder, "The Security Dilemma in Alliance Politics," *World Politics* 36 (July 1984): 461–95.

SELECTED BIBLIOGRAPHY

BOOKS

Adamec, Ludwig, W. *Afghanistan's Foreign Affairs to the Mid-Twentieth Century: Relations with the USSR, Germany and Britain*. Tucson, AZ: University of Arizona Press, 1974.

Amuzegar, Jahangir, *The Dynamics of the Iranian Revolution: The Pahlavis' Triumph and Tragedy*. New York: State University of New York Press, 1991.

Arnold, Anthony. *Afghanistan: The Soviet Invasion in Perspective*. Stanford, CA: Hoover Institution Press, 1984.

Baldwin, David A. *Economic Statecraft*. Princeton, NJ: Princeton University Press, 1985.

Blechman, Barry M., and Stephen S. Kaplan, *Force Without War: U.S. Armed Forces as a Political Instrument*. Washington, D.C.: Brookings Institution, 1978.

Bradsher, Henry S. *Afghanistan and the Soviet Union*. Durham, NC: Duke University Press, 1985.

Brzezinski, Zbigniew. *Power and Principle: Memoirs of the National Security Advisor, 1977–1981*. New York: Farrar, Straus, and Giroux, 1985.

Bunge, Mario. *Causality and Modern Science*. New York: Dover Publications, 1979.

Buzan, Barry, and Gowher Rizvi, eds. *South Asian Insecurity and the Great Powers*. New York: St. Martin's Press, 1986.

Campbell, Donald T. *Methodology and Epistemology for Social Sciences*. Chicago, IL: University of Chicago Press, 1988.

Carr, Edward Hallet. *What Is History?* New York: Vintage Books, 1961.

Carter, Jimmy. *Keeping Faith: Memoirs of a President*. New York: Bantam Books, 1982.

Chubin, Shahram. *Security in the Persian Gulf: The Role of Outside Powers.* Aldershot, England: Gower Publishing Co., 1982.

Chubin, Shahram, and Charles Tripp. *Iran and Iraq at War.* London: I. B. Tauris & Co., Ltd., 1988.

Collins, Joseph J. *The Soviet Invasion of Afghanistan: A Study in the Use of Force in Soviet Foreign Policy.* Lexington, MA: Lexington Books, 1986.

Cordesman, Anthony H. *After the Storm: The Changing Military Balance in the Middle East.* Boulder, CO: Westview Press, 1993.

———. *The Gulf and the Search for Strategic Stability: Saudi Arabia, the Military Balance in the Gulf, and Trends in the Arab-Israeli Military Balance.* Boulder, CO: Westview Press, 1984.

———. *The Iran-Iraq War and Western Security 1984–87: Strategic Implications and Policy Options.* London: Jane's, 1987.

———. *The Gulf and the West: Strategic Relations and Military Realities.* Boulder, CO: Westview Press, 1988.

Crombie, A. C. *Augustine to Galileo.* Volume 2. Cambridge, MA: Harvard University Press, 1961.

Eisenstadt, Michael. "Like a Phoenix from the Ashes? The Future of Iraqi Military Power," Policy Paper No. 36. Washington, D.C.: The Washington Institute for Near East Policy, 1993.

Fouquet, David, ed. *Jane's NATO Handbook.* Surrey, England: Sentinel House, 1988.

Freedman, Lawrence, and Efraim Karsh. *The Gulf Conflict 1990–1991: Diplomacy and War in the New World Order.* Princeton, NJ: Princeton University Press, 1993.

The Gallup Poll: Public Opinion. Wilmington, DE: Scholarly Resources, Inc., various editions (1979–1987).

Gilpin, Robert. *War and Change in World Politics.* New York: Cambridge University Press, 1981.

Halliday, Fred. *Soviet Policy in the Arc of Crisis.* Amsterdam, The Netherlands: Institute for Policy Studies, 1981.

Hammond, Thomas T. *Red Flag over Afghanistan: The Communist Coup, the Soviet Invasion, and the Consequences.* Boulder, CO: Westview Press, 1984.

Harrison, Selig S. *In Afghanistan's Shadow: Baluch Nationalism and Soviet Temptations.* Washington, D.C.: Carnegie Endowment for International Peace, 1981.

Hilsman, Roger. *George Bush vs. Saddam Hussein: Military Success! Political Failure?* Novato, CA: Lyford Books, 1992.

Holden, David, and Richard Johns. *The House of Saud.* New York: Holt, Rinehart, and Winston, 1981.

Jervis, Robert. *Perception and Misperception in International Politics.* Princeton, NJ: Princeton University Press, 1976.

Johnson, Maxwell Orme. *The Military as an Instrument of U.S. Policy in Southwest Asia: The Rapid Deployment Joint Task Force, 1979–1982.* Boulder, CO: Westview Press, 1983.

Keesing's Contemporary Archives. New York: Scribner, various years (1987–1989).

Keohane, Robert O., and Joseph S. Nye. *Power and Interdependence: World Politics in Transition*. Boston: Little, Brown, 1977.

Legum, Colin, et al., eds. *Middle East Contemporary Survey*. Volumes 1978–1990. New York: Holmes and Meier.

Martin, Lenore. *The Unstable Gulf: Threats from Within*. Lexington, MA: Lexington Books, 1984.

McNaugher, Thomas L. *Arms and Oil: U.S. Military Strategy and the Persian Gulf*. Washington, D.C.: Brookings Institution, 1985.

Mughisuddin, Mohammed, ed. *Conflict and Cooperation in the Persian Gulf*. New York: Praeger, 1977.

Noyes, James H. *The Clouded Lens: Persian Gulf Security and U.S. Policy*. Stanford, CA: Hoover Institution Press, 1982.

O'Loughlin, John, Tom Mayer, and Edward S. Greenberg, *War and Its Consequences: Lessons from the Persian Gulf Conflict*. New York: Harper Collins, 1994.

Palmer, Michael A. *Guardians of the Gulf: A History of America's Expanding Role in the Persian Gulf, 1833–1992*. New York: The Free Press, 1992.

Perry, Jack R., ed. *Proceedings of a Conference on Gulf Security*. Charleston, SC: The Citadel, 1983.

Quandt, William. *Saudi Arabia in the 1980s: Foreign Policy, Security, and Oil*. Washington D.C.: Brookings Institution, 1981.

Ramazani, R. K. *The Persian Gulf and the Strait of Hormuz*. The Netherlands: Sijthoff & Noordhoff, 1979.

———. *Revolutionary Iran: Challenge and Response in the Middle East*. Baltimore, MD: The Johns Hopkins University Press, 1986.

———. *The United States and Iran: The Patterns of Influence*. New York: Praeger, 1982.

Record, Jeffrey. *Hollow Victory: A Contrary View of the Gulf War*. Washington, D.C.: Brassey's (US), Inc., 1993.

Ro'i, Yaacov, ed. *The U.S.S.R. and the Muslim World*. London: Allen and Unwin, 1984.

Rubin, Barry. *Paved with Good Intentions: The American Experience and Iran*. New York: Oxford University Press, 1980.

Rubinstein, Alvin Z., ed. *The Great Game: Rivalry in the Persian Gulf and South Asia*. New York: Praeger, 1983.

Safran, Nadav. *Saudi Arabia: The Ceaseless Quest for Security*. Cambridge, MA: Harvard University Press, 1985.

Sick, Gary. *All Fall Down: America's Tragic Encounter with Iran*. Boulder, CO: Westview Press, 1985.

Skoçpol, Theda. *States and Social Revolutions: A Comparative Analysis of France, Russia, and China*. New York: Cambridge University Press, 1979.

U.S. News and World Report. *Triumph Without Victory: The Unreported History of the Persian Gulf War*. New York: Times Books, 1992.

Vance, Cyrus. *Hard Choices: Critical Years in America's Foreign Policy*. New York: Simon and Schuster, 1983.

ARTICLES

Albright, David, and Mark Hibbs. "Iraq's Bomb: Blueprints and Artifacts." *The Bulletin of the Atomic Scientists* (January/February 1992): 30–40.

Armstrong, Scott. "Eye of the Storm." *Mother Jones* (Special Report) 16 (November/December 1991): 31–32.

Bill, James A. "Resurgent Islam in the Persian Gulf." *Foreign Affairs* 63, no. 1 (Fall 1984): 108–27.

Boleslaw, Adam Boczek. "Law of Warfare at Sea and Neutrality: Lessons of the Gulf War." *Ocean Development and International Law* 20 (1989): 239–71.

Christie, John. "A History of the Gulf Cooperation Council." *American-Arab Affairs* 13 (Fall 1986): 1–13.

Chubin, Shahram. "Leftist Forces in Iran." *Problems of Communism* 29 (July-August 1980): 1–25.

Cohen, Stephen P. "South Asia After Afghanistan." *Problems of Communism* 34 (January–February 1985): 18–31.

Crist, General George B. "Bone, Sinew and Muscle for REGIONAL DEFENSE." *Defense/87* (November–December): 36–42.

Dixon, Michael J. "The Soviet Union and the Middle East: An Imperial Burden or Political Asset." *CRS Review* 5, no. 6 (June 1984).

Eilts, F. Hermann. "Security Considerations in the Persian Gulf." *International Security* 5 (Fall 1980): 79–113.

"Empty Reforms: Saudi Arabia's New Basic Laws." *Middle East Watch* (May 1992): 59–62.

Fromkin, David. "The Great Game in Asia." *Foreign Affairs* 58 (Spring 1980): 936–51.

Goldman, Stuart. *U.S.-Soviet Relations after Afghanistan*. Congressional Research Service, Foreign Affairs and National Defense Division, Issue Brief IB80080 (19 November 1980).

Graur, Mina. "The Soviet Union Versus Muslim Solidarity Following the Soviet Invasion of Afghanistan." *Slavic and Soviet Studies* 4 (1979): 74–89.

Grimmett, Richard F. *Trends in Conventional Arms Transfers to Third World by Major Supplier, 1981–1988*, CRS Report for Congress (4 August 1989).

Harary, Frank, "A Structural Analysis of the Situation in the Middle East in 1956." *Journal of Conflict Resolution* 5 (June 1961): 167–78.

Heller, Mark. "The Iran-Iraq War: Implications for Third Parties." *Jaffe Center for Strategic Studies* 23 (January 1984).

Hermann, Charles F. "Changing Course: When Governments Choose to Redirect Foreign Policy." *International Studies Quarterly* 34, no. 1 (March 1990): 3–22.

Jervis, Robert. "Cooperation under the Security Dilemma." *World Politics* 30 (January 1978): 167–214.

Karsh, Efraim, and Inari Rautsi, "Why Saddam Hussein Invaded Kuwait." *Survival* 33 (January/February 1991): 18–30.

Katz, N. Mark. "Soviet Policy in the Gulf States." *Current History* 84, no. 498 (January 1985): 25–28, 41.

Kechichian, Joseph A. "The Gulf Cooperation Council: Containing the Iranian Revolution." *Journal of South Asian and Middle Eastern Studies* 13, nos. 1 & 2, (Fall/Winter 1989): 146–65.

Lake, Anthony. "Confronting Backlash States." *Foreign Affairs* 73, no. 2 (March/April 1994): 45–55.

Lijphart, Arend. "Comparative Politics and the Comparative Method." *American Political Science Review* 65 (September 1971): 682–93.

Maoz, Zeev, "Resolve, Capabilities, and the Outcomes of Interstate Disputes, 1816–1976." *Journal of Conflict Resolutions* 27 (June 1983): 195–229.

Mofid, Kamran, "The Economic Reconstruction of Iraq." *Third World Quarterly* 12, no. 1 (January 1990): 52–54.

Mylroie, Laurie. "The Baghdad Alternative." *Orbis* 32, no. 3 (Summer 1988): 339–54.

Page, Stephen. "The Soviet Union and the GCC States: A Search for Openings." *American-Arab Affairs* 20 (Spring 1987): 38–56.

Quandt, William. "Riyadh Between the Superpowers." *Foreign Policy* 44 (Fall 1981): 37–56.

Ramazani, R. K. "Iran's Islamic Revolution and the Persian Gulf." *Current History* 84, no. 498 (January 1985): 5–8, 40–41.

———. "The Iran-Iraq War and the Persian Gulf Crisis." *Current History* 87, no. 526 (February 1988): 61–64, 86–88.

Record, Jeffrey. "The RDF: Is the Pentagon Kidding?" *The Washington Quarterly* 4, no. 3 (Summer 1981): 41–51.

Sarabi, Farzin. "The Post-Khomeini Era in Iran: The Election of the Fourth Islamic Majlis." *Middle East Journal* 48, no. 1 (Winter 1994).

Seth, S. P. "Afghanistan in Global Politics." *Institute for Defense Studies and Analyses* [New Delhi] (October/December 1980): 189–200.

Sick, Gary. "Iran's Quest for Superpower Status." *Foreign Affairs* 65, no. 4 (Spring 1987): 697–715.

———. "Trial by Error: Reflections on the Iran-Iraq War." *Middle East Journal* 43, no. 2 (Spring 1989): 230–45.

"Symposium on Dual Containment: U.S. Policy Toward Iran and Iraq." *Middle East Policy* 3, no. 1 (1994): 1–43.

Vertzberger, Yaacov. "Afghanistan in China's Policy." *Problems of Communism* (May–June 1982): 6–14.

Waltz, Kenneth N. "Realist Thought and Neorealist Theory." *Journal of International Affairs* 44 (Spring 1990): 21–37.

Yetiv, S. A. "How the Soviet Military Intervention in Afghanistan Improved the

U.S. Strategic Position in the Persian Gulf." *Asian Affairs: An American Review* 18 (Summer 1990): 62–81.

———. "The Outcomes of Operations Desert Shield and Desert Storm: Some Antecedent Causes." *Political Science Quarterly* 107 (Summer 1992): 195–212.

———. "Persian Gulf Security: A Bivariable Analysis." *Defense Analysis* 6, no. 3 (September 1990): 289–98.

———. "The Transatlantic Dimension of Persian Gulf Security." *Naval War College Review* 44 (Autumn 1991): 45–58.

SELECTED OFFICIAL DOCUMENTS
AND SOURCE MATERIAL

Declassified Documents Reference Service. *Retrospective Collection.* Woodbridge CT: Research Publications, 1984.

"Desert Shield/Storm: Air Mobility Command's Achievements and Lessons for the Future." GAO/NSIAD-93-40, January 1993.

"Military Afloat Prepositioning: Wartime Use and Issues for the Future." GAO/NSIAD-93-39, November 1992.

"Military Airlift: Changes Underway to Ensure Continued Success of Civil Reserve Air Fleet," GAO/NSIAD-93-12, December 1992.

"Operation Desert Storm: War Offers Important Insights into Army and Marine Corps Training Needs." GAO/NSIAD-92-240, August 1992.

Soviet Military Power. Washington, D.C.: Government Printing Office, 1987, 125.

Strategic Sealift: Part of the National Defense Reserve Fleet Is No Longer Needed. Washington, D.C.: U.S. General Accounting Office, October 1991.

U.S. Congress. *Rapid Deployment Forces: Policy and Budgetary Implications.* Washington, D.C.: Congressional Budget Office, 1983.

U.S. Department of Defense, Caspar W. Weinberger. *Report of the Secretary of Defense to the Congress on the FY1988/1989 Budget and FY1988-92 Defense Programs,* 12 June 1987.

U.S. Department of Defense. *Conduct of the Persian Gulf War: Final Report to Congress.* Washington, D.C.: Government Printing Office, April 1992.

U.S. General Accounting Office. *Additional Costs to Government, Reflagging Kuwaiti Ships and Protecting Them in the Persian Gulf,* October 1987.

U.S. Congress, House of Representatives

Committee on Armed Services. *Defense for a New Era: Lessons of the Persian Gulf War.* Washington, D.C.: GPO, 1992.

Committee on Foreign Affairs. *Chronologies of Major Developments in Selected Areas of Foreign Affairs* Washington, D.C.: GPO, 1979.

Committee on Foreign Affairs. *Congress and Foreign Policy—1980*. Washington, D.C.: GPO, 1980.

Committee on Foreign Affairs. *The Persian Gulf Crisis: Relevant Documents, Correspondence, Reports*. Report prepared by the Subcommittee on Arms Control, June 1991. Washington, D.C.: GPO, 1991.

Committee on Foreign Affairs. Subcommittee on Europe and the Middle East. *Iraq's Nuclear Weapons Capability and IAEA Inspections in Iraq*, 29 June 1993. Washington, D.C.: GPO, 1993.

Committee on Foreign Affairs, *United States Policy Toward the Middle East and the Persian Gulf*, Hearings Before the Subcommittee on Europe and the Middle East, 17 June and 26 June 1991. Washington, D.C.: GPO, 1991.

Committee on Foreign Affairs. *U.S. Policy Toward Iraq 3 Years After the Gulf War*. Hearing Before the Subcommittee on Europe and the Middle East, 23 February 1994. Washington, D.C.: GPO, 1994.

Hearing before the Subcommittee on Foreign Affairs and the Joint Economic Committee. *U.S. Policy Toward the Persian Gulf*, 10 May 1982. Washington, D.C.: GPO, 1982.

Hearings before the Committee on Foreign Affairs. *Foreign Assistance Legislation for Fiscal Year 1981* (Part I). Washington, D.C.: GPO, 1980.

Hearings before the Subcommittee on Europe and the Middle East of the Committee on Foreign Affairs. *U.S. Policy Toward Iran*, 17 January 1979. Washington, D.C.: GPO, 1979.

Saudi Arabia and the United States. Report Prepared for the Subcommittee on Europe and the Middle East of the Committee on Foreign Affairs. Washington, D.C.: Congressional Research Service [CRS], August 1981.

U.S. Congress, Senate

Hearing before a Subcommittee of the Committee on Appropriations. *Department of Defense Appropriations for Fiscal Year 1989*. Washington, D.C.: GPO, 1988.

Hearings before the Committee on the Budget. *First Concurrent Resolution on the Budget—Fiscal Year 1981*, February-March 1980. Washington, D.C.: GPO, 1980.

Hearings before the Committee on Foreign Relations. *Security Interests and Policy in Southwest Asia*, 6 February 1980. Washington, D.C.: GPO, 1980.

War in the Persian Gulf: The U.S. Takes Sides. Staff Report to the Committee on Foreign Relations, November 1987. Washington, D.C.: GPO, 1987.

AUTHOR'S INTERVIEWS (ON THE RECORD)

Ambassador Richard Murphy, former Assistant Secretary of State for Near Eastern Affairs under the Reagan administration, 26 May 1994.

Dr. Paul D. Wolfowitz, Under Secretary of Defense for Policy, 1989–1993, 26 August 1994.

OFFICIAL STATEMENTS, ADDRESSES, AND TRANSCRIPTS

Address by Ronald Neumann, Director, Office of Northern Gulf Affairs, Department of State. "United States Policy Toward Iraq," Washington, D.C., Meridian International Center, 27 January 1994.

Address by Robert Pelletreau, Assistant Secretary for Near East and South Asian Affairs, to the American Business Community, Abu Dhabi, 8 May 1994.

Address by Fred Smith, Defense Department official, Meridian International Center, Washington, D.C., 18 May 1994.

Carter, Jimmy. *Public Papers of the Presidents of the United States*. Washington D.C.: Government Printing Office, various editions (1979–1980).

Interview with King Fahd. *London AL-HAWADITH*, FBIS: NESA, 14 February 1992.

Interview with National Security Advisor Zbigniew Brzezinski. *Wall Street Journal*, 15 January 1980, 20.

Interview with President Jimmy Carter. "Meet the Press." *New York Times*, 21 January 1980, A4.

Interview with Secretary of Defense Harold Brown. *Wall Street Journal*, 1 July 1980, 22.

Interview with Secretary of State Cyrus Vance. "TV Interview on Iran and Afghanistan." *Current Policy* 125 (January 1980). U.S. Department of State, Bureau of Public Affairs, Washington D.C.

Reagan, Ronald. *Public Papers of the Presidents of the United States*. Washington, D.C.: Government Printing Office, various editions (1981–1983).

Secretary of State Alexander Haig. "U.S. Strategy in the Middle East." *Current Policy* 312 (17 September 1981): 2.

Secretary of State Alexander Haig. "Saudi Security, Middle East Peace, and U.S. Interests." *Current Policy* 323 (1 October 1981): 1–3.

Text of President Jimmy Carter's remarks at a White House Briefing. "Hostages in Iran, Invasion of Afghanistan." 8 January 1980, *Department of State Bulletin* (DSB) 80 (March 1980): 33–35.

Text of the Damascus Declaration. *Journal of Palestine Studies* 20 (Summer 1991): 161–63.

Text of the transcript of the meeting between April Glaspie and Saddam Hussein. *New York Times*, 23 September 1990, A19.

Texts of major U.N. resolutions adopted in 1991. *U.N. Security Resolutions on Iraq: Compliance and Implementation, Report to the Committee on Foreign Affairs by the CRS*, March 1992. Washington, D.C.: GPO, 1992.

Transcript of President Jimmy Carter's State of the Union Address. "Transcript of President's State of the Union Address to Joint Session of Congress." *New York Times*, 24 January 1980, A12.

Transcript of President Jimmy Carter's Speech on the Soviet Military Intervention in Afghanistan. *New York Times*, 5 January 1980, A6.

Witness Statement by General H. Norman Schwarzkopf, Commander in Chief of the U.S. Central Command, before the Senate Armed Services Committee, 8 February 1990.

INDEX

About the Author

STEVE A. YETIV is an Assistant Professor of Political Science at Old Dominion University in Virginia and a research affiliate at the Center for Middle Eastern Studies at Harvard University.

ISBN 0-275-94973-7

90000>

EAN

9 780275 949730

HARDCOVER BAR CODE